CW00801524

Symbols
in
Craft Freemasonry

Symbolism
in
Craft Freemasonry

COLIN F. W. DYER
PAGDC

Master of Quatuor Coronati
Lodge No. 2076, (1975-76)

First published in England 1976
Revised paperback edition 2003
Reprinted 2004
This impression 2006

ISBN 0 85318 233 7

Published by Lewis Masonic

an imprint of
Ian Allan Publishing Ltd,
Hersham, Surrey KT12 4RG.

Printed in England by
Ian Allan Printing Ltd, Hersham,
Surrey KT12 4RG.

---

*The cover images of the three
Tracing Boards
are reproduced by kind permission of
Revd Neville Barker Cryer*

CONTENTS

PREFACE   7

1 THE SPECULATIVE MASON   9
Free and Accepted Masons—free—accepted—rebuilding after
the great fire—the link and later development—speculative—
speculation and symbolism.

2 THE BASIC SYMBOLISM   27
Allegory and symbols—the Antients Grand Lodge work—the
work of the Moderns—William Preston—early catechisms and
exposures—mysteries of ancient civilisations—Jewish influence
—development—justification—the use of numbers.

3 THE LODGE—ITS NATURE AND PURPOSE   58
The lodge room—the situation of the lodge—holy ground—the
entrance—development of lodges—pillars and columns—the
flooring—the construction.

4 THE LODGE—ORNAMENTS, FURNITURE AND
   JEWELS   84
The tracing board—the letter G—the letter G and the square—
geometry—the masonic jewels—Jacob's ladder—the point
within a circle—other symbols.

5 DARKNESS AND LIGHT   105
Light generally—three great lights—the lesser lights—the
Shekinah—the blazing star—furniture—the Sacred law—the
square and compasses—the position of the great lights.

6 THE CEREMONIES   122
Progress—the Holy of Holies—intermediate objects—the basis
of the degrees—the first degree—the second degree—the third
degree.

7 MASONIC CLOTHING   141
Clothing generally—the apron—the installed master's apron and
the past master's jewel—collars.

8 THE WORKING TOOLS   149
Implements generally—the trowel—the gavel and chisel—the
rule—the square—the level and plumb rule—the third degree
tools—masonical aphorisms.

ILLUSTRATIONS

Between pages 16-17

PLATE

1 Part of Rocque's Map of London, 1766, showing the major works of reconstruction in the City under the supervision of Sir Christopher Wren after the great fire of London of 1666.

Between pages 92-93

2 The Frontispiece from the Moderns Book of Constitutions, 1786.

3 The north front of Somerset House.

4 A Lodge Board shewing symbols and emblems of the first and second degrees.

5 A dual Tracing Board designed for the Lodge of Unions.

6 A Master's Tracing Board dating from about 1800.

7 A Master's Tracing Board from Britannic Lodge.

8 First Degree Tracing Board designed by John Harris.

9 A 'split' second degree Harris Tracing Board.

10 Lodge Cloth shewing some emblems and symbols which have now fallen out of use.

PREFACE

T HERE IS no doubt that many men see meanings in different aspects of freemasonry which others do not—symbolism can be very subjective. It is equally clear that there is intentional symbolism in freemásonry in many places, deliberately inserted for reasons which were good to those who made the introduction many years ago. Extreme use of symbolism and the copying of manners and customs of earlier ages were fashions adopted generally in Great Britain during an important period in the development of freemasonry. Finding such practices in the freemasonry of the time was not unusual to the man living in those times (although the symbolism itself might be), any more than the oaths of secrecy incorporated into freemasonry were very different from those used in other aspects of life at the time.

No-one has left a record which is likely to give the definite origins of any great amount of the symbolism intended to be in freemasonry. Many parallel instances of the use of symbols may be found, by which it is possible that freemasonry could have been influenced, while the amount which has been written on the subject would defeat any attempt to read it all—and possibly even to be aware of it. Such writing includes not only matters relating to intended original symbolism incorporated into the practice of freemasonry, but also, in many later writings, aspects which have presented themselves to those who found those symbols already in use.

In this book I have attempted to examine as much as I have been able to find on the reasons for the incorporation of particular symbolism. I have included all of that which seems to me to hang together as a whole, although, even from the reading which I have been able to do, it is apparent that there may be more than one source and some differences in practice in earlier days. In addition, I have tried to include a selection of later writings of thoughtful masons on what they have found of this nature for them in the craft. This does not necessarily mean that I sharè their opinions, but that is no reason for not comparing them with others. Reading on this subject never ends and so much may be omitted because I have not got as far as reading it, while I have deliberately not included items which in my opinion did not bear serious examination, usually because a particular reference or meaning may have been overlooked in their compilation.

In the course of compiling this book I have received valuable

advice and assistance from a number of people. I shall make no
attempt to mention them by name, but I do wish to place on record
my thanks for the help they have given me. I also wish to acknowledge
with thanks the permission of the Board of General Purposes to
utilise material in the Library and Museum at Freemasons' Hall
London.

C. D.

1

THE SPECULATIVE MASON

WHEN A lodge meets, the members come together and exercise their minds not as operative, but as free and accepted, or speculative masons. The rise, development and organisation of speculative masonry as we now know it, took place in the British Isles, and the first attempt at central organisation of any sort took place in England with the formation of the first Grand Lodge in 1717. That was not the beginning of speculative masonry. It had been a movement concerned with a philosophy of the spiritual life of man for an indefinite number of years before that, moralising, or, as our forebears termed it, 'spiritualizing', certain aspects of the trade of building stately edifices for guidance to men in the building of better lives, based on the Fatherhood of God and the Brotherhood of Man.

The description of the members of the order as 'masons' or as 'freemasons' has not been consistent over the years and many examples of each may be found in use at the same period of time. The matter is further complicated by the fact that 'mason' and 'free mason' have, in some circumstances, been alternative names for operative craftsmen from early times in the history of the mason craft. The use of the combined word 'freemason', as distinct from the old uses, 'free mason' or 'free-mason', as a general practice probably goes no further back than the beginning of the nineteenth century, but speculative masons have been 'free and accepted' for very much longer than that. In private lodges under a great number of the independent Grand Lodges of the world, the words 'free and accepted' are in general use in connection with the lodge itself and are incorporated in the title. Private lodges under the United Grand Lodge of England do not as a general rule use 'free and accepted' as part of the lodge title; the Grand Lodge style generally used in formal papers since the *Book of Constitutions* published in 1815 is 'United Grand Lodge of Antient Free and Accepted Masons of England' (although some documents may be worded slightly differently). Curiously, the seal of the Grand Lodge refers to 'Antient Free Masons of England'.

Free

Much has been written in explanation of why masons should call themselves 'free and accepted'. The master tells the candidate that

9

masonry is free and requires a perfect freedom of inclination in every candidate. In that the second part of this statement implies a voluntary application, it is perfectly understandable, but the expression 'masonry is free' does not seem to advance matters very far. There is a general acceptance in many places that the word is used to indicate that the society is open only to free men—men under no form of bondage to others—for, at the time of masonry's first organisation, servitude and slavery were still in existence. While it is true that masonry has always been restricted to men who were free—and until 1848 the qualification in England was actually to have been *born* free—this is unlikely to be the reason for the use of the word in the title. The standard masonic lectures current in the English Constitution state that freemasons are so called because they are 'free to good fellowship and ought to be free from vice.' This thought probably represents a later inclusion by a compiler of an earnest nature searching for a reason to put in his lecture, and, again, is unlikely to be the reason why masons are called free.

At a masonic dinner in London on 24 June 1721 (probably the annual feast on St John's day), George Payne produced an 'old MS of the *Constitutions* which he got in the West of England.' This was what is now known as the *Cooke MS* and it is now in the British Museum. It is a version of the old charges of operative masons and is believed to date from about the year 1400. George Payne was Grand Master of the original Grand Lodge of England in 1718-19 and 1720-21. Up to this time there does not appear to have been a formal constitution for the now four-year-old Grand Lodge but work was started shortly after this production of the *Cooke MS* on *The Constitutions of the Freemasons*, largely the work of James Anderson (but to which Payne also contributed), which was completed, approved and published in 1723. The 1723 *Constitutions* contains a number of short quotations and paraphrases from the *Cooke MS*, while the revised edition of 1738 (also the work of Anderson) contains even more.

This old manuscript mentions the seven liberal arts and sciences, stressing that Geometry is the one that matters and is the 'causer' of all. Although Geometry is accepted as the science of earth measurement, the manuscript goes on to argue that it has developed into masonry, and so Geometry and Masonry are the same thing. Knoop, Jones and Hamer published in *The Two Earliest Masonic MSS*, in 1938, a transcription of the *Cooke MS*, along with the *Regius MS* (which has a number of similarities and is ascribed to about 1390), together with detailed notes on both. They are at pains to point out that this approach was not uncommon among all trades—to prove that the science which was closest to their own work was quite surely the most important; these manuscripts were for the mason craft. They go on:

> The Seven Liberal Arts or Sciences (the word Science here means solely 'branch of knowledge') constituted the initial item in the mediæval arrangement of knowledge, and in its educational system. The Romans held that the arts were either *artes liberales*, or *ingenuæ*, the arts of free men, as opposed to the *artes illiberales*, or *sordidæ*, the arts, crafts, or employments of slaves or of the lower classes.

William Preston in his lectures of the end of the eighteenth century reflects this thought that masonry and geometry meant the same thing to those concerned. In his questions, after establishing that the candidate was passed for the sake of Geometry, he goes on to say why:

> Because originally Masonry and Geometry must have been synonymous terms as they were taken for the sciences in general; but in the progress of civilisation and improvement in knowledge, Geometry was limited to a certain part of science though still considered as essential to all, and symbolic of knowledge.

Geometry, then, was one of the 'free sciences', and as masonry was synonymous with Geometry, those whose special studies embraced this particular science, might be referred to as 'free masons'. G. W. Speth advances this view as the reason men so described themselves when not actually engaged in the operative trade, but chose to follow the study of 'free Geometry' for moral or philosophical reasons. The connection with the very early organisation of speculative masonry of the *Cooke MS* may have been a reason for the growing up of this practice of calling speculative masons 'free'.

In Britain, the organisation of various trades into guilds (or 'gilds') for their common protection has a history going back for many hundreds of years. As an example, in the City of London, where a continuation of this system lives on in the form of Livery Companies with social, educational and charitable objects, some of these companies can trace an existence going back a minimum of eight hundred years. Some, such as the Goldsmiths and Fishmongers, still have trade responsibilities. Guilds of this kind could exercise control among their members over standards of work, admission to the trade, and perform the functions of a charitable organisation for members and dependants who fell on hard times. More important still, by working with the leading citizens who ran the borough or city, they could control the complete trade in a town. In order to trade within a town, the tradesman had to have the 'freedom' of the town, that is, the official permission or licence, or freedom, to trade, within the boundaries administered by the city fathers. If, in addition, the tradesman had to have the freedom of his guild and one would not be granted without the other, there was complete control, both as to who might trade and as to the standards of work imposed. Apprenticeship and trade education would then lie within the province of the guild; the apprentice was registered and on properly finishing his indentures, would be admitted a freeman. So there arose a grading of guild membership. A master was properly a tradesman who undertook contract work and who employed others. The guild itself had an organisation normally of the most influential members, while the exercise of full authority on the guild's behalf might take up much time, and so these influential inner members took it in turns to give up this time from their own businesses to serve as Warden or as Master of the guild. Here is the basis of a multi-grade system, based essentially on that most important right, the freedom to exercise a trade—to be free of the city and to be free of the company. So a free mason might mean that in any given city such a man might be a member of the trade guild and have the right or privilege of exercising his trade in that city, subject to the control of his guild.

Robert Freke Gould in his *History of Freemasonry* (1886) examines a number of possibilities in considering the rise of the use of the description 'freemason' for those concerned with speculative masonry. He also points out the difficulty caused by the old usage of 'free mason' as an operative term, when considering whether references relate to operative or speculative masons. He holds to the view that the custom of the masons of London was largely responsible by styling themselves 'free masons' because of the practice of that City to require its craftsmen to hold the freedom; he also quotes from the 1633 edition of Stow's *Survey of London*, 'the masons, otherwise termed "free-masons" ', and refers to even earlier records of the Corporation of London which in 1376-77 relate to 'fre masons' and 'masons' as if they were the same trade. This, however, only shows the rise of the use of 'free' and carries no evidence of its application *particularly* to speculative masons.

The London Company of Masons, the City guild related to the craft, was known until the early sixteenth century as the Fellowship of Masons, when the name was changed to the Company of Free Masons. In 1655 the name was again changed to the present title. Gould provides strong evidence of the existence in London in the late 1600s of a Society of Freemasons, separate from though probably associated with the London Company of Masons. As will be seen later when considering the inference of 'accepted', some such speculative society was in existence from much earlier in the same century in connection with the London Company. Bernard E. Jones in his *Freemasons' Guide and Compendium* suggests that this speculative offshoot of the London Company of Masons continued with the name 'freemason' after the Company finally changed its name in 1655 with the consequent identification of the speculative brethren as 'freemasons'.

Soon after the formation of the first Grand Lodge in London in 1717, masonry achieved a certain place in London society so that joining became one of the fashionable things to do. This gave rise to a plague of 'exposures' purporting to reveal all the secrets of the new society and culminating in one of greater length than the others, in 1730, by Samuel Prichard, called *Masonry Dissected*. Several pamphlets in defence of the new society also appeared and one, *A Defence of Masonry*, was published from an anonymous author in December 1730. This must have had some authenticity as it was reproduced in 1738 in both Smith's *Pocket Companion for Free-Masons* and the official *Constitutions* of Grand Lodge prepared by Anderson. In the course of this pamphlet the author refers to the parallel of the Livery Companies of the City of London in their organisation with that of masonry; not only is it a parallel, but an obvious establishment to copy:

> There are a *Master*, two *Wardens*, and a number of *Assistants*, to make what the *Dissector* may call (if he pleases) a *perfect Lodge*, in the City Companies. There is the Degree of *enter'd Prentice*, Master of his Trade or *Fellow-Craft*, and *Master*, or Master of the Company. There are Constitutions and Orders, and a successive and gradual Enjoyment of Offices, according to the several Rules and Limitations of Admission.

In considering the use of the word 'Master' in this quotation, it is well to bear in mind that it was written at the time when the three-degree system of masonry was emerging from the old two-degree system, and a parallel with modern practice should not be drawn. In the use of the London Company as an example, it may be that they were the only true example to be found, so far as England is concerned. Knoop, Jones and Hamer give the following account of the character of medieval industry in England;

> In most mediæval industries production was on a small scale, and was directed by independent craftsmen or 'little masters' employing one or

two journeymen or apprentices who had some hope of becoming, in time, independent masters themselves, but the stone-building industry was generally organised on a different basis. There were, no doubt, some stonemasons working on their own account or with one or two assistants, undertaking small jobs of repair or of construction. The method of having parts of larger works done by task or 'in gross' was not uncommon in the second half of the fourteenth century. On the other hand, the letting of masonry contracts for whole buildings appears to have been exceptional at this period. Larger building jobs were generally executed by what we should now call the 'direct labour' system: the employer—commonly the Crown or the Church—appointed certain officials, such as the master mason and a clerk of the works, to organise and administer the building operations, to arrange for supplies of materials and to engage the necessary craftsmen and labourers. Those responsible for the buildings also commonly worked quarries and organised the transport of the stone by land or water as the case might be.

The master mason or the mason-contractor, as the case might be, is the 'master' frequently mentioned in our MSS. The employer for whom the building was being erected is the 'lord.' Whether the 'direct labour' system or the contract system was employed, the industry was organised on a capitalist basis and the majority of masons were, unlike many workmen in other industries, life-long wage earners.

Another respect in which the stone-building industry differed from contemporary industries was in the matter of craft gilds. Nowhere except in London have any masons' craft ordinances of the fourteenth of fifteenth centuries been traced, though indirect evidence points to some organisation at Norwich in 1440. At York, Beverley and Coventry masons took part in Corpus Christi or in Whitsun pageants in the fifteenth century and they probably did so at Chester. Such participation points to some kind of organisation, but not necessarily to a craft gild. Even in London it seems probable that there was no formally established masons' craft gild until some date between 1356 and 1376. This absence of craft gilds is probably explained, in part at least, by four features of the industry to which attention has already been drawn: (i) the fact that many stone buildings were erected outside the boroughs, whereas craft gilds were municipal institutions; (ii) the fact that the industry had a capitalistic organisation which could not easily be reconciled with the more or less democratic character of a craft gild; (iii) the fact that the Crown, Church and Municipality, who would have to approve craft ordinances, were the chief employers of masons and, as builders, would probably prefer to deal with unorganised labour; (iv) the fact that the impressment of masons was of frequent occurrence, this being difficult to reconcile with well-organised craft gilds among masons.

Many attribute the appellation 'free' as coming from a particular part of the old mason craft which used as their material, free-stone—a fine-grained sandstone or limestone—and argued that those who worked in this material were of a superior class. Joseph Fort Newton, in *The Builders*, takes a lead from *The Cathedral Builders: The Story of a Great Masonic Guild*, a book by Leader Scott on the Comacine Masters, whom Newton sees as a direct link in the history of free-masonry from earliest times. Newton's object (from an historical standpoint) is to attempt to justify the long continuous existence of freemasonry which is depicted in Anderson's *Constitutions*—that is, the rather fanciful descent of modern freemasonry from the moral and spiritual 'mysteries' of thousands of years earlier by direct traceable connection. Newton quotes from Leader Scott:

> . . . . we may admit that they were the link between the classic Collegia and all other art and trade Guilds of the Middle Ages. They were Freemasons because they were builders of a privileged class, absolved from taxes and servitude, and free to travel about in times of feudal bondage.

Some of the lectures dating from the late eighteenth century also refer to this freedom from taxes, but relate it to the builders working for King Solomon.

Accepted

I have referred to Robert Freke Gould's evidence adduced in support of there having been a separate Society of Freemasons in the late 1600s. Throughout most of that century (Edward Conder the Company's historian says 'before 1618') there is known to have been, in the London Company of Masons itself, an inner conclave of a different character from the normal company arrangement. Member-ship of this inner conclave was not automatic even for those entrusted with the normal government of the guild and it represented a sort of spiritual movement towards a better life such as has been found to rise at intervals through the world's history. It is likely that the rise of this organisation was merely an early indication, a herald, or forerunner, of the much stronger philosophical movement which showed itself in a number of ways in the following century—which became known as the Age of Reason—and during which freemasonry developed to such a great extent. An important factor of this different, moral, inner conclave of the Masons' Company was that there could be admitted to membership those who were not practising operative masons but were responsible citizens with a suitable outlook on life. These other citizens were 'accepted' as masons for the purpose of membership of this inner group, which ultimately became known as 'the Acception.'

One of the pamphlets in defence of Freemasonry published in 1730 (and attributed by some to Martin Clare, later Deputy Grand Master) was *The Perjured Free Mason Detected*. It contains the following:

> . . . . I understand that you are only admitted to the first steps of a Free Mason, but are not yet taken into the full Confidence of the Society.
>
> . . . . after having approv'd your self honest, and given the Society some year's Experience of your Fidelity, as well as of your Improvement in Knowledge, and the Science of a Mason, you may at length attain to the full Degree of an Accepted Mason, but not yet I assure you.

The inference of these two passages could be that admission to the society (*i.e.* initiation) made the candidate a *Free* Mason, but that he only became an *Accepted* Mason after he had taken some further ceremony. If this is so, the expression 'free and accepted' could in those days only be applied to those who were complete— those who had taken the degree of 'free' and that of 'accepted'. This seeming two degree grading would not be inconsistent with early known gradings, for it is believed that up to the 1720s there may have been only two degrees, while in later years the degree of Master Mason was regarded as a special mark of favour above that of full admission.

Later in that century the view on this seems to have changed, for, as an apprentice was not considered free, being bound to his principal, so he could only be accepted and not free until he became a craftsman. This seems to be borne out by the opening and closing in the first degree which was approved by Grand Lodge in August 1815; the word 'mason' is used throughout although 'freemason' occurs in the opening and closing of the second degree.

Effects of rebuilding after the Great Fire of London.

Many serious masonic historians discount most of James Anderson's historical claims for the craft including his discovery that Sir Christopher Wren was Grand Master. The rebuilding of the City of London after the great fire of 1666 did bring an immense congregation of people connected with the building trade, not just of craftsmen alone,

PLATE I

PART OF ROCQUE'S MAP OF LONDON, 1776

Shewing the major works of reconstruction under the supervision of Sir Christopher Wren in the City of London after the great fire of 1666, demonstrating the concentration of those concerned with building during the period in which this took place. Other places of interest are also marked.

The buildings indicated by numbers are those referred to in the Book of Constitutions of 1756. A key is given on the following pages. The dates against each building indicate the period during which work was progressing on it and are taken from the publication of the Wren Society. The finishing dates given coincide except in two cases (and then only of one year's difference) with those given in the Book of Constitutions.

Wren's major work was the construction of the present St. Paul's Cathedral. The clearing of the site of the old, fire-damaged, building was done between 1673-75, in which latter year the new building was started. The present cathedral was first used for services in 1697, although it was 1708 before it was substantially completed. Both the Book of Constitutions and the Wren Society record the laying of the final stone in 1710. Over fifty churches were rebuilt (or subject to major repair) as well as several other important structures. Those marked 'x' in the key are still standing (although they may have been overhauled since), while the tower is still standing in those marked 't'. The site of St. Mary, Aldermanbury ('o') is now laid out as a garden, the church having been rebuilt in Fulton, Missouri, USA. Those buildings marked 'd' have not survived; new structures having been erected later on the same sites. Most of the buildings were of stone; where other material was used, the fact is indicated in the key.

The streets in which were the meeting places of three of the four lodges concerned in the formation of the Grand Lodge in 1717 are also shown, indicating how close they were to the main work going on just before that event. The four lodges held a joint meeting in 1716 at the Apple Tree Tavern in Charles-street (2), where the lodge which is now Fortitude and Old Cumberland, No. 12, then met. Another met at the Crown in Parkers-lane (1)—this expired in 1736. The lodge which later became the Lodge of Antiquity, now No. 2, met at the *Goose and Gridiron* in St. Paul's Churchyard itself (12), and it was at this hostelry that the first Grand Feast was held to inaugurate the new Grand Lodge on 24 June 1717.

(Parkers-lane is now called Parker-street; Charles-street is now part of Wellington-street).

1667-69	The Royal Exchange	43d
1667-68	St. Dunstan-in-the-East (major repairs)	60t
1667-70	St. Sepulchre-without-Newgate	6x
1668	The Custom House	61d
1670-71	St. Christopher-le-Stocks (major repairs)	40
1670-72	St. Mary-at-Hill (mainly stone)	58x
1670-72	St. Michael, Cornhill (mainly stone)	50x
1670-73	St. Mary-le-Bow (brick and stone)	24x
1670-73	St. Olave, Old Jewry (mainly brick)	33t
1670-74	St. Dionis Backchurch (mainly stone)	57
1670-75	St. Michael, Wood-street	22
1670-76	St. Mildred, Poultry	35
1670-77	St. Lawrence Jewry-next-Guildhall	29x
1670-77	St. Mary, Aldermanbury	28o
1670-77	St. Mary Woolnoth (major repairs)	4id

Continued overleaf

1670-80	St. Bride, Fleet-street (church only)		5x
1670-90	St. Edmund the King, Lombard-street		48x
1671-74	St. George, Botolph-lane		56
1671-76	St. Magnus-the-Martyr (church only)		52x
1671-77	St. Nicholas Cole Abbey		14x
1671-77	The Monument (commemorating the start of the fire)		51x
1671-80	The steeple of St. Mary-le-Bow		24x
1672-76	St. Stephen, Walbrook		36x

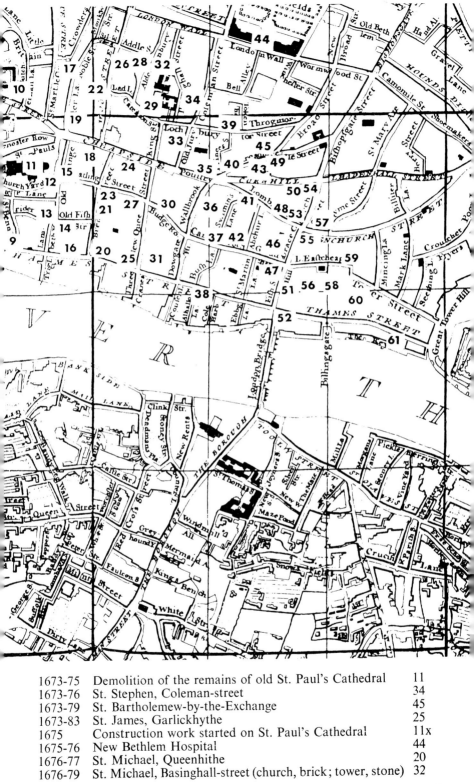

1673-75	Demolition of the remains of old St. Paul's Cathedral	11
1673-76	St. Stephen, Coleman-street	34
1673-79	St. Bartholemew-by-the-Exchange	45
1673-83	St. James, Garlickhythe	25
1675	Construction work started on St. Paul's Cathedral	11x
1675-76	New Bethlem Hospital	44
1676-77	St. Michael, Queenhithe	20
1676-79	St. Michael, Basinghall-street (church, brick; tower, stone)	32

Continued overleaf

1676-80	St. Anne and St. Agnes, Aldersgate	17x
1677-79	St. Swithun London Stone	37
1677-81	St. Peter-upon-Cornhill (church, stone; tower, brick)	54x
1677-83	All Hallows-the-Great, Thames-street	38
1677-83	St. Benet, Paul's-wharf	9x
1677-84	St. Martin, Ludgate	7x
1677-84	All Hallows, Bread-street	23
1677-87	Christ Church, Newgate	10t
1678-82	St. Antholin, Watling-street	30
1680-82	St. Clement Danes	3x
1680-83	St. Augustin, Watling-street	15
1681-83	St. Mildred, Bread-street (one front stone)	21t
1681-85	St. Benet, Gracechurch	55
1681-85	St. Matthew, Friday-street	18
1681-86	St. Mary Abchurch (brick, some stone)	42x
1682-85	St. Alban, Wood-street	26t
1682	some work on St. Mary Aldermary	27x
1683-85	St. Mary Magdalen (mainly stone)	13
1683-86	St. Clement, Eastcheap (brick and stone)	46x
1683	St. James, Piccadilly	x
1684	Steeple of St. Dionis Backchurch	57
1684-87	St. Margaret Pattens (brick and stone)	59x
1684-88	St. Michael, Crooked-lane	47
1685-92	St. Andrew-by-the-Wardrobe (mainly brick)	8x
1686-90	St. Margaret, Lothbury	39x
1686-94	All Hallows, Lombard-street	53
1686-94	St. Michael Paternoster Royal (mainly stone)	31x
1686-95	St. Mary Somerset	16t
1687	St. Andrew, Holborn (church only)	4x
1693	further work on St. Benet Gracechurch	55
1695	Steeple of St. Augustin, Watling-street	15
1696	further work on St. Christopher-le-Stocks	40
1697	The first services held in the new St. Paul's Cathedral	11x
1697	Steeple of All Hallows, Bread-street	23
1698	further work on St. Dunstan-in-the-East	60t
1698	further work on St. Michael, Crooked-lane	47
1698-99	Spire of St. Bride, Fleet-street	5x
1701	further work on St. Mildred, Poultry	35
1701	further work on St. Michael, Cornhill	50x
1702	further work on St. Anne and St. Agnes, Aldersgate	17x
1703-05	Steeple of St. Magnus-the-Martyr	52x
1704	Tower of St. Andrew, Holborn	4x
1705-06	further work on St. Michael, Queenhithe	20
1706	further work on St. Margaret, Lothbury	39x
1708	St. Paul's Cathedral mainly completed	11x
1710	reputed, the last stone of St. Paul's Cathedral laid	11x
1711	probable further work on St. Mary Aldermary	27x

In addition, in London, there were also built—Christ's Hospital, Marlborough House, and the College of Physicians in Warwick-lane, as well as work at Temple Bar, all under Wren's control. There was other work going on, both in the City of London and in Westminster under the control of others. In addition to works in London itself, Wren was also responsible for Greenwich Hospital and Greenwich Observatory, Chelsea Hospital, the Sheldonian and other works at Oxford, among others.

into a confined area of less than a square mile over a period in excess of forty years. The whole of this was under Wren's supervision during the complete period until the final completion of St Paul's Cathedral in 1710. It is possible that the building of this one edifice, occupying the time from the start of the demolition of the old building in 1673 to the laying of the last stone on the lantern in 1710 (although the building had been in use since 1697), may tend to dazzle us in this day so as to overlook the other work that went on. The fire destroyed 13,200 houses, 89 parish churches, the Royal Exchange, Guildhall, Bridewell, the two Compters, 52 halls of city livery companies, as well as other public buildings. Much of the private building was probably not under Wren's control and the artificers employed may not have been masons. In the substantial buildings with which he was directly concerned, masons were likely to be employed and the final incorporation of the Company of Masons of the City of London by Letters Patent of Charles II in 1677 may well have occurred because of this concentration of craftsmen and others engaged in the rebuilding.

A start was made in 1668 with the building of the Custom House while the Royal Exchange, commenced in 1667, was completed in 1669. Between 1670 and 1700, 52 churches were either rebuilt completely or subject to major reconstruction; some of them were tackled in two stages and in four cases the second stage was not completed until after 1700; of these churches well over half were built entirely in stone while at least another 15 were either mainly in stone or in a mixture of brick and stone. Thus Sir Christopher Wren was in direct contact with a very large body of men engaged in the building trade, much of it in stone, during a period of over 40 years shortly before a gathering of free-masons decided to start a formal Grand Lodge, meeting almost in the shadow of all this new building work. Anderson makes no reference to this in his *Constitutions* of 1723, and only passing reference in the 1738 edition. Much fuller detail is included in the 1756 edition by Rev. John Entick and continued in John Noorthouck's edition of 1784.

The Link and Later development

Thus we find, in London, a Society of Freemasons associated with the London Company of Masons in the later years of the seventeenth century. This society continued to use the name 'free' after it had been dropped by the operative Company, and it was also known as

the 'Acception'—a society of free and accepted masons of a speculative character. There was at the same time an accumulation of
persons for over 40 years concerned with the building work in the
restoration after the great fire, and especially on the new St Paul's
Cathedral completed in 1710. The first Grand Lodge was organised
(among other things to find a Grand Master) in London, in 1717.
When this new body sought a coat-of-arms, that of the London
Company of Masons was adopted and when, a few years later, a
constitution was being considered, it was sparked off by, and based
on, the discovery of a copy of an old charge relating to the mason
trade. It may have been coincidence but it all hangs together remark-
ably well.

There is less significance in the adoption of the arms of the Masons
Company than there might be today. In those days it was not the
practice to ask for permission to use the arms of others and in many
cases arms were used to provide a form of identification, as with a
trade. The attitude of the College of Arms was also probably different. What appears to have been taken by the Grand Lodge was
the general pattern of the arms rather than a faithful copy, and
different colouring was probably used. The arms of the original
Grand Lodge were never sanctioned by the College of Arms; it seems
likely that it was not until well into the twentieth century that
sanction of any kind was sought.

In his 1738 *Constitutions* (but, curiously, not in that of 1723),
Anderson claims that the search for a new Grand Master in 1717 was
as a result of the neglect of Sir Christopher Wren. Any evidence that
exists about Wren's connection with free and accepted masons is
slight and not particularly reliable. It would have been perfectly
possible for him to have taken an interest in the speculative side of
the craft as well as in the operative—after all, he had been in daily
contact with the large number of people involved for forty years.
He may even have neglected them after 1710—but then he was over
85 years old when the Grand Lodge was formed!

There is no doubt that, as a moral movement, similar and parallel
bodies were arising elsewhere than in London at the same time as the
development of the Acception. Each may have had slightly different
ideas on the 'spiritualizing' of its own trade. One of the earliest
recorded initiations, that of Elias Ashmole in 1646, was not in
London but in Warrington in Lancashire, but some association with
the London Acception may be assumed from Ashmole's record of
his having been admitted into that fellowship at Masons' Hall,
London, in 1682. Particular mention may be made of Scotland with

its very early growth of independent lodges with some speculative content.

Although it is not possible to give a starting date to free and accepted masonry in England, the timing of the happenings referred to earlier suggests that if formal symbolism started to arise in connection with it, that was likely to be in the late 1600s, and that with the development which took place in speculative masonry in the 1700s, a great deal more was probably added in those days. There is unlikely to be a continuous history of a speculative movement giving direct succession over thousands of years, but that need not prevent those of a speculative turn of mind from knowing about the organisation of the earlier 'mysteries'—and, if deemed of value, to copy from them. When such a moral movement appears to have arisen in connection with a particular trade, as this did, it is most likely that in seeking to moralise or 'spiritualize', examples would be taken from that trade.

Membership of the old trade guilds could be acquired in three ways—by patrimony, son following father in a guild; by servitude, formal apprenticeship registered (or 'entered') with the guild; by redemption or purchase. This last might be necessary for setting up in another town from that in which a tradesman had been apprenticed and trained—as in the case of William Preston who was apprenticed in Edinburgh and moved to London; in 1794 he obtained the freedom of the Stationers' Company in London to enable him to operate in that City. There was no national registration council, the guild arrangements were essentially local in nature, and a safeguard might be necessary before someone unknown could be allowed to purchase his way into a trade in a town. Documents could easily be forged and so some further proof was preferable. In trades, such as that of building in stone, where a particular professional standard was required, some other means of identification came into use. This had to be of a secret nature because it was the immediate key to a privilege. It did not constitute the secrets of the trade itself, they could only be acquired over a long apprenticeship, but it represented a protection to those secrets. Moral movements are not always popular and may be held up to ridicule, so what more reasonable than that the Acception might also adopt similar forms for their own protection. Even today the secrets of freemasonry are not, of themselves, important knowledge; they too represent a protection and also a cover or a reminder of a much deeper meaning which can only be acquired over a long experience and, in many cases, is not really capable of direct communication.

Speculative

In the sphere of free and accepted masonry there are many generally used illustrations of principles, emblems with particular significance or meaning, and hieroglyphics or characters. These are to symbolise —and to remind the members of—the moral principles which relate to membership of the order. These were and are the true symbols of free and accepted masonry and if explanation of these symbols and symbolism is sought, then the reason they were first incorporated in the masonic system must be the true explanation. That is why they are there, and the original teaching may be as valid today as when they were originally used in the lodge. In a number of cases the true reason may have been lost in the passage of time, while in other cases, change, whether deliberate and legitimate or not, may have caused a symbol to lose completely its original significance—but the original meaning may still be known and provide a useful masonic illustration.

These original symbols found a place in our lodge and its work during the development period of speculative masonry because our forebears in the Craft speculated on the principles they were trying to teach and they attempted to illustrate those principles in a simple manner. In 1770 John Ladd published *The Science of Free-Masonry Explained*, including thoughts which he had collated over a period, and in this he writes:

> Speculative knowledge is that which arises from contemplation; it is inferred and confirmed by a due reasoning from principles; of this kind are all the demonstrative truths to which we give the name of Science.

William Preston, at about the same period, wrote:

> Speculative Masonry comprehends the hidden order of the Universe and secret things, both of heaven and earth, more particularly those of a spiritual and intellectual nature. Operative Masonry directs our works to perfection, Speculative to happiness. One directs us to discern and use the gifts of nature, the other enables us to investigate the order and system of the universe and adapts to its constant rules our ideas of justice, the only means by which man can live with comfort and happiness in the world.

Current dictionaries give the meaning of 'speculative' as 'thoughtful' or 'philosophic'. The true speculative mason therefore thinks about the craft and meditates and contemplates on its meaning for him and for mankind. Those who call themselves freemasons are not operative masons; they are free and accepted, or speculative. This definition places 'speculative' as an *alternative* name or description to 'free and accepted'. The craft has acquired the qualifying 'free and accepted' as a matter of history, but those who choose to become members of it are bound by this alternative title to do more than just remain passive members; they should think about the underlying principles of the society they have joined.

In the later years of the eighteenth century many of the masonic writers were concerned to invoke the mason to be more speculative in his approach and to involve himself in finding the meaning of the craft of which he was a member. In the second edition of his *Illustrations of Masonry* published in 1775, William Preston develops this theme of personal involvement:

> To make a daily progress in Masonry is a duty incumbent on every member of this society, and is expressly required by our general laws. What end can be more noble than the pursuit of virtue; what motive more alluring than the practice of justice; or what instruction more beneficial than an accurate elucidation of symbolical mysteries, which tend to embellish and adorn the human mind? Everything that strikes the eye more immediately engages the attention and imprints on the memory those circumstances which are accompanied with serious and solemn truths. Hence masons have universally adopted the method of inculcating the tenets of their Order by typical figures and allegorical emblems. This practice has secured their mysteries from descending into the familiar reach of every inattentive and unprepared novice, from whom they might not receive due veneration.

If the symbols are already there in the craft and we know their original meanings; if they came there by the thoughtful speculation of our brethren of a much earlier age; and if that earlier age has produced so much speculative writing which has become incorporated into the structure of the craft; how are we to carry out the injunction set upon us by William Preston—and emphasised on the night of his initiation to every new member of the order? Is not all the speculation done? What is there left to do?

First we may look at the symbols which exist in the craft, consider what is their purpose and what is their real meaning and what they teach us. *The Concise Oxford Dictionary* defines a symbol as a 'thing regarded by general consent as naturally typifying or representing or recalling something by possession of analogous qualities or by association in fact or thought' or a 'mark or character taken as the conventional sign of some object or idea or process.' We shall find

both kinds of symbol to engage our attention in our lodges, not
only those things which, by association or thought, represent or
recall the principles intended for our instruction, but also devices or
marks which have a special significance. Our forebears in masonry
often referred to such things as 'hieroglyphics'; Wellins Calcott, in
A Candid Disquisition published in 1769, states what he means by
hieroglyphics in a masonic connection:

> Hieroglyphics are properly emblems or signs of divine, sacred or
> supernatural things, by which they are distinguished from common
> symbols, which are signs of sensible or natural things.

Speculation and Symbolism

I have already said that symbols incorporated in the lore of the craft
were put there by our ancient brethren for a particular purpose and
to express a particular thought or precept. This thought or precept
may be very valuable to us in this generation, but we must bear in
mind that no particular age has a monopoly of original, deep or
interesting thought and it is proper that those of succeeding generations of masons in reconsidering those original symbols should also
be considered. Many later writers have expressed their thoughts on
the significance to them of the established symbols of the Craft.

I have attempted to draw a distinction between the original
meaning of the symbols found in masonry and what constitutes true
masonic speculation. Much of the later writing which gives us the
benefit of speculation has been published under the general heading
of symbolism, and in many cases has endeavoured to show speculative
interpretations as if no original meaning existed. Where this speculative work is valuable in producing a new view and a new way of
showing an old truth, the name under which the author publishes
it is of little consequence. The immediate object is to study our
symbols and to speculate on them. J. S. M. Ward, in *An Interpretation
of Our Masonic Symbols*, writes:

> We may go outside the Lodge and, gazing on nature, perceive that
> all around us God teaches us by symbol and by allegory. The sun
> which rises in the heavens is but a faint image of His glory. It shadows
> forth His creative power, and in its rising and setting is an allegory of
> mortal life and death, and even more of the resurrection. The corn
> planted in the ground has for us the selfsame message, and the humble
> beasts of the field can teach us many a lesson.
> The great laws of nature are His laws, and the more we study them

the more we realise that they are not the outcome of blind chance, but the proof of a profound and all-embracing Intellect, beside which the intellect of the wisest man is as the foolishness of a little child. Assuredly one of the chief objects of our life on earth is that we may endeavour to understand, albeit but dimly, the meaning of His great symbols. Thus there is a deep significance in the injunction laid on every Mason ' to make a daily advance in Masonic knowledge'. This means that it is our duty to study and learn to interpret the meaning of our symbols and allegories, for thereby we shall be better fitted to interpret the great allegory of nature.

We must not forget that in the making of Masonry many different traditions and lines of teaching have blended in the course of ages, and so it is quite possible for one man to expound one line of interpretation, and another a somewhat different one. What is more, both may be right, and all that has happened is that, for the sake of clarity, the one has concentrated on one aspect, and the other on a second. To make my meaning clear. It is possible to give a Christian interpretation to the whole of Craft Masonry, including all its symbols, and, in view of the long period of time Masonry was avowedly Christian, no one can deny the general correctness of that interpretation. But before Christianity existed systems similar to our own were known and venerated, and some of their symbolism and teaching has undoubtedly linked up with Freemasonry. It is therefore natural that a non-Christian interpretation should also exist and be just as correct.

There is one fact which must always be borne in mind when studying the meaning and origin of all customs, ritual practices and symbols and that is that, as time passes, men are apt to forget the true origin and meaning and invent new and ingenious explanations. They weave new legends round old customs, or import them from another school of belief. This tendency can be traced in Masonry in many ways. More than one meaning lies hidden in our silent emblems, and the ostensible explanation given in the ceremony is usually neither the original nor the most profound meaning attached to it.

The following extracts from *Leaves from Georgia Masonry*, published under the auspices of the Grand Lodge of Georgia relate to the general question of symbolism and speculation:

Symbolism is the key to all mysteries, to all ancient and modern religions, to all esoteric knowledge. Without an understanding of the meaning of symbols, one will never appreciate the beauty of life, or understand what his own religion is trying to teach him. But as the knowledge of the meaning of symbols comes to him, he becomes more and more a free man, or initiate.

Words are inadequate to carry or convey spiritual truths, for all the words have a material origin, and, originally, a material meaning.

Masonry, however has no monopoly of the truth, nor of the wisdom of the ancient sages; nor, indeed, could it or any other organisation truly claim a monopoly of these inestimable gifts. This wisdom and the great truths of life are concealed about us; in every man these truths are hidden in his heart, so that when he sees one of them, he is not surprised, for he seems to recognize an old acquaintance. But men cannot see these truths when they live by false standards or darken their judgment by errors or vices.

These truths are hidden in the allegories of the world, even in the fairy tales that are told to children. But men cannot hear the spiritual meaning so plain to the adept until their ears are tuned to the harmony of the spiritual; and every fault, folly, vice, or error clogs the musical strings of the soul so that it cannot respond to its true harmonic but produces discord instead.

These secrets of priceless worth are writ large on the face of the Book of Nature, that wondrous tome of many pages made and written by the Great Creator Himself, but the worthy alone are able to learn the letters.

2
THE BASIC SYMBOLISM

V ERY EARLY in his masonic experience the initiate is brought into contact with the symbolism of the Craft. In English practice, whatever meaning the initiation ceremony may have had for him, the new member cannot make any progress at all without actually *saying* that masonry is a system of morality, *veiled in allegory and illustrated by symbols*. Nor are these words merely repeated from dictation by someone else; they are among the earliest words which the candidate is expected to learn by heart. Being heard so often by those who attend masonic meetings, they remain in the mind and understanding of every mason. Again, so far as English practice is concerned, the precise words used—whatever they may be for the lodge concerned —only came into formal ritual use as part of the work settled by the Lodge of Reconciliation between 1814 and 1816 for use in lodges under the new United Grand Lodge of England. They, or similar words to the same effect, are found in masonic lectures before that time and they represent the thoughts of our predecessors included into the basic practice during the development of speculative masonry.

In present day use, 'allegory' is generally understood as 'narrative description of a subject under the guise of another suggestively similar.' This definition is that of the *Concise Oxford Dictionary*— which also gives as a meaning, 'emblem', a word almost synonymous with 'symbol'. George Savage in his *Dictionary of Antiques* (1970) goes beyond this in considering the use of the word in the seventeenth and eighteenth centuries, that is, in the period when masonic procedures were developing:

> Allegory—A subject which recalls another by reason of its analogous context. For instance, a bunch of grapes, because of the time of the year in which it is harvested, is symbolic or allegorical of Autumn. Allegorical subjects were very popular during the 17th and 18th centuries. The gods of classical mythology all had objects sacred to them. The laurel was sacred to Appollo (Helios); the vine to Bacchus (Dionysius); the lightning bolt and the eagle to Jupiter (Zeus); the lionskin and club to Hercules (Heracles); and the caduceus to Mercury (Hermes), the names in brackets being the Greek equivalents of the Roman names first given. These attributes, standing by themselves, were symbolic of

the gods who bore them. In Christian art both the lamb and the fish symbolized Jesus Christ. Groups of this kind were termed trophies. Symbolism was carried to great lengths, especially in the eighteenth century, when sets of porcelain and bronze figures represented the Seasons, Continents, Elements (Earth, Fire Air and Water), etc., the meaning of which could only be deduced from the symbols they carried. Thus, flowers represented Spring; a sheaf of corn, Summer; grapes, Autumn; and a brazier, Winter. Everyone was expected to be sufficiently well acquainted with this kind of symbolism to be able to identify the meaning.

In addition to stressing that the eighteenth century meaning of 'allegory' enables it to be classed with 'symbols' under the general consideration of symbolism, it suggests an attitude of mind towards this subject in our eighteenth century forebears who were responsible for most of the masonic development of ritual, procedures and lodge forms. That attitude of mind must be always in consideration when looking at the rise of so much of the symbolism in the Craft today.

If the ritual of the ceremonies contains any formal explanation of the intended symbolism, then that must *appear* to have some form of sanction. This particularly applies in ceremonies from former times, up to the time of the formal approval by Grand Lodge of 1816. Prior to that time, explanatory lectures represented an essential part of the ceremony, although carried out at the meal table after the short ritual ceremony. The explanations in the lectures were of the symbolism of the short previous ritual ceremony, the symbolic structure of the lodge itself, and the principles and teachings of the order. Although the present day ceremonies in the English practice do not necessarily include such lectures, there are standard lectures still in use which are directly descended from those in use in England before the union of the Grand Lodges in 1813.

It is, therefore, from a study of old ritual forms and lectures that an indication may be found of the symbolism originally put into the ceremonies and the lodge, although so far as present-day practice in England is concerned, it is as well to bear in mind the considerable change in the detail of lodge work as a result of the ceremonies and lectures having been settled afresh after the amalgamation of 1813. The two former Grand Lodges which amalgamated, the original Grand Lodge of 1717, sometimes known derisively as the 'Moderns' from the accusation that they had forsaken the ancient principles; and the Grand Lodge first organised in 1751, largely from brethren with Irish connections and known sometimes as 'Atholl' (from having successive Dukes of Atholl as Grand Masters) or 'Antients', had some differences in practices, procedures and symbolism. In the rearrangement which took place, much of this earlier symbolism was continued, from whichever side it came. Some, however, was discarded, and where there were differences in interpretation, some solution by compromise was found. Necessary adjustment to suit the new procedures sometimes resulted in quite new moral references in the ceremonies—as, for example, the inclusion of the working tools in the three degree ceremonies in the manner as at present generally given in English lodges, which dates only from 1816. Some changes slipped by without the alteration in symbolic reference being fully appreciated, giving rise to situations not completely explicable without reference to what was previously done.

The Antients Grand Lodge Work

In the decade of the 1760s a series of 'exposures' of masonic practice was published, purporting to give lodge working under this Grand Lodge. The number of editions which were published—of two, particularly—of these exposures of the 1760s over the next sixty years shows that the books were much used as aides–memoires, so that they were either fairly correct in what they published, or they had the effect of influencing lodge work because nothing of an official nature was printed. Some manuscript lecture books from a little later in that century which are based on the same system as that given in the exposures have survived. These give more information and a good deal more about the underlying symbolism. The lecture forms used by this Grand Lodge appear to have been fairly simple and straightforward in construction. In the first and second degrees, a first part or section went through a direct description of the ceremony; this was followed by a second section, (sometimes more) normally termed 'the reasons', which explained from a symbolic angle why the particular parts of the ceremony were conducted in that manner. There was also some expansion of explanation on the lodge itself and on other aspects.

It is worth noting that the four figures on the coat of arms adopted by the Antients Grand Lodge—a man, a lion, an ox and an eagle were the old Church symbols for ss Matthew, Mark, Luke and John.

The Work of the Moderns

One of the exposures of the 1760s claimed also to give the work of this other Grand Lodge, although there appeared from this to be no difference between them. It is probable that they *were* different in a number of respects—in fact the importance of these exposures probably lies in their influence in use as 'ritual books' in later years, rather than in what they appear to portray as the work of 1760-62. A few Lodges may have worked in this way, but, as A. C. F. Jackson says in his paper on these exposures in *Ars Quatuor Coronatorum*, volume 84, there was probably no standard form at that time. In 1770, Thomas Dunckerley is believed to have been commissioned by Grand Lodge to produce a standard system of work for the Moderns Lodges; it appears clear that he did produce a system, because of occasional reference to one by his name, but there is no direct evidence as to what it was or that it was taken into exclusive use. However, in the 1790s there is some detailed evidence as to how some Moderns Lodges were working, and, as there are several manuscripts and prints on much the same basis, this was probably the most accepted system under the Moderns Grand Lodge. The fullest printed book was *A Master Key*, by John Browne, in the form of a series of lectures in cypher, the key to which was obtainable from the publisher subject to suitable safeguards. The lectures contained a description of the ceremonies of the three degrees, with explanations of the meaning of the various ritual acts as the description progressed, and with the symbolism of the lodge itself and the moral principles of masonry. In addition, Browne gave separately a fairly full ritual procedure for the ceremonies. William Finch published *A Masonic Key* in 1801 (with many later editions under other names); the basis of this was similar to Browne's, although even from the first edition the lectures were differently arranged. Finch incorporated a good deal of his own and others' speculative thought, particularly in the later editions which are, in places, quite different. While every lodge did not work in exactly the same way, even by 1800, the systems were probably based on the same procedures and used the same *basic* symbolism, often borrowing from each other.

William Preston

William Preston produced a lecture in the first degree which was demonstrated in the presence of the Grand Master of the Moderns Grand Lodge at a gala in 1772. This was followed by the publication of his book, *Illustrations of Masonry*, and by the development of lectures for the other two degrees. The *Illustrations* went through a number of editions, the last before Preston's death being the twelfth in 1812. Preston was a great speculative mason as the constant variations and additions to successive issues of his book show. The *Illustrations* did not contain the actual text of Preston's lectures or even the whole content of them. The questions of his first and second lectures were first printed in 1790 and 1792, respectively, and then in cryptic form; the answers, which provide the substance of the teaching, were not printed and are found separately in manuscript form. Although in his later years Preston operated under the Moderns Grand Lodge, he claims to have selected the best from any source, old or new, and he undoubtedly took material from sources connected with the other Grand Lodge while he was also influenced by, and probably involved in, the mystical studies fashionable at the time. As a consequence his lectures represent a different system from either of the others and, because of the way he thought and collected, there is much of value in his work so far as the symbolism of masonry in those early days is concerned.

These are the sources from which may be derived ideas on the original symbols incorporated into masonic systems, and these are the sources meant when it is stated later that such an explanation is to be found in the old lectures. This does not mean even then that this was necessarily the original source, but merely that it had at some time been incorporated. Much that later became accepted parts of lecture systems can be traced to earlier writers, of whom John Ladd, William Preston and Wellins Calcott (who was a past master of the Lodge of Regularity, now No 91) have already been mentioned. *The Spirit of Masonry*, published in 1775 and the work of William Hutchinson, also provided inspiration for much that is included. Hutchinson was a well known writer and historian in the north-east of England and was a past master of the Lodge of Concord at Barnard Castle. Although he has no proved connection with the Craft, some of John Milton's passages may be found in the lectures, even to this day, although this is likely to be from the beauty of his writing and has no connection with masonic symbolism.

The Early Catechisms and Exposures

Masonic symbolism did not *start* in the later years of the eighteenth century, it merely developed and blossomed in that period to a point where it becomes recognisable as a system with some degree of completeness. All the time that there has been speculative masonry, symbolism has existed in it and probably also in certain aspects of the operative Craft. There are masonic catechisms—the forerunners of the lectures—traceable back to the seventeenth century. Many of these may be found collected together for easy reference in *The Early Masonic Catechisms* by Knoop, Jones and Hamer (with a second, revised and enlarged edition [1963] by Harry Carr.) *The Edinburgh Register House Manuscript* of 1696, *The Chetwode Crawley Manuscript* of about 1700 and *The Kevan Manuscript* of about 1714-20, all of which are very similar, contain references to the numbers of masons in a lodge, the situation of a lodge, jewels, lights, and points of fellowship, all in a manner which shows the practice recorded in them to be the source from which the lectures later developed. There is not nearly so much detailed explanation found in these manuscripts as is found in those of a date later in the eighteenth century. *The Sloane Manuscript* of about 1700, *The Trinity College Dublin, Manuscript* of 1711, and, particularly, the *Dumfries No. 4 Manuscript* of about 1710, all have more or less the same thing, although not necessarily in the same way. The Dumfries document, which is undoubtedly of Scottish origin, has several differences from the others, incorporating the seven liberal sciences, the three great lights as English practice now knows them and differently from that shown in the 1720s and 1730s, and the names of the pillars, as well as several others. This may merely emphasise that there was a deal of local development quite early in the rise of speculative masonry.

From the 1720s there were a number of 'exposures' of various sorts, and answers to them. Prichard's *Masonry Dissected* of 1730 was the last detailed exposure for some time to be put out in England, and, from the number of editions published, must have been used as a handbook in English masonry for over thirty years. Compared with the exposures of the 1760s these earlier pamphlets appear very incomplete, but again there is sufficient to show that what happened in the later period was development of what had existed earlier and that much of the *basis* of the later rich symbolism was already there in use, although not so fully explained or justified.

The Mysteries of Ancient Civilisations

When the free and accepted form of masonry began to have a separate existence from the operative craft, it used symbols and emblems to remind the members about the underlying moral and spiritual principles of the society. In the period of this development, as has already been shown, the general use of symbols would have been common practice and everyday use, and so its incorporation into any thoughtful institution, such as that of speculative masons, would not have been extraordinary. There have been in the past—

and in the distant past and in different parts of the world—moral systems, nowadays generally referred to as 'the Mysteries', which, on examination, appear to have characteristics similar to those of freemasonry and to have made use of symbols in their operation. Dr James Anderson, who compiled the *Books of Constitutions* of the Grand Lodge of England published in 1723 and 1738, included a fanciful record of continuous masonic succession going back to the oldest of these Mysteries. Anderson's story was taken up by later writers so that this direct descent may well have been generally believed among average masons. Certainly there is clear proof that the masons of the eighteenth century had made considerable study of the Mysteries of ancient times and may well have been influenced by them, or have copied from them in the type of symbols incorporated, in the development of speculative masonry. One of the instances from which such proof can be drawn was in the address given by George Downing on his installation as Provincial Grand Master for Essex on 15 May 1797:

> The most famous mysteries on record are those in Persia, which are celebrated in honour of the God Mythra, and those at Eleusis, in Greece, in honour of the Goddess Ceres.
> Many arguments might be adduced to prove that both these were corruptions of Freemasonry, and hereafter I shall not want the inclination, if I do not want the opportunity to discuss them. At present, however, I shall content myself with pointing out the similarity which subsists between the initiatory rites practised by the professors of those mysteries and by our Brethren, both ancient and modern; more especially in the allegorical part of their ceremonials.

George Downing was a lawyer, a conveyancer, by profession and probably dabbled a little in what we should now call masonic research. He was particularly friendly with Rev Thomas Maurice, who in 1798 became Assistant Keeper of the Manuscripts in the British Museum and published several works, specialising in the history and religions of the East. Even in more recent times, Joseph Fort Newton, in *The Builders*, has raised again the question of continuous history and endeavoured to show new evidence and a new bridge, but, although from a speculative aspect his is a wonderful book, there is still no real proof to show that there is any direct historical connection between modern speculative masonry and the old Mysteries.

W. L. Wilmshurst in *The Meaning of Masonry* (1922) had a good deal to say about the Mysteries of the ancient civilisations:

In all periods of the world's history, and in every part of the globe, secret orders and societies have existed outside the limits of the official churches for the purpose of teaching what are called 'the Mysteries': for imparting to suitable and prepared minds certain truths of human life, certain instructions about divine things, about the things that belong to our peace, about human nature and human destiny, which it was undesirable to publish to the multitude who would but profane those teachings and apply the esoteric knowledge that was communicated to perverse and perhaps to disastrous ends.

. . . . It is, of course, common knowledge that great secret systems of the Mysteries (referred to in our lectures as 'noble orders of architecture', i.e., of soul building) existed in the East, in Chaldea, Assyria, Egypt, Greece, Italy, amongst the Hebrews, amongst Mohammedans and amongst Christians, . . . [and] among African races they are to be found. All the great teachers of humanity, Socrates, Plato, Pythagoras, Moses, Aristotle, Virgil, the author of the Homeric poems, and the great Greek tragedians, along with St John, St Paul and innumerable other great names—were initiates of the Sacred Mysteries. The *form* of the teaching communicated has varied considerably from age to age; it has been expressed under different veils, but since the ultimate truth the Mysteries aim at teaching is always one and the same, there has always been taught, and can only be taught, one and the same doctrine. What that doctrine was, and still is, we will consider presently so far as we are able to speak of it, and so far as Masonry gives expression to it. For the moment let me merely say that behind all the official religious systems of the world, and behind all the great moral movements and developments in the history of humanity, have stood what St Paul called the keepers or 'stewards of the Mysteries'. . . . .

All that I wish to emphasize at this stage is that our present system is *not* one coming from remote antiquity: there is no direct continuity between us and the Egyptians, or even those ancient Hebrews who built, in the reign of King Solomon, a certain Temple at Jerusalem. What *is* extremely ancient in Freemasonry is the spiritual doctrine concealed within the architectural phraseology; for this doctrine is an elementary form of the doctrine that has been taught in all ages, no matter in what garb it has been expressed. Our own teaching, for instance, recognizes[1] Pythagoras as having undergone numerous initiations in different parts of the world, and as having attained great eminence in the science. Now it is perfectly certain that Pythagoras was not a Mason at all in our present sense of the word; but it is also perfectly certain that Pythagoras was a very highly advanced master in the knowledge of the secret schools of the Mysteries, of whose doctrine some small portion is enshrined for us in our Masonic system.

---

[1] *Wilmshurst's use of 'recognizes' probably gives an erroneous idea: our teachings may be based on such a theory but I doubt if there is any positive influence.*

In his preface to the 1784 *Constitutions* of the Moderns Grand Lodge, which he edited, John Noorthouck wrote:

..... speculative masonry, of which the practical art is only considered as the substratum. The history of operative masonry is therefore meerly (*sic*) introductory to that of free-masonry; but claims the greater regard, as the first elements of the latter are borrowed from it. So long then as the two professions remained united in the same persons, and until the records of the latter become distinguished; stone and mortar appear the most conspicuous objects in the foreground of the picture. But when speculative masons became a separate correlative body of men, we then have no farther concern with practical masonry, than the reference that free-masonry has to the art on which it is founded.

Free and accepted masonry was certainly in existence at the beginning of the eighteenth century (and certainly existed earlier) and its main tenets were clear, but its symbols and detailed practices were few and rough, with some different local ideas in different places. At the end of the eighteenth century there was a complete system (probably still with some differences in different places) of three Craft degrees in detail, along with supporting lectures explaining the aims and symbolism of the craft. Although it has no part in this book, there were also in existence, and active, a system of a number of additional masonic degrees, in most cases practised in the Craft lodges themselves or associated with them. This whole development of the basic principles of a hundred years earlier had taken place during an Age of Reason, when those who practised free masonry and who must have activated this development have shown that they were aware of the old Mysteries and their practices in some detail and were prepared to claim direct descent from them. Without, perhaps, more than a mere mention of the direct historical descent, many writers have made direct comparison with the old Mysteries of the systems of the free and accepted masons, for somehow, from the comparatively rude speculative state of 1700, the fuller system developed by 1800 had much more of the old Mysteries in it.

There must be more than a possibility that the knowledge of these old Mysteries provided source material which was put into this development. In the pamphlet of 1730, *A Defence of Masonry*, which has been referred to earlier, there is reference to the Mysteries:

I could not avoid immediately thinking of the old Egyptians, who concealed the chief Mysteries of their Religion under Signs and Symbols, called Hieroglyphicks. And so great was their Regard for Silence and Secrecy, that they had a Deity called Harpocrates, whom they respected with peculiar Honour and Veneration. A learned Author has given a Description of this Idol: Harpocrates, the God of Silence, was formed with his Right-hand placed near the Heart, cover'd with a Skin before, full of Eyes and Ears, to signify by this, that many things are to be seen and heard, but little to be spoken. Among the same People, their great Goddess Isis . . . . . . had always the Image of a Sphinx placed in the Entrance of her Temples, that their Secrets should be preserved under sacred Coverings, that they might be kept from the Knowledge of the Vulgar as much as the Riddles of Sphinx.

Pythagoras, by travelling into Egypt became instructed in the Mysteries of that Nation, and here he laid the Foundation of all his symbolical Learning. The several Writers that have mentioned this Philosopher, and given an Account of his Sect and Institutions, have convinced me fully, that Free-Masonry, as published by the Dissector, is very nearly allied to the old Pythagorean Discipline; from whence I am persuaded it may in some Circumstances very justly claim its Descent. To mention a few.

Upon the Admission of a Disciple, he was bound by a solemn Oath to conceal the Mysteries from the Vulgar and Un-initiated.

The principal and most efficacious of their Doctrines were (says Jamblichus) ever kept secret among themselves; they were continued unwritten, and preserved only by memory to their Successors, to whom they delivered them as Mysteries of the Gods.

They conversed with one another by Signs, and they had particular Words which they received upon their Admission, and which were preserved with great Reverence as the distinction of their Sect: For (it is the judicious Remark of Laertius) as Generals use Watch-Words to distinguish their own Soldiers from others, so it is proper to communicate to the Initiated peculiar Signs and Words as distinctive Marks of a Society.

The Pythagoreans professed a great Regard for what the Dissector calls the four Principles of Masonry, a Point, a Line, a Superficies, and a Solid; and particularly held that a Square was a very proper Emblem of the Divine Essence. The Gods, they say, who are the Authors of every thing established in Wisdom, Strength and Beauty, are not improperly represented by the Figure of a Square.

Many more Instances might be produced, would the Limits of my Design admit; I shall only observe, that there was a false Brother, one Hipparchus, of this Sect, who, out of Spleen and Disappointment, broke through the Bond of his Oath, and committed the Secrets of the Society to Writing, in order to bring the Doctrine into contempt. He was immediately expelled the School as a Person most infamous and abandoned, as one dead to all Sense of Virtue and Goodness; and the Pythagoreans, according to their Custom, made a Tomb for him as if he had been actually dead. The Shame and Disgrace that justly attended this Violation of his Oath threw the poor Wretch into a Fit of Madness and Despair, so that he cut his Throat, and perished by his own Hands; and (which surprized me to find) his memory was so abhorred after Death, that his body lay upon the Shore of the Island of Samos, and had no other Burial than in the Sands of the Sea.

The Essenes among the Jews were a sort of Pythagoreans, and corresponded in many Particulars with the Practice of the Fraternity, as delivered in the Dissection. For example: When a Person desired to be admitted into their Society, he was to pass through two Degrees of Probation before he could be perfect Master of their Mysteries. When he was received into the Class of Novices, he was presented with a white Garment; and when he had been long enough to give some competent Proofs of his Secrecy and Virtue, he was admitted to further Knowledge; but he still went on with the Trial of his Integrity and Good Manners, and then was fully taken into the Society. But before he was receiv'd as an establish'd Member, he was first to bind himself by solemn Obligations and Professions, to do Justice, to do no Wrong, to keep Faith with all Men, to embrace the Truth, to keep his Hands clear from Theft and fraudulent Dealing, not to conceal from his Fellow-Professors any of the Mysteries, nor communicate any of them to the Profane, though it should be to save his Life; to deliver nothing but what he received, and endeavour to preserve the Principle that he professes. They eat and drink at the same common Table, and the Fraternity that come from any other Place are sure to be received there; they meet together in an Assembly, the Right-hand is laid upon the Part between the Chin and the Breast, and the Left-hand let down straight by their Side.

The Cabalists, another Sect, dealt in hidden and mysterious Ceremonies. The Jews had a great Regard for this Science, and thought they made uncommon Discoveries by means of it. They divided their Knowledge into Speculative and Operative. David and Solomon, they say, were exquisitely skilled in it, and no body at first presumed to commit it to Writing; but, what seems most to the present Purpose, the Perfection of their Skill consisted in what the Dissector calls Lettering of it, or by ordering the Letters of a Word in a particular manner.

The last instance I shall mention, is that of the Druids in our own Nation. They were the only Priests among the ancient Britons. In their Solemnities they were clothed in White, and their Ceremonies always ended with a good Feast. Pomponius Mela relates of them, that their Science was only an Effort of Memory, for they wrote down nothing, and they never fail'd to repeat many Verses which they received by Tradition. Cæsar observes, that they had a Head, who had sovereign Power: This President exercised a sort of Excommunication, attended with dreadful penalties upon such as either divulged or profaned their Mysteries.

The passage is reproduced without the italics in which many words, possibly for emphasis, appear in the original, and without the reference notes. I have also omitted the original latin of the two passages which the author put in, and have included only the translation. The only claim to descent in this passage, taken from Chapter III of the pamphlet, is from the system of Pythagoras. The Dissector referred to is Samuel Pritchard, the author of *Masonry Dissected*, to which this pamphlet was a reply. The pamphlet seems to accept what Pritchard says and to attempt to justify such a system by showing that such practices were common in the ancient Mysteries, on which the author of the pamphlet was uncommonly well read. In the original pamphlet he indicates the classical authors that he quotes, by direct mention, and also, in the separate notes, his sources. In addition, he includes mentions of then current works of reference. That this depth of study was undertaken by some of those involved in the masonry of those times may well indicate, not merely justification, but actual influence of the old Mysteries on the development of masonry which was taking place. The pamphlet was reproduced in the 1738 edition of Dr Anderson's *Constitutions* and that is, no doubt, the source which many later writers used and from which they developed ideas contained in it. William Preston (born 1742, initiated 1763, died 1818) used the Egyptian reference, in part, word for word, and based some of his historical references to the Druids on their mention in the pamphlet. Rev George Oliver (born 1782, initiated about 1803, died 1867) also takes up the Egyptian and Druidical themes and develops them in several of his books.

It was not just to the author of the 1730 pamphlet that the old Mysteries were known. The masonic writers of the last part of the eighteenth century included much of a moral and esoteric nature which actually became incorporated in the ceremonies as they were practised at the end of the century. These authors showed a similar depth of knowledge, very often referring to points other than those contained in the pamphlet. William Hutchinson's *Spirit of Masonry* contains the following:

.... we find those sages and select men, to whom were committed, and who retained, the light of understanding and truth, unpolluted with the sins of the world, under the denomination of magi among the Persians; wisemen, southsayers, and astrologers among the Caldeans; philosophers among the Greeks and Romans; bramins among the Indians; druids and bards among the Britons; and with the chosen people of God SOLOMON shone forth in the fulness of human wisdom.

Jewish Influence

In the references to the old Mysteries quoted from the pamphlet *A Defence of Masonry*, it is probable that those to the Essenes and Cabalists are the most significant. These were both Jewish sects whose practices were well documented. Dr Anderson in his *Constitutions* of 1723 spends a great deal of space on Jewish history and especially on the building of King Solomon's Temple, which was almost the central theme of Anderson's masonry. It is not surprising that the practices of Jewish sects, which had moral aims thought to be similar to those of masonry, might influence masonic development. Nor was Anderson the only mason in the century following to show interest in Jewish matters and the Hebrew language. Two, especially, spring to mind—Laurence Dermott, for many years Grand Secretary of the Antients Grand Lodge, and the Duke of Sussex, first Grand Master of the United Grand Lodge. Dermott became a major influence in the Antients Grand Lodge very soon after its inception in 1751 and was one of its officers for over forty years. He had some acquaintance with the Hebrew tongue and called the Constitutions of his Grand Lodge by a Hebrew name—*Ahimon Rezon*—although no-one now seems very certain of what he meant to convey. The Duke of Sussex was a very religious man and a considerable student of Hebrew; the catalogues of his library when sold after his death show a great number of books relating to Jewish history, many of them manuscripts in Hebrew and some on the subject of the Cabala.

The periodical resurgence of questions relating to the Jews in Britain during the seventeenth and eighteenth centuries may have contributed to an interest in their history. It was the year 1656 that saw the resettlement of the Jews in this country. Even then they were regarded as aliens, but a proposal regarding the naturalisation of Jews in 1753 caused another upsurge of interest which continued until the turn of the century. *A Defence of Masonry* mentions *Antiquities of the Jews* by Flavius Josephus; there had been editions in English of this work in 1655 and 1670, while another was published in 1737 and re-issued about 1800. That there was other reference to Josephus's work in the later years of the century is shown by at least three of the 'additional' degrees which arose at that time having their ritual story based on incidents in his book.

The details of the practices of the Essenes mentioned in *A Defence of Masonry* give food for thought on their quotation at least as justification for masonic practice. A communal and convivial meal after formal work and the welcoming of visitors are points of similarity; the summary of principles expressed is also relevant along with the wearing of a white garment by the novice. The most interesting reference, particularly in view of the date of the pamphlet, 1730, is to the new member having to pass through two degrees of probation before becoming a perfect master of their Mysteries—that is, a system of three degrees. Early references which can be interpreted as giving grades or degrees in masonry in England indicate a system of two degrees only. It is not until the middle of the 1720s that reference to a system of three degrees is found. This is hardly five years before the date of the pamphlet, while in addition, there is stress on the nature of the third degree from this time on which indicates a greater similarity to the system of the Essenes. If the influence or justification seen in the practices of the Jewish Essenes was as great as was shown in the 1730 pamphlet, it is possible that it may have influenced the change from two degrees to three in the English System.

The Cabala (or Kabbala) with which the Cabalists were associated is a traditional aspect of Jewish religion and has a tendency towards mysticism. Towards the end of the eighteenth century a distinct tendency towards mysticism may be seen in some areas of English masonry. From the interest shown in things Jewish at that time, and from the references available, some influence from the Cabala seems probable. Although his writings do not provide the original source from which I make this suggestion, Dr William Wynn Westcott in a paper to Quatuor Coronati Lodge in 1887 (*Ars Quatuor Coronatorum*, Vol. 1) also put forward this proposition, although he goes very much further. He was regarded by his associates as an extreme and a mystic so far as his views on symbolism are concerned. Although also attributed to Pythagoras, the essential passing on of secrets by oral process and a ban on commiting them to print or writing was one of the Cabalistic points which is parallelled in the masonry of the period. The Duke of Sussex showed himself at the time of the Union of the two old Grand Lodges to have this principle very much in mind, and adherence to it has prevented any formal record of what was decided on as standard ritual practice after the Union. For over fifty years this principle was very strictly followed by those in authority in the United Grand Lodge, and, although relaxed in the 1870s merely by failure to proceed against those offending, it was not until after 1945 that more liberal views appeared to prevail.

The Cabala had a tradition of reserving certain knowledge to such persons as could be shown to be wise, in the same way as, with the Essenes and eighteenth century masonry, the third degree contained the root of the Mystery. One of the outstanding aspects of Cabala which may have found a reflection in this development of masonry is in the reading of meaning into numbers; this is examined later in this chapter. An examination of William Preston's second lecture shows unmistakable signs of cabalistic influence and he attempts to show special significance in certain numbers. In writing of this lecture, Percy James, who was something of an authority on Preston's lectures, says in a paper included in *Ars Quatuor Coronatorum*, Vol. 83:

> . . . . . the Second Lecture traces the new Fellowcraft's course to the Middle Chamber in a series of discussions upon factual matters which become more and more technical, abstract and mystical. It is based on a metaphysical notion of King Solmon's Temple, which is looked upon as a sort of Masonic university, with excursions into Platonic Theory and Cabalism. In places it is difficult to understand; more often it is hard to see what it has to do with Speculative Masonry. At times, it must be confessed, it becomes pure nonsense.

Preston spent the years from 1772, when his first lecture was first given, until, probably, the turn of the century in actually compiling his lectures—his first syllabuses for both the first and second lectures were published about 1796-97. This is the period in which I believe that this concept of mysticism, of which the Cabala is an example, most influenced English masonic development, and if it affected one of the calibre of William Preston, some of its influence may have had a lasting effect.

Development

W. L. Wilmshurst, writing in the twentieth century, speaks of the great moral movements which periodically arise in world history and classes masonry, in its speculative nature, as one of them. He says that these movements, throughout history, tend to exist outside of formal religion. Lest it should be suggested that masonry has at any time been a religion in itself or a substitute for formal religion, it should immediately be stated emphatically that this is not so. The very tenets of masonry require a member of the Craft to be a religious man in the sense of holding some religious belief. During the time when the guild system was in full swing and when free and accepted masonry was developing in the British Isles, that religion represented automatically the Christian faith, and, so far as the English guilds were concerned in the years after the Reformation, that faith according to the tenets of the Church of England as that was the established Church. So in guild histories there are many references to religious connection, to the patronage of a particular saint, and certainly to formal attendance at regular church services. The Acception too developed with an automatic link with the Church so far as the individual members were concerned, and when moral teaching or spiritualising was concerned, it was in terms of the highest principles of the Christian faith. This regarded the Holy Bible as its Sacred Writings, and not only the New Testament which dealt with the foundation of that faith, but also the Old Testament which included the Sacred Writings of the Jewish religion and a great deal of the history of the Hebrew people.

If, by requiring the previous fulfilling of certain qualifications and conditions, societies seek to be selective in those they admit to membership, they must introduce means of showing existing members that the qualifications and conditions are fulfilled with respect to proposed new members. If membership involves the knowledge of certain protective secrets restricted to members, there must be some means, and preferably some formal means, of making the communication to new members and of ensuring that they are completely understood. In addition, there is a duty to ensure that such secrets restricted to a group in membership, in fact remain secret; this may best be done by requiring some formal binding promise from those to whom the communication is made. Where, as in the case of the developing free and accepted masonry, the society wished to accentuate certain teachings, tenets and principles for the better conduct of life, what better than that they should consider the moral application of aspects of the workaday world and use the principles of the trade with which they were associated, that of building, to illustrate and instruct in the building of a good life. Where a particular religion was second nature to all the members and a closer knowledge of the Bible not just a desirable, but considered a necessary, attribute of the good man, it was natural that if further inspiration and illustration were required, they should be taken from the Bible or from the well known tenets of the common religion. If there were to be several grades of membership, separate initiation into the secrets of each would be necessary.

This was how freemasonry developed, but all this did not happen overnight; it probably took well over a century. Douglas Knoop and G. P. Jones, who have made a special study of the earlier aspects of masonry, gave as their opinion in *The Genesis of Freemasonry* (1949):

It was almost certainly not until the second half of the eighteenth century that Freemasonry had become so modified in character that it could justly be defined as a peculiar system of morality, veiled in allegory and illustrated by symbols.

From masonic records in the latter half of the eighteenth century, it is clear that there were general standards with regard to the principles, practices and teachings of masonry by that time. The need to meet together for ceremonies, business and instruction gave rise to some standard forms of lodge layout. All were not identical, as records show, and although the main business and instruction was carried out at the dining table, the ceremonies were carried out where possible in another room as this excerpt from the minutes of Old Kings Arms Lodge in 1801 shows:

> ... it shall be incumbent for every member to continue in the Lodge Room until the Steward for the time being shall have announced to the Worshipful Master that the Supper Room is arranged for his and the Brethren's Reception.

Some thought had to be given to the use of uniform dress or badge, both for the indication of membership itself, and of the grade; in the case of the badge, the old connection with an operative trade seemed readily to have provided an answer. In the same way, the application of a moral principle through the medium of an aspect of that trade meant the use of the materials and implements of the trade. In time the implements would come to represent the principle and it was an easy progress to look for other illustrations to remind the younger members of the tenets of the craft—hence the use of the beehive as a constant inspiration to industry and of the serpent to represent the attribute of wisdom, so much to be desired.

The eighteenth century was a period of enlightenment when philosophy was in vogue through Europe and was aptly named the Age of Reason. Masonry does not live in a vacuum, it is influenced by and is a part of the world scene in every age, and, as a philosophical movement, it is not surprising that it rose and developed to such an extent during this particular time in history.

In his Prestonian Lecture for 1969 which he called *External Influences on the Evolution of English Masonry*, J. R. Clarke emphasises 'the inevitably great influence of contemporaneous thought and events on its evolution'. In commenting on this lecture, Alex Horne wrote about this development period:

First we note the general interest in architecture and antiquities, which somehow tied the one to the other; and which gave the young man on his Grand Tour an intimate contact with European architecture especially the ecclesiastical, and perhaps some insight into its symbolical character, with its moral, religious, and philosophical implications. Then we note the birth, or perhaps only the prominent development, of a literature devoted to religious, mystical and occult thought—mostly of an allegorical character, Kabbalistic, Rosicrucian, Alchemical, Hermetic; influences emanating from the Gnostic and Neo-Platonic periods, and religious thinking from the 'heretical' schools. And there was the purely intellectual and scientific influence of the Royal Society, and the philosophical writings of Hobbs, Hume, Locke and Francis Bacon. All this must have caused a ferment of thought and inspiration from which the newly-aborning Speculative spirit could not have insulated itself, had it tried to do so.

The last twenty or thirty years of the eighteenth century were noted for the rise of interest in mythology, the occult, and kindred subjects, and for some extremes in the study of alchemy and the propogation of theories in this whole field. From the point of view of influence on Masonry the most important of these was undoubtedly Swedenborgianism, a new form of Christian religion developed from the teachings of Emanuel Swedenborg (1688-1772). Writing of the man himself in *The Swedenborg Rite* (1870), Samuel Beswick says:

... he was obedient in heart and soul to the call, and preferred those spiritual associations which he claims were opened to him in the year of his call, 1745. In that year he claims to have had a divine call to become the Herald of a New Dispensation of goodness and truth to mankind; and to have had his spiritual sight opened, so as to be able to see and openly converse with the spirits of departed persons; and to have had his mind enlightened so as to see rationally all the great facts and laws of the unseen world, and that inner and divine sense within the literal rendering of the Scriptures, which essentially constitutes Divine Revelation.

It was not the rise of this sect itself which affected Masonry; the Masonry of the day was religiously based and those who embraced the teachings of Swedenborg attempted to influence the religious aspect of their Lodges so as to reflect the beliefs of the sect. A branch of the sect was established in London in 1788. Another way in which Masonry was affected was by a multiplication of rites based on Swedenborgian ideas, particularly on the continent, and the involvement of such people as Cagliostro, Mesmer, St Martin and many others, some of whom brought continental masonry into disrepute. The whole of the Swedenborgian teaching is based on symbolism, as this note, again by Samuel Beswick, indicates:

It proposes to teach the symbolism of nature as a science, by presenting the most suitable symbols to the eye and senses in the most attractive forms and combinations. There is a strict correspondence between the varied forms and phenomena of nature in the material world, and the varied forms, powers, forces and phenomena of mind—which correspondence cannot be seen, understood and taught, without a scientific and systematic knowledge of the symbol and the thing symbolized, between the predicates of which there is a correspondence. The Rite assumes that the science of correspondence is a key by which we can at any time unlock the secret and hidden forces of nature, 'the invisible things of creation may be understood by the things that are made.' And because it applies to every department of nature, it is not inaptly designated the 'science of sciences.' This is the corner-stone of every system of Freemasonry: exclude it and you destroy symbolic teaching. The symbolism of Freemasonry has never yet been studied as a science; and certainly it has never been taught as a science. The idea of dealing with symbolism as a science had no existence in the minds of those who revised the monitorial lectures and work in 1717.

The Rite to which Beswick refers is the Swedenborgian Rite using the same structure and principals as regular masonry but including additional degrees. The latter part is a statement of opinion based on an unproved and unprovable assumption that speculative masonry in a number of different orders and additional degrees existed very widely in Europe in the seventeenth century, but the promulgation of these beliefs among those who had influence in English lodges of the time must have had an effect.

G. P. G. Hills wrote a paper on '*Notes on Some Masonic Personalities at the End of the Eighteenth Century*' which is included in *Ars Quatuor Coronatorum*, Vol. 25, and states that the objects of masonry at that time were confused by the introduction of these matters. In commenting on this paper in the same volume, E. H. Dring writes:

There were from 1780 to 1795 a large number of books published on Mythology and kindred subjects . . . . The references to the Eleusinian Mysteries were no doubt instigated by the appearance of Taylor's well known book, *The Eleusinian Mysteries*, published about 1793-4, and that no doubt gave rise to this allusion or suggestion of tracing Freemasonry to these Mysteries. It is not the first time that theory has been suggested, by many dozens of times. It is still one of the most popular suggestions of people who have not the slightest knowledge of classical mythology or Oriental legends, but try to trace the origin of Freemasonry to the Eleusinian rites.

At that time there were also a number of continental societies of a quasi-masonic nature which dealt in these matters; they attracted a masonic membership from this country. Hills goes into this aspect in his paper by a slight examination of the papers of General Rainsford, which are in the British Museum, and he shows that among the interested Englishmen was James Heseltine. Heseltine was Grand Secretary of the Moderns Grand Lodge, 1769-83, Senior Grand Warden in 1785 and Grand Treasurer 1785-1804. He was also friendly with William Preston and when the latter started the Order of Harodim in the late 1780s, for the purpose of working the lecture system associated with his name, Heseltine was associated with the venture from its early days. He is listed among the 1791 officers as one of two Vice Patrons. Preston's lectures in the second and third degrees reflect very much this influence of his times. There can be little doubt that these studies had some influence on the development of masonry at that time, although the purging influence of the reforms after the union of Grand Lodges in 1813 may have got rid of the most offensive introductions.

Many great works of reference to satisfy the enquiring mind were first published in this period and were undoubtedly read and noticed by those developing and speculating on the principles of freemasonry. Dr Johnson's *Dictionary* was first published in 1751; Alexander Cruden's *Complete Concordance of the Old and New Testaments*, after a first edition in 1737, was published in two further editions in 1761 and 1769; the *Encyclopaedia Britannica* first appeared—in three volumes—in 1768 to 1771, with a second edition in ten volumes between 1777 and 1784 and an even larger third edition between 1788 and 1797. At the opening of this century, Newton and Wren were at work, to be followed by Hawksmoor and Vanbrugh, the Adam brothers, Chippendale and Sheraton, Reynolds and Gainsborough, Pope, Goldsmith, Dr Johnson, Sheridan, Wordsworth and many others in England. Masonry could not be neglected in development as a philosophy in times such as these, but it is in the second half of the century, particularly, that saw the publication of many works on masonry of a speculative character. These were very probably the culmination of work over twenty to thirty years and at the same time they reflected the thoughts and practices of speculative masons unknown, of the 1730 to 1760 era; several of the writers concerned refer to both these points. Development of any sort was rapid in this atmosphere, the climate was right, the men were there, along with the material—much of it in the form of greater knowledge through the works published during that time.

The free and accepted masonry of the earlier 1700s had been exported to France where it had been independently developed with the aid of the inventive characteristics of the Gallic race and some of these new forms had been re-imported at different stages later in the century. Masonry had been centrally organised in Ireland under a Grand Lodge there from the 1720s; events of the 1740s brought many Irish immigrants to England, and particularly to the London area. Those who were masons in Ireland brought their masonry with them, along with any small developments which had taken place in twenty years and more in Irish masonry of a speculative nature. Certain deliberate changes had been made in the original English procedures, so that many of the Irish immigrants felt that they could not join with lodges under the original English Grand Lodge, and so in the 1750s they formed a second Grand Lodge in England.

All of these things had their influence on the development of English masonry; development in other countries was often very different especially in the Netherlands, Scandinavia, Germany and France, although in places politically dependent on Great Britain, the lead tended to be taken from one or other of the home Grand Lodges. The tendency in England was for a standard short ceremony followed by standard forms of instruction by means of lecture—for the majority seemed to prefer to teach from the works of those who taught well rather than use their own words to explain something which they might not, in any case, be too sure about. There was much latitude on precisely what was taught and in what words, but it was quite common, until well on in the nineteenth century, for the work of an established writer to become part of the teaching used in lodges.

Justification

There is evidence in practically all manuscripts relating to the ceremonies of the late 1700s, including the instructional lectures used after the formal ritual ceremony, that certain Scripture texts were particularly associated with the ceremonies. The texts always had some relationship with part of the ceremony against which they were listed, but vary slightly from document to document. They appear to

have been set down as a sort of Scriptural justification for the particular part of the ceremony and it appears likely that they were
actually intended to be read in the lodge immediately before a ritual
act. In certain other aspects of masonry in the present day something
of the same sort is often found, and the recitals of the Chaplain in the
ceremony of consecration of a new lodge come to mind as one
example, although there are others in some additional degrees. In
some Craft lodges which have retained parts of an old working, there
is often a tradition for Scripture readings or chantings to be given
during perambulations or before ceremonial actions. That is not to
say that in all instances where formal singing or music is incorporated
as part of a lodge ceremony that this relates to an ancient practice;
it is well known that in a number of cases such practices came about
during a period of innovation long after the time to which reference
has been made.

Dr Oliver, when writing on the question of masonic symbols
generally, goes into this question of the number of instances found in
the Old Testament of the use of signs and symbols—and not just by
men, but by God Himself giving symbolic signs to man. He instances
'the tree of Life; Jacob's Vision; the manna; the brazen serpent; the
scape goat; the Sun of righteousness' among others and points out
that these 'are symbols of a nature too plain and unequivocal to be
mistaken.' It is not only in justification that Scripture references are
found in a masonic context, the use of Bible stories for the illustration
of moral and procedural points also became an essential part of
speculative masonry.

Of the Scriptural texts found in the old manuscripts, those which
relate to the use of the badge are almost the most numerous. First is
the justification found in *Genesis*, Chapter 3, v 7, 'and they sewed fig
leaves together and made themselves aprons.' In case fig leaves
might not have been thought suitable masonic adornment, another
material is found to be suitable in verse 21 of the same chapter—
'unto Adam also and to his wife did the Lord God make coats of
skins and clothed them.' As everyone was not to wear the same plain
apron, a further text justifies decoration, for at *Numbers*, Chapter 15,
vv 37-40, there is:

And the Lord spake unto Moses, saying,
Speak unto the children of Israel, and bid them that they make them
fringes in the borders of their garments throughout their generations,
and that they put upon the fringe of the borders a ribband of blue:
And it shall be unto you for a fringe, that ye may look upon it and

remember all the commandments of the Lord, and do them; and that ye seek not after your own heart and your own eyes, after which ye used to go a whoring:
That ye may remember, and do all my commandments, and be holy unto your God.

In this passage our forebears found not only justification for the symbolism itself, but also for the apron to be a real symbol in the accepted sense—a reminder to follow the commandments of God.

The story of the signs given by the Lord to Moses to convince the Egyptians as recounted in *Exodus*, Chapter 4, appears to have been intended to be read before the communication of signs. *Judges*, Chapter 12, tells the story of the use of a difficult word used as a test word to find out the Ephraimites. The meaning of this word involving corn is not given in the same story, but is referred to in a book published early in the eighteenth century. I took this from the eighth edition, published in 1757, of Volume I of *Spectacle de la Nature or Nature Display'd, translated from the Original French by Mr Humphreys:*

The Harvest . . . . . made the sixth Constellation be characterised by the Figure of a young Female Reaper, bearing an Ear of Corn. The Symbol is taken from those young Damsels who gained their Living by gleaning after the Reapers; and nothing could better mark out that Season of the Year when Providence supplies the Rich and Poor with their necessary Provisions. The *Chevalier* will be pleased to take note that the Ear of Corn which she has in her hand is called *Shibboleth* in the Hebrew Language, and in the *Arabic, Sibbul* or *Sibbula.*

Incidentally, the new Revised Standard Version of the Bible confirms that the number of Ephraimites slain was 42,000. Other texts given are both *Genesis*, Chapter 21, vv 9-10 and *Job*, Chapter, 9 v 23, in relation to free men as opposed to bondmen; both *Exodus*, Chapter 3 and *Joshua*, Chapter 5, on the need to remove the shoes on holy ground; and others in relation to the giving of a word.

The use of metal tools, and particularly tools of iron, is the subject of several of the quotations referred to in these old manuscripts. *I Kings*, Chapter 6, v 7, is part of the story of the building of King Solomon's Temple. The lectures reflect the wonder expressed that the actual construction was carried out without the aid of metal tools. The old lectures go on to say that the use of metal tools would pollute the Temple. This view on iron tools in confirmed by other texts given—notably *Exodus*, Chapter 20, v 25 and *Deuteronomy*,

Chapter 27, vv 5-6. This matter of pollution by the use of metal is taken as the justification for the symbolism of depriving a candidate of *all* metals, as indeed the ceremony states, rather than just valuables. The importance and nature of the Charity charge at the north-east corner has tended to obscure this further piece of original symbolism which still survives in our present ceremonies to remind us of the ancient belief in the polluting qualities of metal.

The Use of Numbers

The numbers three, five and seven appear to have a special significance in present day ceremonies. The work at the end of the eighteenth century before the union of the two former Grand Lodges in 1813 showed a much more pronounced use of special numbers. In the old lectures it is particularly noticeable that three and seven recur persistently. To a lesser degree they are joined by five, eleven, fifteen, and sometimes by four and twelve. With a building with four sides it is difficult to avoid the use of that number and symbolic justification in the number of Gospels was quickly found, while twelve was the number of both the tribes of Israel and the Apostles. The remainder are all odd numbers and of these, three is the most persistent. At various times there are, for example, three knocks; steps; lights; pillars or columns; staves on a ladder (Faith, Hope and Charity); principal officers and Grand Masters of old times; as well as three degrees. There are also many instances of the deliberate use of three words together—squares, levels and perpendiculars; sign, token and word; mature age, sound judgement and strict morals; hail, conceal and never reveal; secrecy, fidelity and obedience; and many more. The number three dominates the Craft.

In one version of the old lectures dating from the 1790s there is one passage with a particularly strong reference to three. It refers to an obligation taken 'my left hand supporting three, my right hand covering three', while it is described as consisting of 'three points and three penalties'. The candidate was entrusted with three secrets and was given three charges and three duties. The number is mentioned on each occasion and this constant use is not by accident. Another passage brings in seven in conjunction with three but this appears to be an attempt to relate three and seven and seems contrived. It does indicate that at that particular time in masonic development there was this extreme interest in certain numbers, and it was about the same time that particular numbers started to be associated with the three degrees and that the staircase developed into a symbol related to those same numbers.

The author of *A Defence of Masonry* as early as 1730 had something to say about three, which he notes occurs so frequently in Prichard's exposure of that time. He finds 'that the Ancients, both Greeks and Latins, professed a great veneration for the same number' and after quoting some instances goes on:

> Whether this Fancy owes its Original to the Number Three, because containing a Beginning, Middle, and End, it seems to signify all Things in the World; or whether to the Esteem the Pythagoreans and other Philosophers had for it on account of their Triad or Trinity; or lastly, (to mention no more Opinions) to its Aptness to signify the Power of all the Gods, who were divided into three classes, Celestial, Terrestrial, and Infernal; I shall leave to be determined by others. The Gods, as Virgil asserts, had a particular Esteem for this number.

The same author has something to say on the question of the number seven:

> I instantly recurred to the old Egyptians, who held the Number of Seven to be Sacred; more especially they believed that whilst their Feast of Seven Days lasted, the Crocodiles lost their inbred Cruelty; and Leo Afer, in his Description of Africa, says that even in his Time the Custom of Feasting so Many Days and Nights was still used for the happy Overflowing of the Nile. The Greeks and Latins professed the same Regard for that Number, which might be proved by many Examples.

In this instance the author seems to be calling the ancient Mysteries in aid, but a number of early manuscripts refer to seven as the number of perfection and suggest that this is taken from the Bible as the Creation 'from chaos to perfection' is recorded as taking place over six specific periods followed by one of rest. *The Dumfries No. 4 Manuscript* catechism of about 1710 refers to the Trinity as the justification for three—in this case for three staves of a ladder. Throughout the eighteenth century there is constant reference to the triangle with its three sides—and through this, the number three— as being emblematic of the Trinity; there were even triangular buildings in honour of the Trinity. In this period, masonry in England had not abandoned its Christian principle of religion in favour of a non-sectarian view. One such triangular building is the Triangular Lodge at Rushton near Kettering, which was built by Sir Thomas Tresham about 1593-5. Everything is arranged in threes and all measurements are exactly divisible by three. The building has three floors, three gables on each side, there are separate devices in each of its three sides, arranged in threes. Just below the gables on each side are quotations from the Vulgate, each containing 33 letters. There are in addition a number of figures of a pious nature used as decoration.

It is often claimed that because James Anderson in his *Constitutions* included a note under 'Concerning God and Religion', that 'it is now thought more expedient only to oblige them to that religion in which all men agree, leaving their particular opinions to themselves', that masonry was not based on the Christian faith from the early days of an organised grand Lodge. So far as a study of the lectures, rituals and procedures of the eighteenth century is concerned, those which have survived show that nothing could be farther from the truth, for the whole is based on a Christian way of life. Anderson was a non-conformist minister and the upholding of the orthodox protestant faith as practised in the established Church of England was a matter of some importance in the days of George I; this could have been the reason for his wording. On the other hand, at the time the *Constitutions* were written, there had been a great movement towards Unitarianism, and many thinking masons consider that this may have influenced Anderson. Unitarianism proved to be something of a passing fashion, which probably accounts for the strictly orthodox religious approach found in later eighteenth century papers. In spite of this strong religious flavour in English practice, right up to the final 'dechristianisation' in 1816, it had been found possible to admit into the English Craft those of different religious beliefs as if Anderson's statement had that meaning.

It is interesting to note the different uses mentioned in some of the old manuscripts; for example, one of the early years of the eighteenth century refers to the staircase having three steps, demonstrating that the practices of masonry which had settled down a century later were still very much in a state of development. Once a three degree system became established by the 1730s, the introduction of the odd number five as intermediate to three and seven may have been automatic. In the early days there is no doubt that three was regarded as a general masonic number, while seven related to completeness or perfection. In particular, seven, the number of perfection, became associated with the third degree, which, in the middle 1700s, before the advent of the many additional degrees, was the special and perfect degree of the Craft.

Most of the old catechisms refer to the number required to make 'a full and perfect lodge' or 'a true and perfect lodge', or some such similar expression. The answers varied, but the use of three, five and seven is fairly constant, often in alternative. Thus the *Edinburgh Register House Manuscript* of 1696 has;

> What makes a true and perfect Lodge?
> Seven Masters, five entered apprentices . . . . .
> Does no less make a true and perfect Lodge?
> Yes, five Masons and three entered apprentices &c.
> Does no less?
> The more the merrier, the fewer the better cheer.

The pamphlet *A Mason's Confession* of about 1727 has:

> What makes a just and perfect Lodge?
> Five fellow crafts and seven entered apprentices.—N.B. They do not restrict themselves to this number, though they mention it in their form of questions, but will do the thing with fewer.

Here is a suggestion that the numbers were merely a matter of symbolism and not necessarily followed in practice, which could also be the reason for the wording in the *Edinburgh Register House Manuscript*. The prevalence of odd numbers may be noted, and *The Grand Mystery of Free-Masons Discover'd* of 1724 gives a reason for this:

> How many make a Lodge?
> God and the Square, with five or seven right and perfect Masons . . . .
> Why do Odds make a Lodge?
> Because all Odds are Mens advantage.

The theme of 'Odds' being male is also found in other manuscripts and seems to show that the use of odd numbers where possible was symbolic that free and accepted masonry was restricted to men and that a more general use of even numbers would show feminine influence. *A Defence of Masonry* includes a classical quotation translated as 'Unequal numbers please the Gods.' Even to-day it may be noted that all salutes given to rulers in the Craft of various grades are in odd numbers from three to eleven.

There is plenty of justification in the Bible for the use of these numbers if one is looking for justification. Cruden's *Complete Concordance*—which was available by the middle of the eighteenth century—stresses the recurrence of the number seven in the Bible and he says:

> Besides the known significance of this word it is also used in Scripture as a number of perfection. In the sacred books, and in the religion of the Jews, a great number of events and mysterious circumstances are set forth by the number seven.

Cruden then follows with reference to the Creation; the Sabbath; Jacob's seven years for each wife; that seven multiplied by seven was celebrated as a jubilee; Pharaoh's dream was in sevens; the branched candlestick; the seven trumpets; and the seven days to surround the walls of Jericho. Cruden does not give nearly the same significance to three, although he lists nearly as many instances of Biblical use as for seven, which run to almost two closely printed columns. Abraham, Isaac and Jacob are probably the most significant historical use of three in the Jewish faith. As might be expected the use of five is not so great, although it appears to have some significance in David's five stones, five loaves of bread and Benjamin's five changes of raiment; the probability is that it was a convenient bridge to three and seven.

With the influence of Jewish history and the Essenes and Cabalists, it is of interest to note that the *Encyclopaedia Judaica* refers especially to three and seven—three, because of its inherent completeness and seven, as having an especially important role in antiquity. In the Cabala, there was particularly strong use of groups of three. Many writers have referred to the influence of Pythagorean systems on masonry, but the *Jewish Encyclopedia* (1903) refers to the similarity of the Pythagorean idea of the creative powers of numbers and letters with that which is the foundation of one of the text books of the Cabala. Dr Wynn Westcott suggests that the use of five may have come from Pythagorean influence and refer to the pentalpha, or five pointed star used in masonry which he calls 'the emblem of health, the Pythagorean emblem.' Wynn Westcott also asserts that the development of the number of steps in the winding staircase probably came from a Hebrew, and possibly a Cabala, source. It is clear, as already mentioned that the number of stairs was not always fifteen and that this is the total of the figures three, five and seven, associated with the three degrees. Wynn Westcott says:

> Three, five and seven amount to fifteen, which is equivalent to JAH, God; Yod and He, ten and five; every Hebrew word is also a number, and the reverse.

In the various lecture versions in the times up to the union of the Grand Lodges in 1813, there was no consistent numbering of sections on this sort of basis. When the new system which is still used appeared in its more or less final form in 1817, the lectures of the three degrees had seven, five and three sections respectively, the minimum numbers which the lectures claimed were required to form a lodge in each of those degrees. This was the first time this numerical pattern appeared in lectures and it must have been deliberate. The Duke of Sussex was Grand Master at the time and was intensely interested, not only in the re-organisation of the ritual and lectures, but also in the Hebrew language and the Cabala; he may have been responsible. The number pattern found in the Jewish religion has other important numbers. Those who were influenced by Cabalistic and other Jewish uses appear only to have taken what suited them.

It certainly appears that the special number features we have today in masonry are the result of several influences. There seems little doubt that the original inclusion of three as a dominant number was of a religious origin when masonry was essentially Christian, but that other strong reasons were found later to support its continued use. Seven may also have come from a Biblical origin, though whether religious or historical it is not possible to determine, but again additional reasons were found for its use. The incorporation of five may have been first a matter of convenience or it may have arisen from the Pythagorean or Cabalistic influence; there is no doubt that both of these had an effect on the use of numbers in masonry, much of which is still there.

Later writers have attempted to develop ideas on this use of numbers, particularly Dr Oliver, and in more recent times W. L. Wilmshurst. He commented at length on three and seven, using much of what others had written, but he goes into great detail of the significance of four. Most of this would appear to be speculative rather than original symbolism:

A man's first entry into a Lodge is symbolical of his first entry upon the science of knowing himself. His organism is symbolised by a four-square or four-sided building. This is in accordance with the very ancient philosophical doctrine that four is the arithmetical symbol of everything which has manifested or physical form. Spirit, which is unmanifest and not physical, is expressed by the number three and the triangle. But Spirit which has so far projected itself as to become objective and wear a material form or body, is denoted by the number four and the quadrangle or square. Hence the Hebrew name of Deity, as known and worshipped in this outer world, was the great unspeakable name of four letters or Tetragrammaton, whilst the cardinal points of space are also four, and every manifested thing is a compound of the four basic metaphysical elements called by the ancients, fire, water, air and earth.

The question of the ancient philosophical doctrine related to the numbers three and four occurs a number of times in later writers concerned with a more mystical approach to masonic symbolism. In particular does it arise on the question of the modern apron design, where the basic square shape is regarded as representing the material and the triangular flap the spiritual. This design is very much later than the period when most of the symbolism arose and I have found no trace of such thoughts in earlier writings, either in connection with the apron or the Tetragrammaton, which is used by late eighteenth century writers for illustration, and is usually enclosed in a triangle surrounded by a glory. But that does not prevent contemplation of this nature on what we find in masonry to-day.

Masonry in the United States was founded mostly on principles set forth in British lodges before the union of 1813 and has developed on slightly different lines since they became independent two hundred years ago. The same influence of numbers is found and the following extract from *Leaves from Georgia Masonry*, on the numbers in relation to the staircase, sums up a good deal that has been considered:

The number three is a sacred number, that mysterious number which 'plays so great a part in the traditions of Asia, and the philosophy of Plato, image of the Supreme Being . . . . . to the Philosophers, the most excellent and favourite number; a mysterious type, revered by all antiquity, and consecrated in the Mysteries; wherefore there are but three essential degrees among Masons; who venerate, in the triangle, the most august mystery, that of the Sacred Triad, object of their homage and study.' Three also referred to harmony, friendship, peace, concord, and temperance; and was so highly esteemed among the Pythagoreans that they called it perfect harmony. The appearances of this mysterious number in the Masonic signs, symbols, and ceremonies are almost innumerable, and it will be a good exercise for you to see how many times you can discover this symbol in them.

Having climbed up the first three steps, and laid the foundation of your Masonic building, you see now a flight of five steps, replete also with profound meaning. For five is also a sacred number ever found in connection with two, and with seven. Jesus is said to have fed the multitude with five loaves and two fishes, and of the fragments there remained twelve baskets, that is five and seven. The five steps show on one side the five orders of architecture, and on the other the five human senses. Now when you hear of a 'sacred' number, you think probably that that means nothing to you personally, but stop and consider for a that that means nothing to you personally, but stop and consider a moment. This number five is engraven in your being more than once. Examine yourself, and you find five fingers, five toes, and five avenues through which the outside world can communicate with that mysterious being who sits in the center of your consciousness and receives and translates—no man knows how—the various messages carried to the brain by the nerves from the outside world.

Seven is a particularly sacred number, having appeared in the religious and philosophical system of the entire ancient world. It also is engraved in your very being, for at the age of seven you first showed understanding, at the age of fourteen puberty is generally reached, at the age of twenty-one manhood is recognized, at the age of twenty-eight full growth attained and at the age of thirty-five, physical vigor is highest, at forty-two, this begins to decline; at forty-nine man should have reached the height of intellectual strength; and at seventy he has reached the ordinary limit of human life. These figures are not merely arbitrary, but the result of study and observation of men everywhere.

So, seven days constituted the entire period of creation, seven colors are found in the rainbow, of which three are primary; seven days in the week; seven lamps in the great candlestick of the Tabernacle and Temple; the seventh year was a Sabbath of rest, and the year after the seven times seventh year was the year of Jubilee; Jericho fell when seven priests, with seven trumpets, made the circuit of the city on seven successive days—once each day for six days, and seven times on the seventh; and time is lacking to give you all the instances of the use of seven in sacred literature and in the esoteric writings. 'The seven eyes of the Lord,' says Zechariah, 'run to and fro through the whole earth.' The ladder of the ancients (supposed to be that which Jacob saw in his dream, with the angels ascending and descending) symbolised the seven mystic spheres: the Moon, Mercury, Venus, the Sun, Mars, Jupiter and Saturn; down which the souls of men came in their progress towards the earth, taking from each planet its particular characteristic; and up which men must climb back towards God, leaving at each planet the earthly or lower attraction which they no longer need; the seven-fold purification being symbolized by the seven steps of King Solomon's Temple, which also symbolized the purification mentioned in the Kabalah and the Hermetic writings.

3

THE LODGE — Its Nature and Purpose

Behold the lodge rise into view,
The work of industry and art;
'Tis grand, and regular, and true,
For so is each good Mason's heart.
Friendship cements it from the ground,
And secresy shall fence it round.

A stately dome o'erlooks the east,
Like orient Phoebus in the morn;
And two tall pillars in the west
At once support us and adorn.
Upholden thus the structure stands,
Untouch'd by sacrilegious hands.

from *An Ode on Masonry*, c 1738 by BROTHER BANCKS.

ANY MASTER Mason would recognise a lodge room as such, by its shape, by its layout, and by the articles he would find there. Yet there may be differences between one lodge room and another, according to the views of the lodges that meet in them; these differences may be in the absence or presence of particular items of furniture or adornment or in their precise positioning, and may be accentuated by the nature and proportions of the room itself. Some masonic premises are in permanent use as meeting places for Craft lodges, some are converted for that use for the time of the lodge meeting, having been given over to quite a different use yesterday and will be used for something else tomorrow.

In many places where a room is rented for the occasion, it must be dismantled as soon as the lodge is closed and re-arranged for the service of a meal for the brethren. In setting up a room for a lodge meeting, certain basic furniture is essential and its presence is taken for granted; it would not be considered proper to meet and to open the lodge without these adjuncts. These essential items have become part of masonry and are incorporated in our lodges for particular reasons. In many cases they each act as a reminder or symbol, either of some desired masonic attribute or of some happening or personage connected with the Craft. Our lodges did not just *happen* that way, they developed into these forms. In many cases the basic beliefs and goals of the Craft found expression in the lodge in these symbols, while in others, necessary furniture such as seats and tables in the course of time took on a significance which tended to render them symbolic and even caused specialist designs to be used. Thoughtful brethren, separated from each other by distance, have endeavoured to find in their lodges symbolic expression for their masonic aims. Because of this separation and through lack of central direction and control or of communication, the actual symbol used might be different in each case, although there is no doubt that, over the years, a good deal of borrowing went on from inter-visiting of lodges. It must be emphasised that many differences of symbolism in lodges, both now and in times past, derive from this separate development of symbolism, in lodges and in areas.

All this relates to the lodge meeting room, but is that all that a mason means by a lodge? When a new lodge is formed, in these days there is a formal ceremony by which it is both consecrated and constituted. In the ceremony of consecration of a lodge certain elements associated with the ceremony are poured on to a board (usually a first degree tracing board) symbolising the new lodge—the lodge board. These elements are used symbolically as is stated in the ceremony—corn as a symbol of plenty and abundance, wine to symbolise joy and cheerfulness and oil for peace and unanimity. Salt is normally used as a symbol of the constitution of the founders themselves into a new lodge and represents the friendship and fidelity which should be the attribute of every lodge. These particular elements are used because they seem to have the authority of Bible use and in particular, corn, wine and oil were the payment made by King Solomon to Hiram, King of Tyre, for the supplies sent for the building of the Temple of Jerusalem, as set out in II *Chronicles*, Chapter 2.

The old lectures and catechisms from the earliest times have dealt with the symbolic attributes of a lodge and today many of them are still contained in the lectures and in the explanation of the first degree tracing board. Doctor Oliver summarised the nature of a lodge from the old lectures:

A Lodge of Masons consists of a certain number of brethren who are assembled together to expatiate on the mysteries of the Craft; having the Holy Bible open on the pedestal to teach them the sacred principles of religion and justice; on which rest those two expressive emblems the Square and Compass, to remind them of the duties they owe to society and to themselves; the *Book of Constitutions* where they may study the general statutes of Masonry; the Bye Laws, to point out their duty as members of an individual Lodge; and the Warrant, by virtue of which, having been issued by the Grand Lodge, and enrolled in the archives of the Province where it is situated, at the general quarter sessions of the peace, the brethren meet to transact the business of Masonry.

The form of the Lodge is an oblong square, situated due East and West; supported by three pillars, and standing on holy ground. Its dimensions are unlimited, and its covering no less than the spangled canopy of heaven. To this object the Mason's mind is continually directed; and in those blessed regions he hopes at last to arrive by the aid of the theological ladder, which Jacob in his vision beheld reaching from earth to heaven; the three principal rounds of which admonish us to have faith in God, hope in immortality, and charity to all mankind.

From these general principles it appears that a Mason's lodge is a microcosm or miniature world, over which the glory in the centre sheds its refulgent rays, like the sun in the firmament, to enlighten the brethren in the paths of virtue and science. In the Lodge, the practice of social and moral virtue is as essential towards the brethren, and invested with the same degree of approbation or censure, as the performance of our public duties as Christians and citizens of the world at large.

A Mason sitting in his Lodge, surrounded by the characteristic symbols which are distributed on all sides, feels that he is a member of the universal lodge of nature; created by the author and source of *Light* and redeemed by divine love or *Charity*. He seriously reflects on the incumbent duties that bind him to practice the permanent virtue and morality which these emblems embody and recommend; in the hope that when he is finally summoned to give up his accounts, he may be transferred from his lodge on earth to the Grand Temple above; there to enjoy for ever the bright system of Freemasonry in its perfect and glorified state of ineffable Light, unbounded Charity, and undisturbed Peace.

The brethren used to attend lodge meetings 'to expatiate on the mysteries of the Craft'—to consider the teachings of masonry, discuss its precepts and its symbolism, perhaps as expressed in one version of the old lectures:

What did you come into the Lodge for?
  I came there to conquer my passions, correct my vices and improve my morals.
What qualifications does a man require to be a Mason?
  Silence and Secrecy.

What constitutes the character of a Mason?

To walk humbly in the sight of God, to do Justice and to love Mercy.

What are the qualifications suitable for the dignity of the Craft?

To afford succour to the distressed, to give bread to the poor, and to put the misguided traveller into his way.

What does Masonry order us to guard against?

Blasphemy, Drunkenness, Lewdness, Swearing, Evil plotting, Lying and Controversy.

Then what does Masonry require?

Ability, attendance and a good appearance.

If a Brother should be lost, where would you seek him?

Between the square and the compass.

Why so, Brother?

Because all honest and good Masons are there, or ought to be there.

What sort of man should a Warden be?

He should be well acquainted with the private as well as the public rules and orders of the Craft; he ought to be strictly honest, humane of nature, patient in injuries, modest in conversation, grave in counsel and advice, and above all constant in amity and faithful in secrecy, which may we all be, God, of His infinite Goodness, grant.

There is no mention in the older manuscripts and prints of masons and lodges meeting to work ceremonies as the principal reason, yet that seems to be the major work of English lodges today. The esoteric ceremonies in earlier times were very short indeed and were often carried out by a small team of officers meeting for that special purpose some time before the full meeting of the lodge. Many instances may be found of a lodge called for say, five o'clock, with a note stating 'makings four o'clock, passings half past four' for example. The actual work done when the lodge met was, apart from business matters, the rendering of the catechisms known as the lectures— instructive in the symbolism and principles of the craft. This pattern of work was not necessarily consistently in vogue over a long period, but it seems to have been that of about twenty years before the union of 1813 in many places. In these days much of the instruction and symbolism is incorporated in the ceremonies themselves, so that they are, in themselves, instructive, and contain a good deal of the true teaching of masonry. The ceremonies which developed after 1813 were longer than those of earlier date and incorporated both the esoteric and the instructive; this also brought about the change from work at table to a separation of lodge work and meal.

If the ceremonies are worked in an understanding manner, with the Master—or other brother in the chair for the work—having, by his own study, found the true meaning to convey to the candidate, then some 'expatiation' may well take place. Ceremonies are not a test of merit for the Master, their importance lies in the meaning for the *candidate*, and not just in the words themselves. If the working is perfunctory, then no true masonry is worked. In the same way the members of the lodge, by their interest in the proceedings, must take a part in the effect of the ceremony. But a lodge is still not complete and fulfilled without some time given to discussion and contemplation on the meaning of masonry.

William Hutchinson, in the *Spirit of Masonry* (published 1775), tells of what a right thinking mason should see in his lodge when he attends:

> The Lodge when revealed to an entering Mason discovers to him a representation of the World in which, from the wonders of nature, we are led to contemplate her great original and worship him for his mighty works; and we are thereby also moved to exercise those moral and social virtues, which become mankind, as the servants of the great architect of the world; in whose image we were formed in the beginning.

We go then to contemplate God's works and to worship Him. Such worship would be normal in a Temple, and Hutchinson's words find an echo in a part of the lecture—'The universe is the Temple of the Deity whom we serve'. Is it to be wondered that the places where lodges meet are generally known as masonic Temples, when they represent to the mason this vast area for the worship of God?

Symbolically therefore, a masons's lodge represents a Temple, and this is represented by a symbolic shape, according to Oliver's interpretation, an oblong square. This was a reference to the old lectures mainly current in the lodges under the former Antients Grand Lodge. The candidates made progressive steps in the three degrees, on the first, second and third steps of 'a right angled oblong square'. The lecture went on to explain that this 'Great, Grand and Glorious Oblong Square' had a proportion in length which was three times its breadth, and represented the Temple of King Solomon, which had these proportions. And indeed *I Kings*, Chapter 6, at the second verse, confirms this:

> And the house which King Solomon built for the Lord, the length thereof was threescore cubits, and the breadth thereof twenty cubits, and the height thereof thirty cubits.

So the groundplan was sixty by twenty cubits—an oblong square (meaning that it had square corners) with the proportions of the sides at three to one. It is natural that the religious outlook of our forebears should cause them to look to Holy Writ for some symbolic justification for the Temple they were seeking to represent, and what more famous—or indeed well documented—example could they need than that built by King Solomon. They saw in the detail of its construction opportunities to symbolise the building of a spiritual life, and to draw speculative conclusions from its many features. Dr Oliver, stating that he quotes an earlier author, in the *Revelations of a Square*, says:

> The Society adopted the Temple of Solomon for its symbol, because it was the most stable and the most magnificent structure that ever existed, whether we consider its foundation or superstructure; so that of all the societies men have invented, no one was ever more firmly united, or better planned, than the Masons. Its chief aim is to conciliate and tame the passions, to establish among men the spirit of peace and concord, which may render them impenetrable to the feelings of hatred and dissension, those bitter enemies which poison the best of our days; —to inculcate sentiments of honour and probity, which may render men more attentive to their respective duties;—to teach a dutiful obedience to the orders of parents and princes;—to support towards one another the tender relation of Brothers, by which name they address each other; —and, in a word, to form an admirable sect, whose only aim is liberty, love, and equality. If this interpretation should not be to the taste of the candidate, or if he feels any repugnance to adopt it, they well know how to reply in a manner still more artificial. The Temple of Solomon, then, signifies nothing more than a temple sacred to the Virtues, which are practised by the Society in the greatest perfection; a dungeon destined for the vices, where these monsters groan under the most rigorous confinement . . . . The edifices which Freemasons build are nothing more than virtues or vices to be erected or destroyed; and in this case heaven only occupies their minds, which soar above a corrupted world. The Temple of Solomon denotes reason and intelligence.

On the significance in masonry of King Solomon's Temple, *Leaves from Georgia Masonry* has the following comments:

> The Temple of Solomon is a symbol to teach, among other lessons, that no labor or care is too great to fit our hearts and minds as living temples for the dwelling places of the Most High. That we must not profane the Holy of Holies of our own heart by bad thoughts or improper desires, but must keep it pure as He is pure.
> The two pillars at the entrance signify the principles of fixity and motion, attraction and repulsion, which hold the universe together and guide the stars in their courses.

The mosaic pavement symbolizes among other things the most secret doctrine as to the constitution of matter, and teaches us that life is made up of bright and dark, good and evil, while the blazing star in the center teaches, among other things, that he who fixes his eyes on the heavens and guides his steps by the divine light will be little troubled by what goes on around him upon the earth.

The Situation of the Lodge

A masons' lodge is always placed *symbolically* due east and west. Many masons believe that the layout should be physically so and in their plans and designs will go to untold lengths to achieve this, even at great inconvenience. Christian churches are, wherever possible, set in this way, and with the religious background of masonry, no doubt this had some influence on the physical practice for masons' lodges, but many cases can be found of churches laid out on a different line where convenience made this necessary. Indeed this is no new problem and is referred to in the 1754 *Book of Constitutions* of the Moderns Grand Lodge, which was edited by Rev John Entick. The reconstructed St Paul's Cathedral was built due east and west and so is at a slight angle to the approach up Ludgate Hill, a matter which has produced planning problems in recent rebuilding schemes. St Clement Danes church, which divides the Strand in London so that traffic passes both sides, is also, by being built east and west, not quite along the same line as the street. Of these, Entick says:

As the appearance of St Paul's Cathedral is injured by its oblique position with the street by which we approach to it; so the public highway through the Strand, is most absurdly contracted by superstitiously fixing St Clement's church due east and west, instead of complying with the direction of the street! In confined situations, no ideal consideration ought to take place of general convenience.

But, *symbolically*, Lodges *are* due east and west with the entrance in the west. Rev J. T. Lawrence has suggested that, as the Inner Guard is the assistant to the Junior Warden in being in charge of the door, that door should be placed in the south so that the control is more obviously in the Junior Warden's charge, with his assistant near him. This suggestion quite overlooks the original symbolism, which is still followed, and also overlooks a change during the development of lodges, made for a completely different reason.

Some reasons for an east-west layout are contained in the old lectures and are still there today, and in the explanation of the first degree tracing board—this board being an emblematical representation of the lodge. The most important reason is again taken from Holy Writ, that King Solomon's Temple was placed that way, but more than this, that it was placed on that axis because God told Moses to place that way the tent or tabernacle used by the Israelites as a place of worship during their wanderings in the wilderness. Furthermore, King David, who was not permitted by God to build the Temple himself, passed on the necessary instructions to his son, Solomon, to whom the actual construction was divinely entrusted. *Exodus*, Chapter 27 gives details of the structure of the tabernacle, which was to have a length of one hundred cubits on an east-west line, and a breadth of fifty cubits—or double square in plan. William Hutchinson writing in 1775, quoted Josephus, the Jewish historian, on the subject of the tabernacle and its influence on the symbolic origins of a masons' lodge. Thomas Sandby's Grand Temple for the Moderns Grand Lodge, dedicated in 1776, was in the approximate form of a double cube—it was about 78 feet long and about 38 to 39 feet in both width and height.

King Solomon's Temple was placed east-west with the sole entrance, through the porch, in the east. Most papers and articles on the design and layout of the Temple agree on these points. *Ezekiel*, Chapter 8, v 16, is often quoted as justification:

> And he brought me into the inner court of the Lord's house, and behold at the door of the temple of the Lord, between the porch and the altar, were about five and twenty men with their backs toward the temple of the Lord, and their faces toward the east.

Although masonry has kept the east-west axis in its lodges consistent with that of King Solomon's Temple, it has changed the orientation, so that the entrance to lodges is in the symbolic west. This has caused a good deal of havoc with some of the symbolic orientation, particularly in the case of the winding staircase leading to the middle chamber, which, in King Solomon's Temple, went off to the south from just inside the porch and ultimately led towards the *west*. In a masons' lodge it must lead towards the pedestal in the east, and so has to start from the north towards the south to be in the same *relative* position. The other reasons in the old lectures tell us why this is, and they have a profound effect on the symbolism of the lodge. The first such reason is religious, that it was the custom of Christian churches to be placed east and west; the others are that knowledge originated in the east and spread its divine influence to the west, and that the sun rises in the east and sets in the west. The change of orientation may well have been because churches of the established religion were placed with the sanctuary and altar in the east and the main entrance usually in the west. There is again a possibility that it was influenced (as some other points have been shown to be) by the Cabala; in the *Jewish Encyclopedia* there is a reference to an essential doctrine of one particular school:

> His כבוד ('majesty') also called הסימורך כבוד which has size and shape and sits on a throne in the east, as the actual representative of God. His throne is separated by a curtain פרגוד on the east, south, and north, from the world of angels; the side on the west being uncovered.

The *Encyclopaedia Judaica* refers to adjacent buildings, with walls parallel to the walls of the Temple proper and constructed on all sides except the front—presumably the east end. The *Encyclopaedia* suggests that the entrance to these adjacent buildings was on the south side, although it suggests also that these buildings may have had more than one entrance. The *New Standard Jewish Dictionary* (W. H. Allen, 1970) says that there were a number of entrances to the outer precincts, although its other comments agree with those of the *Encyclopaedia Judaica*. From a ritual point of view there is an apparent conflict in that there is stress that there was but *one* entrance to the Temple proper, that through the porch at the east end, yet when the fellowcrafts depart on their search in the third degree, they do so in three lodges, from the *three* entrances of the Temple. The only reasonable explanation of this apparent discrepancy is that the craftsmen left not from the Temple proper, but from the surrounding buildings through three of those entrances, or that the entrances used on this occasion were three of the gates into the court around the Temple. The same comment applies to the trials experienced by HAB at the three entrances (old lectures do not all agree on the positioning of these entrances). It seems likely that 'poetic licence' was used by those who compiled this allegorical story.

The old lecture reference to the course of the sun during one day is a constant reminder of the organisation of a daily life, a reference to the fact that time for us is not endless on earth, and that the function of the master in the east was to open the lodge and put the brethren to employment. But the master's place in the east was more than just that, for the east was the source of knowledge and wisdom and the master's duty included the instruction of the brethren in masonry. Thus, the lodge layout sets out for us the basic symbolism of the masonic system—an entrance, both into the lodge and into the Craft, in the west; progress by degrees, demonstrated by steps (of different sorts in different places) towards the east. In the east was that fount of knowledge, the master, the representative of King Solomon, and the mastership is still the highest honour that a lodge can bestow on any of its members.

Dr Oliver had this very much in mind:

The W M should always bear in his memory, that to him the brethren look for instruction—on him depend the welfare and success—the credit and popularity of the community. His situation, as the chief pillar of the Lodge, is most important; and if he fail in the satisfactory discharge of its duties, he inflicts a fatal blow, not only on the Lodge, which will be the first victim of an ill placed confidence, but on the order of Free-masonry itself, which will suffer in public estimation, should its principal officer prove incompetent to the high office he has undertaken;—should fail through inattention, neglect, or incapacity, to improve the brethren in wisdom and knowledge; or to vindicate and defend the purity of the order against the attacks and surmises of those who ridicule or condemn it, simply because they do not understand its object, and are incapable of comprehending its beauty and utility.

In many lodges, both in normal lodge practice and in the ceremonies, this symbolism is still strong. The seats of the senior brethren are those nearest the east. In the progression through the ceremonies in many lodges two hundred years ago, symbolic steps were taken, not to the Master's pedestal, but, in succeeding degrees further towards the east. This appears to be preserved in some ritual workings today by the candidate taking the later part of the proceedings—the Charge, Lodge Board explanation, etc.—in a progression towards the east. Thus the Charge after Initiation is given with the candidate at the left of the Senior Warden where this practice prevails, the tracing board of the second degree is explained in the centre of the lodge and the explanation of the traditional history and the third degree board is given with the candidate in front of the Master's pedestal in the east.

A masons' lodge is said to be supported by three pillars. These represent Wisdom, Strength and Beauty. Much has been written about them which it will be more appropriate to set out later in the chapter, but they are now often shown in a lodge as three columns, each surmounted by a candlestick, and placed by the seats of the master and the two wardens. In the old lectures of the Antients there is some reference to this connection—the seating of the wardens in the south and west did not become the practice of the Moderns lodges, officially, until 1810:

Who does the Pillar of Wisdom represent?

The Master in the East, because he gives instructions to the Craft to carry on the work with good order and harmony.

Who does the Pillar of Strength represent?

The Senior Warden in the West, because he pays the Labourers their wages, which is the strength and support of the business, and dismisses them from their work that they may go home and take their natural rest and pray for the light of an ensuing day.

Who does the Pillar of Beauty represent?

The Junior Warden in the South, because he stands in the South to observe the sun approaching its highest meridian, which is the Beauty of the day, to call the brethren from labour to refreshment and to bring them again to their work after the sun has passed its highest meridian, that the Master may have pleasure and profit thereby.

Holy Ground

The dedication of King Solomon's Temple to God is recorded in *I Kings*, Chapter 8; therefore a masons' lodge must similarly be dedicated to God. The lodge was also dedicated to King Solomon, according to the old lectures, while records of obligations used up till about 1816 have as their wording 'dedicated to God and his service and the Holy Apostle St John'. This dedication to St John is of some antiquity and references to it occur in some of the older documents. Hence, the Craft degrees were often known as St John's masonry, and an unattached mason (a very common occurrence in the early days) as a St John's mason. If a lodge were dedicated to God then it must stand on dedicated or holy ground. There are many references and reasons in the old lectures relating to lodges standing on holy ground. These relate to Moses and the burning bush (*Exodus*, Chapter 3,) Joshua and the Angel (*Joshua*, Chapter 5), the consecration of the first lodge and of Solomon's Temple, and the symbolic holding of lodges on high ground (such as Mount Moriah) or in valleys. This last led to a symbolic Valley of Jehosaphat, referred to by William Hutchinson in 1775:

We place the spiritual lodge in the vale of JEHOSAPHAT, implying thereby, that the principles of Masonry are derived from the knowledge of God, and are established in the JUDGMENT OF THE LORD; the literal translation of the word JEHOSAPHAT, from the Hebrew tongue, being no other than those express words.—The highest hills and lowest vallies were from the earliest times esteemed sacred, and it was supposed the spirit of God was peculiarly diffusive in those places:— *Ezekiel* xliii. 12. 'Upon the top of the mountain, the whole limit thereof round about shall be most holy.'—It is said in the *Old Testament*, that the spirit of God buried Moses in a valley in the land of Moab; implying that from divine influence he was interred in such halloed retirement. —On Elijah's translation, the sons of the prophets said to Elisha, 'behold now there be with the servants fifty strong men; let them go, we pray thee, and seek thy master, least peradventure the spirit of the Lord hath taken him up, and cast him upon some mountain, or into some valley.' Hence was derived the veneration paid to such places in the earliest ages. . . . .

The Entrance

With the seat of Wisdom and of King Solomon in the east of a lodge and the progress of the new initiate to start from an entrance in the west, there is an immediate analogy of progress in King Solomon's Temple, from an entrance at one end, through a middle chamber (symbolised in the second degree), to the Holy of Holies at the far end. The most important features in that progress were the two great pillars which stood at the entrance. After the Master, the two most important officers in the lodge were his Wardens; what more natural than that the Wardens of a lodge should be identified with those pillars. Before 1810 many lodges, and particularly those under the Grand Lodge formed in 1717 (the Moderns), placed both Wardens in the west with the symbolic entrance to the lodge between them. Thus, when entering a lodge, which was a representation of King Solomon's Temple, the candidates quite genuinely came between the symbolic pillars at the entrance, as represented by the two Wardens, with the representation of the King himself, in the person of the Master, situated in the east. This arrangement still applies in some constitutions.

In the first half of the eighteenth century there are several references to masons' processions, the Wardens each having a column in his hand—for these columns were the Wardens' symbols of office, the two columns of King Solomon's Temple. Until nearly the end of the eighteenth century they were the only pillars in a masons' lodge and were regarded also as the depository of those essential attributes of a lodge, wisdom, strength and beauty, for they were the pillars 'whose base is Wisdom, whose shaft is Strength, and whose chapiter is Beauty'. Traditionally the Junior Warden has responsibility for the apprentices and the Senior Warden for the craftsmen. This may be the reason why, in some rites tracing from the old French system of the earlier 1700s, the wages are paid to the workmen at the foot of the appropriate column. In English masonry, this was one of the features of William Preston's system in the days before the Union of Grand Lodges, but it has not survived.

Dr Oliver was nearly as great a collector of the works of earlier writers as was William Preston, and he writes thus of the two pillars at the entrance:

Ancient tradition says that the shafts were covered with astronomical and masonic figures, characters, and calculations; and the hollow space in the interior served as archives of Masonry, and to hold the constitutional records. Each had 'a vase rising from the cylindrical shaft, ornamented with lotus flowers. The bottom of the vase was partly hidden by the flowers; the belly of it was overlaid with network, ornamented by seven wreaths—the Hebrew number of happiness.' They were further adorned with chapiters of five cubits in height; enriched with network, chains, lilies, and pomegranates; emblematical of unity, fortitude, peace, and plenty. They had a double row of the latter, each containing a hundred pomegranates; and on the summit were placed two spherical balls to represent the earth and heavens, as symbols of the universality of Masonry. It is difficult, say the lectures, at this distance of time, to state the precise ornaments and combinations of these emblems. But our traditions give us to understand that the chapiters respectively represented the whole system of creation celestial and terrestrial. This conjecture is founded upon the symbolical reference of these ornaments; which, how descriptive soever they may be of the union, the strength, the peace and plenty which the people of Israel enjoyed under the mild sway of that wisest and best of kings,—are emblems of far more extensive signification. The network refers to the strong and beautiful texture of the universe. The chains denote the orbits which the planetary bodies describe round the sun; and their revolutions on their several axes. The opening flowers point out the mild irradiation of the fixed stars; and the pomegranate was invariably used throughout all antiquity to denote the secret power by which the works of nature were originated and matured.

Development of lodges

In the second half of the eighteenth century, and into the nineteenth until the Union of the two former Grand Lodges in England in 1813, there was often a great deal of confusion of thought on the symbols of masonry. In this sixty or seventy years lodges developed from either a group round a simple floor drawing at the end of the room in which the tables were already laid for the meal (which formed the main purpose of meeting along with instructional work actually at table) or, at best, a small separate room with a removable floorcloth on which the lodge symbols had been drawn or placed. They went through the era of representing the symbolic lodge artistically on a board around which the working lodge could be formed; to the time, well on in the first half of the nineteenth century, of the rise of separate and purpose-built lodges or, alternatively, the furnishing of rooms especially for the purposes of masonry, even on a temporary basis. In a number of lodges, by the ruling in 1810 in England on the position of the Wardens in the South and West for all lodges, the Wardens tended to lose some of the significance of their positions as representing the two great pillars. Instead, they became identified, along with the Master, more with the three original Grand Masters, King Solomon, King Hiram of Tyre and Hiram Abiff. The growth of the symbolism of the three pillars of Wisdom, Strength and Beauty, and the identification of those attributes with the three original Grand Masters and with three of the orders of architecture, caused those orders to be identified with the Master and Wardens.

The three lesser lights were originally placed in their positions around the centre of the lodge—around the tracing board when it came into use to symbolise the working lodge—to enable the symbols to be seen and explained. The lights showed the due course of the sun from its rising in the east, through its meridian in the south to its setting in the west and with the responsibilities of the Master and Wardens becoming identified with those points of the compass, the lights also moved closer to those officers and had become established in those positions in England by the early 1800s. These lights have become identified with the Master and Wardens, and because of the wording of the ritual which also identifies the lights with the sun, moon and Master symbolically, the practice has arisen in some places of mentioning them in a different order, placing the south first. This quite overlooks their original symbolism, to show the due course of the sun (in the northern hemisphere), and they must, to preserve this, be seen to be in the east, south and west, in that order.

With this moving of the lights closer to the seats of the principal officers, and the identification of the architectural orders used on the pillars supporting the lights with those officers, two curious departures from the old symbolism may be noted in many places. The first of these is the placing of the appropriate architectural column and capital on the distinguishing column of the Warden. Masonic

equipment manufacturers disregard the original reason for distinguishing the Wardens by columns as the pillars at each side of the
entrance, and when properly designed, they should have the lilywork,
network and pomegranates of those at the entrance of the Temple,
along with the two spherical balls (or bowls as they are described in
both *I Kings*, Chapter 7, and *II Chronicles*, Chapter 4, although
this anachronism about maps of the globes seems to have existed,
from the earliest recording in masonry). They are still the emblems
of office of the Wardens and a constant reminder that our system is
based on the Temple of King Solomon.

In our ceremonies the pillars at the entrance of the Temple have
been transferred to the second degree and are no longer found on
the first degree tracing board. The Lecture symbolism of the first
degree is concerned with the Master and the Wardens representing
Wisdom, Strength and Beauty, and with the original three Grand
Masters and their architectural symbols. It was not until after 1813
that the Ionic, Doric and Corinthian orders were identified with
Wisdom, Strength and Beauty respectively and allocated to the
Master and two Wardens. In 1790, when new chairs for the Grand
Master and Grand Wardens were ordered by the old Moderns
Grand Lodge to celebrate the accession of George, Prince of Wales,
as Grand Master, the chairs were adorned with the three orders,
although not in the way that was settled after 1813. William Preston's
Lectures, which pre-date the Union, also refer to the Ionic pillar
representing beauty and the Corinthian, wisdom. We now identify
the three pillars in the formal lectures with the Master and Wardens as
representing the three original Grand Masters and attribute to them,
because of their share in the work of building the Temple, Wisdom,
Strength and Beauty. It seems likely that the method of the Antients
was adopted at the Union.

Pillars and/or Columns

The seventh chapter of the first book of *Kings*, verses 15-22:

> For he cast two pillars of brass, of eighteen cubits high apiece; and a
> line of twelve cubits did compass either of them about.
> And he made two chapiters of molten brass, to set upon the tops of the
> pillars: the height of the one chapiter was five cubits, and the height of
> the other chapiter was five cubits:
> And nets of checker work, and wreaths of chainwork, for the chapiters

which were upon the top of the pillars; seven for the one chapiter, and seven for the other chapiter.

And he made the pillars, and two rows round about upon the one network, to cover the chapiters that were upon the top, with pomegranates: and so did he for the other chapiter. And the chapiters that were upon the top of the pillars were of lily work in the porch, four cubits. And the chapiters upon the two pillars had pomegranates also above, over against the belly which was by the network: and the pomegranates were two hundred in rows round about upon the other chapiter. And he set up the pillars in the porch of the temple: and he set up the right pillar, and called the name thereof Jachin: and he set up the left pillar, and called the name thereof Boaz.

And upon the top of the pillars was lily work: so was the work of the pillars finished.

This is taken from the *Authorised Version* of the Bible, current in the seventeenth and eighteenth centuries and most of the nineteenth. The description of the pillars is also given in *II Chronicles*, Chapter 3: vv 15-17. The description is much shorter and slightly different in the dimensions, giving what is assumed to be the combined height of the two pillars as thirty-five cubits, or seventeen and a half each. This description is the basis on which most modern workings operate and as it appears in most older illustrations and lectures. One of the old lectures explains the discrepancy in height between the two descriptions by stating that the pillars were made eighteen cubits each, but half a cubit was sunk in the earth so that they only stood seventeen and a half. As masons adopted the Temple as the symbolic emblem of a lodge, it was natural that these pillars should find a place in masonic ritual and symbolism. There has always been difference of opinion as to what is 'right' or 'left' in connection with them. The reference to *Ezekiel*, Chapter 8, already mentioned, is taken as some authority for saying that the porch and entrance of the Temple was at the east end. A passage from Whiston's translation of Josephus's *Antiquities of the Jews* published in 1735 is quoted in one of the old lectures and shows that the masons of the eighteenth century had no doubts on the question of left and right pillars:

The Hebrews express the East by before, the West by behind, the North by the left hand, and the South by the right hand, according to the position of a man who has his face to the rising sun.

Although we have changed the orientation of our lodges, most ritual workings consider the left and right pillars as if looking out, as this description seems to imply.

74   SYMBOLISM IN CRAFT FREEMASONRY

W. L. Wilmshurst explains that the literal translation of Jachin, which he states to be an abbreviation of *Jehoiakin*, is 'God establishes' and that Boaz, biblically translated, means 'strength' or 'energy'. He suggests that symbolically, the left hand pillar represents the spirit and the right hand, the body, or matter, so that the combination of the two represents the complete man, neither pillar being complete without the other. He also stresses the use made in our language of such expressions as 'pillars of society' and suggests that masons can find a moral there. William Hutchinson, in the *Spirit of Masonry* (1775), saw something also in the translation from the Hebrew of the names of the pillars:

> The pillars erected at the porch of the Temple, were not only ornamental, but also carried with them an emblematical import in their names. Boaz being in its literal translation, in thee is strength; and Jachin, it shall be established; which by a very natural transposition may be put thus: O Lord, thou art mighty, and thy power is established from everlasting to everlasting.

The Encyclopaedia Judaica gives for the inscription on the columns:

> May the Lord establish (*Yakhin*) the throne of David and his kingdom for his seed for ever.
> In the strength (*be'oz*) of the Lord shall the king rejoice.

Dr Oliver also wrote about the three supporting pillars (the quotations he gives are from Noorthouck's edition of the *Book of Constitutions* of the Moderns Grand Lodge, of 1784):

> These particular Pillars are emblematical of three great Masonic characters, whose united abilities rendered an essential service to true religion, by the construction of a primitive Temple, then first dedicated to the exclusive purpose of religious worship; for they jointly possessed the essential properties which characterise the three great sustaining Pillars of our Lodge; the one had Wisdom to contrive; another had Strength to support; and the third possessed genius and ability to adorn the edifice with unexampled Beauty. The result of this union was 'a building which highly transcended all that we are capable to imagine, and has ever been esteemed the finest piece of masonry upon earth, before or since.' 'This magnificent work was begun in Mount Moriah, on Monday the second day of the month Zif, which answers to the twenty-first of our April, being the second month of the sacred year; and was carried on with such speed, that it was finished in all its parts in a little more than seven years, which happened on the eighth day of the month

Bul, which answers to the twenty-third of our October, being the seventh month of the sacred year, and the eleventh of king Solomon. What is still more astonishing, is, that every piece of it, whether timber, stone, or metal, was brought ready cut, framed, and polished to Jerusalem; so that no other tools were wanted nor heard, than what were necessary to join the several parts together. All the noise of axe, hammer, and saw, was confined to Lebanon, and the quarries and plains of Zeredathah, that nothing might be heard among the masons of Sion, save harmony and peace.'

These Pillars refer further to the three governors of the Lodge. The pillar of Wisdom represents the W M whose business is to exert his judgement and penetration, in contriving the most proper and efficient means of completing the intended work, of what nature soever it may be. The pillar of Strength refers to the S W whose duty is to support the authority, and facilitate the designs of the Master with all his influence amongst the Brethren, and to see that his commands are carried into full and permanent effect. The pillar of Beauty is the J W whose duty it is to adorn the work with all his powers of genius and active industry; to promote regularity amongst the Brethren by the sanction of his own good example, the persuasive eloquence of precept, and a discriminative encouragement of merit. Thus by the united energies of these three presiding Officers, the system is adorned and established firm as a rock in the midst of the ocean, braving the malignant shafts of envy and detraction; its summit gilded with the rays of the meridian sun, though stormy winds and waves beat eternally on its basis.

In *The Keystone*, Rev J. T. Lawrence writes on the historical aspect of the pillars and includes speculative thoughts of which the following is an extract:

Wisdom, Strength and Beauty form the most important . . . triad in which the moral precepts of the Craft are enshrined . . . and are represented by three of the most essential articles of furniture in the Lodge, which are always on view, sharing the attention of the brethren with the Master and his Wardens. . . . . They are meant to support the Lodge, through its principal officers, and they can do it with dignity when they are allowed to stand well out, challenging the regards of all in the Lodge. Of the Triad, it scarcely needs to speak of the first two components. The intelligence of the human race recognizes the absolute necessity of both in every transaction of life. Wisdom without strength would be useless, and strength without wisdom would be a menace. The two together will conquer most difficulties. What we have not yet got to the point of comprehending is that God has meant the universe to gain its last support from the Pillar of Beauty. Two pillars by themselves will support nothing, any more than two legs will support a chair or a table. A third is absolutely essential. So far the great majority of the human race have failed to recognize more than the principle of utility—the combination of strength and wisdom. In His own works the Creator teaches us something different. He not only gives us the rain, but also the rainbow, which has nothing but its beauty to recommend it. The flower which yields honey to the bee delights us with its fragrance and its beauty of form. The fruit-tree has its blossom first of all, and its fruit not only affords sustenance, but gratifies both the eye and the palate. The commonest dewdrop glistens like a diamond, and even the puddle at the roadside reflects all the glories of the pillared firmament.

Out of that which is most uncomely the rarest beauties of colour and form and taste are extracted. That which is devised by Eternal Wisdom and formed by Eternal Strength might, were that all, repel us, or make us afraid.

But God's designs would not thus be carried out. His works have to appeal to our senses and attract us, and therefore nothing leaves Him which is not endowed with Eternal Beauty as well. If anything that God has made presents itself in an unattractive form, it is the fault of those to whom it had been entrusted. Part of the curse which our first parents incurred when they left Eden was that a world, hitherto fair and lovely, should henceforth produce thorns and thistles, and henceforth it has been only by the sweat of his brow that man has been able in any degree to restore the lost beauties of Paradise. As we have seen, we find encouragement and help on every hand. In unmistakable language Nature speaking for God Almighty, tells us that Beauty, no less than Strength, and Wisdom, are Divine attributes.

It may well be remembered that that which is devised by wisdom and formed by strength will of itself become beautiful if God's designs are left without interference. Not necessarily at once. The very word 'strength' means that something has had to be overcome, that there has been a struggle; and the word 'wisdom' means that that strength has been wisely directed. No; that which savours of strife and overcoming cannot be immediately beautiful. Beauty—physical, mental, or moral— comes later, and it assuredly will come. And the reverse is equally true, that beauty will not come of itself. It is born out of strife and warfare. Every access of beauty tells of some antecedent strife. Look at the land, for instance. Wisdom has directed the course of certain operations and their applicability to that particular piece of ground, and then strength obeys the dictates of wisdom; and then follows a period of strife. Blasting operations are going on; the plough is cutting it up; excavations are being made. And then out of it all there arise beautiful architectural forms, temples and palaces, and the habitations of men; or it may be the beauty of the orchard, or that of the corn-field, slashed with the scarlet of the poppy. Previous to all this that piece of land was called 'waste ground'.

There was a time in the world's history when the law of gravity was unknown. Our forefathers could not comprehend what kept the earth in its place—on what it was founded. The existence of pillars seemed to suggest one explanation, and so the Old Testament is full of this idea:

The Pillars of the earth are the Lord's and He hath set the world upon them (I Sam ii.8).

The earth and all the inhabiters thereof are dissolved: I bear up the pillars of it (Ps lxxv.3).

He shaketh the earth out of her place, and the pillars thereof tremble (Job xxvi.7).

Note, also, the poetic expression 'the pillared firmament'. Thus the pillar acquired a quasi-sacred character, and many ancient nations practised pillar worship. Even the Hebrews were not free from the superstition. Jacob set up a pillar at Luz or Bethel (Gen 28:18) to commemorate his wonderful vision, and afterwards another at Galeed (Gen 31:46), as a memorial of his treaty with Laban. Joshua set up a pillar at Gilgal to commemorate the miraculous crossing of Jordan (Josh 4:20); and Samuel erected one at Mizpeh (I Sam 7:12). The original altar in almost every form of sacrificial worship was an unhewn stone.

These stones were not erected in accordance with caprice. There must have been some special manifestation of supernatural power—a battle won, a signal deliverance, a vision, and then the place thus consecrated became, like Luz, a *Beth-El*—that is a stone of God. Then the stone was consecrated, either by the pouring of oil or by the blood of a sacrificial victim. The stone set up by Samuel to commemorate a victory over the Philistines, referred to above, he called *Eben-ezer*—a word which, like Bethel, has survived, and is found in the nomenclature of today.

In the writings of J. S. M. Ward some confusion will occasionally be noted between the architectural columns representing Wisdom, Strength and Beauty, and the two Wardens' columns. The effects of history have been touched on elsewhere, but in some lodges a column similar to those of the Wardens is provided for the Master, in the Ionic style. This shows later speculation and thought arising out of the conversion referred to rather late in masonic history in England, and seems to lose sight of the fact that the Wardens' columns are, historically, their essential emblems of office. Ward writes:

The contributions of the three Gr Ms to the great Temple, according to some of our rituals, were as follows: Solomon had the Wisdom to design it; Hiram King of Tyre supported him with his Strength, and more especially in the materials he contributed; while it was adorned with Beauty by the skill of H A B.

In some parts of Cornwall, and in the working of most of the German Lodges, the W M lights his light first with the words, 'Wisdom in the East.' The S W takes his light from the W M's light, and as he lights it says, 'Strength in the West,' and the J W follows with 'Beauty in the South.'

When we come to look at the deeper meaning underlying these respective officers, and the old Solar tradition, we can have no doubt that it is these attributes which apply respectively. Wisdom comes from the East. That is the age-long burden of every religion in the world. Wisdom comes out from the dawn, the abode where the High Gods dwell. From the point of view of the triune nature of man, it is the Divine Spirit which gives him Wisdom; the Soul, or S W, which stands for strength; while Beauty refers to the physical beauty of the body of man. In like manner the sun at its meridian is in its greatest glory and beauty, and helps to make beautiful all things on which it shines. The sun at dawn and at eventide, though beautiful in itself, has not that direct vivifying effect which it has at meridian.

The J W's column is down when the Lodge is at work, indicating that the work of the Lodge concerns the body but little, whereas the S W's column is up, indicating the exact reverse. When we call from labour to refreshment, however, we put aside for a time the spiritual food of the soul and attend to the just needs of the body, and this fact is carefully emphasised in the position of the columns. But in Lodges where the Master's column is used it remains up alike in labour and refreshment, to remind us that both must be controlled by the spiritual faculties in obedience to Divine laws.

There is so much confusion over pillars and columns that it may be worth considering how the three columns may have got into masonic symbolism at all, for they had somehow ousted the two old pillars from the first degree by the end of the eighteenth century. The three columns which support a lodge are three of the five noble orders of classical architecture. In the earlier years of that century, it had become the practice to give lectures in lodge concerned with building, and in particular in relation to architecture. Inigo Jones in the 1600s had visited Italy and came back to England very much influenced by the work of Palladio in a neo classic style. This became very popular in England and from the 1720s it achieved a further burst of popularity led by William Kent so that a number of continental developments passed England by. The whole background of this style was that perfection in art can be obtained by rules and that a system of ideal proportions could be laid down. The idea was not new, it dated back to Vitruvius, but this later revival seemed to fascinate the English—so much so that Chippendale included a treatise on the

Five Orders as a preface to his *Gentleman and Cabinet Maker's Directory*, published in 1754. With this extreme preoccupation with one special style at this time in masonic history, and the giving of lectures in lodges, it is hardly to be wondered that the Five Orders have found a special place in English masonry and that three of them have been taken for this special use. On this point, William Preston says in his lecture:

Of the number of these pillars, how many are truly ancient?
Three.
Name them.
The Doric, Ionic and Corinthian.
What do these three represent?
These differ materially from each other and equally show invention and particular character. The Tuscan and Composite Orders have nothing but what is borrowed and differ only by accident; the Tuscan being plainer than the Doric, and the Composite more ornamented, if not more beautiful, than the Corinthian.

Explain these orders.
In these orders we trace the gradual progress of science. In the Doric columns we behold the emblems of strength. In the Ionic, the emblem of shape and figure, and in the Corinthian, the emblem of wisdom and united talents.

The attributes which Preston gave to the three orders was that generally followed by the Moderns before the change at the time of the Union to that used at present in most English lodges.

J. S. M. Ward also writes on the carpet or flooring, and on the four tassels traditionally shown at its corners and which also appear at the corners of the first degree tracing board:

The inner meaning of this carpet is the chequered way of life—the alternations of joy and sorrow, of good and evil, of day and night, which we all experience in the course of our lives. Indeed, it may be said to stand for all opposites.
But what probably strikes the initiate more than anything else about this carpet are the four tassels which are woven into the pattern at the four corners. We are told that these represent the four cardinal virtues, but this is a late gloss, probably invented towards the close of the eighteenth century, and there seems no particular reason why they should represent the four cardinal virtues more than the four elements, or any other particular four. We find the true origin of these tassels, as of many more obscure points in our ritual, if we study the mediæval methods employed by the Operative masons when laying out the

ground plan of a new building. The master mason, or architect, as we should call him to-day, commenced his work by striking the centre of the piece of ground on which the building was to be erected, and from it he plotted out the square or rectangle on which the containing walls were subsequently to rise. To do so, he extended ropes from the centre pin to the four angles, and pegged these down at the corners of the building; by the simple use of square and triangle he was able to check the four corners and ascertain if they were true. As the walls rose, from time to time a piece of wood was extended from the corner inwards, and a plumb line dropped down to make sure that the walls were perpendicular and the angle as true on its upper tiers as it was at the base. A dim remembrance of these corner plumb lines lingered on well into the middle of the nineteenth century in Speculative Masonry, for I have met several old provincial Brethren who remember seeing, not merely woven tassels on the carpet, but actual tassels hanging in the four corners of the Lodge room; and in the ritual used in the old days it is these hanging tassels to which the four cardinal virtues were attached— implying, of course, that the four cardinal virtues were guides to enable a man to maintain an upright life. Like many other old and interesting customs, these tassels seem to have disappeared, and we are left with a symbolic representation of the four ends of the ropes which crossed the ground plan of the building.

W. L. Wilmshurst saw more in the 'square pavement for the high priest to walk on', which is the original of the lodge floor:

It is not merely the Jewish High Priest of centuries ago that is here referred to, but the individual member of the Craft. For every Mason is intended to be the High Priest of his own personal temple and to make it a place where he and Deity may meet. By the mere fact of being in this dualistic world every living being, whether a Mason or not, walks upon the square pavement of mingled good and evil in every action of his life, so that the floor cloth is the symbol of an elementary philosophical truth common to us all. But, for us, the words 'walk upon' imply much more than that. They mean that he who aspires to be master of his fate and captain of his soul must walk upon these opposites in the sense of transcending and dominating them, of trampling upon his lower sensual nature and keeping it beneath his feet in subjection and control. He must become able to rise above the motley of good and evil, to be superior and indifferent to the ups and downs of fortune, the attractions and fears governing ordinary men and swaying their thoughts and actions this way or that. His object is the development of his innate spiritual potencies, and it is impossible that these should develop so long as he is over-ruled by his material tendencies and the fluctating emotions of pleasure and pain that they give birth to. It is by rising superior to these and attaining serenity and mental equilibrium under any circumstances in which for the moment he may be placed, that a Mason truly 'walks on' the chequered groundwork of existence and the conflicting tendencies of his more material nature.

Our thoughtful brethren of the eighteenth century speculated not only on individual objects in their lodges, but on the whole structure of masonry. When they said 'the rule of three I understand, the key of the Lodge is at my command', they meant that they had a full understanding of all three degrees and could understand the construction of a right angle. In an interesting Lecture form which seems to have been practised mainly in Lancashire towards the end of that century, there is a closing section to the Third Part—that of the third degree—which illustrates their thinking:

You say you have wrought as an head Architect, both as Master and Undertaker; could you undertake to build a Lodge?
   Yes, I could and would undertake it if the materials were found and properly prepared.
What materials are requisite to build a Lodge?
   Truth, Justice and Charity, with which this Lodge and every other Lodge is or ought to be well stored with.
If you have the materials, how would you lay off your foundations to square them?
   I would take the proportions of 3 4 and 5, which answers to the great Eureka of Masonry commonly called the 47th proposition of Euclid's Elements of Geometry.
What does it demonstrate?
   It demonstrates that the square on the hypotenuse of a right-angled triangle is equal to the sum of the squares on the other two sides.
How do you prove it?
   The square of 5 is equal to the sum of the squares of 3 and 4—the square of 3 is 9, and the square of 4 is 16 so that 16 plus 9 is equal to 25, the square of 5, by which proportions Masons take off right angles, squares and perpendiculars.
What is understood by the square of 3?
   By the square of 3 is understood the three points of my entry— Preparation, Admission and Obligation.
How do you apply the square of 4?
   To the four cardinal virtues, which two squares are equal to the square of 5, which are the five points of fellowship, so that the five points of fellowship are equal to the three points at my obligation or entry, and the four cardinal virtues.
Now Brother, as you have squared off your Building, you lay the foundation; what are the tools necessary to carry on your work?

First, compass and rule to lay off my designs upon the trassel board, then Truth to level the foundation, next Justice plumbs the upright and Charity squares the covering.

What cement is used?

Love and Friendship cements and Unity gives the bond.

How do you ornament it?

With Regularity, Virtue and Concord.

What do you furnish it with?

The four cardinal Virtues.

What are they?

Justice, Prudence, Temperance and Fortitude.

How do you place them?

Justice in the East, Prudence in the West, Temperance in the South and Fortitude in the North.

What do you dedicate it with?

Corn, Wine and Oil.

Why do you dedicate it with Corn, Wine and Oil?

Because Corn, Wine and Oil were the merchandizes which Solomon, King of Israel, sent Hiram, King of Tyre, in return for the cedar and cypress wood he received from him to build the Temple.

To whom will you dedicate your Lodge?

To God and the Holy Apostle, St John.

Why do you dedicate it to God?

Because all places where God is worshipped are dedicated to him, and to him all upright and good men are dedicated.

Why do you dedicate it to the Holy Apostle, St John?

Because St John taught and preached Brotherly Love as the capestone of religion, for Love is the fulfilling of the law.

Now Brother, your Lodge thus built, cemented, ornamented, furnished and dedicated, how is the door secured?

Silence locks the door, and deposits the Key.

Where is the Key deposited?

In every true, just and honest Mason's heart.

Now Brother, after it has been thus finished and locked up, how does it stand?

As every honest Mason stands, upright on the Square, fronting the four cardinal points of Heaven with extended arms, ready to receive and comfort the worthy and deserving from all the four points.

When Silence shut the door of your Lodge, what charge did she give you?

She required me to do Justly, love Mercy, to walk humbly with my God, and to remember my three duties that I might be a welcome guest whenever I returned.

When you return, how do you expect to be readmitted?

By three principal Steps, or Graces.

What are they?

First, Faith, which is an assent of the mind to all things delivered in the Holy Scriptures as the Testimony of Almighty God: secondly, Hope, which is the anchor of the soul, sure and steadfast, by which we look for salvation, through the promises and goodness of God: thirdly Charity, which is the Love of God and unlimited Benevolence to all mankind, by the true observance of which, we shall be enabled to ascend the Heavenly Grand Lodge, where there is fulness of joy and pleasure to flow for evermore, which God grant may be our happy lot.   Amen.

4

THE LODGE — Ornaments, Furniture and Jewels

THE SYMBOLISM of many of the articles found physically in a lodge is also that related to the first degree tracing board, in fact, it would be fair to say that the hieroglyphics of the tracing board were developed first, in an era before it was either customary or possible to lay out lodges actually furnished with the necessary emblems. The articles found in the lodge have been developed from the representations found on tracing boards. But on the tracing board for the first degree there are a number of items which do not appear in the lodge itself. In these days it is no longer common to find a pentangle or five-pointed star set out as 'the blazing star or glory in the centre' described in the lectures and formerly found in the middle of the mosaic carpet. It was in this pentangle that the letter G was displayed in former times in the second degree, to indicate that the lodge was working in that degree. It is noticeable that this G does not appear even now on the first degree board but is in the second, and in some places in the third also. Except in some specially built lodge rooms, it is unusual to find Jacob's ladder displayed anywhere but on the Tracing board, and the same may be said of the point within a circle set between two parallel lines under the Volume of the Sacred Law.

The Letter G.

The letter G still looms large in our second degree, for we find it in the explanation of the tracing board as a symbol which specially struck the attention in the middle chamber, where it appeared in substitution for certain characters. There are references to this letter being in the centre, and particularly in the centre of the building. In many masonic buildings the letter may be found hanging, usually in the centre of the room but sometimes over the master's pedestal, as a permanent feature. It belongs properly to the second degree and if its symbolism is strictly followed it should be displayed only in that degree. In the days when the first and second degrees formed a group quite separate from the third and the symbols relating to both the former were displayed in both, the only difference between the first and second was the additional display of the letter G when the lodge was opened in the second. It was not there when work was done in the first degree and it was its being displayed which converted the symbols into those of the second degree, for the apprentice would still require all he had learned on the way for his use as a craftsman, plus this little something extra.

In the present day most lodges make do with a display of the second tracing board to convert the lodge from an apprentices' lodge to a fellow crafts', and this, as the explanation of the board tells us, displays the letter G (or should do so, quite clearly). Some lodges display only the second degree board with its symbols relating only to that degree, and thus unconsciously demonstrate the three quite separate degrees as a structure into which we have drifted since 1813. Some lodges add the second degree board to the first already displayed, thus perpetuating the old relationship. This consideration of the letter G and its significance to our ancient brethren tends to point to the position of the tracing board being properly on the floor in the centre of the lodge, where most lodges seem to place it when it is explained, but recent years have shown a practice of displaying all the boards upright, either against a pedestal or in a special frame or holder.

The letter G has had a considerable significance in masonry in many parts of the world and it is to be found in use in several constitutions placed between the square and compasses united, as part of the major symbol signifying masonry. William Hutchinson, writing before 1775, places it in a pentangle or pentalpha or five-pointed star, surrounded by a glory, as his main frontispiece. He stresses that although the letter G must, in the mason's mind, signify God, yet to give it only that simple significance is to deprive it of much of its importance as a masonic symbol. By its representation of God as the Grand Geometrician it represents Geometry 'which contains the determination, definition, and proof of the order, beauty and wonderful wisdom of the power of God in his creation.' Some constitutions say that, to them, the symbol is that of an excellent mason; there is certainly some earlier justification for this in the English Constitution, for the old Moderns Grand Lodge working included in the third degree a reference to an excellent mason. Old tracing boards for the third degree may still be found including a G, which presumably has this significance while it is also found in this connection in Preston's works, certainly until shortly after the Union.

Present day lectures give the significance of the letter G on the tracing board as denoting God, the Grand Geometrician, but if reference is made to John Browne's *Master Key*, reflecting the practice of lodges under the Moderns Grand Lodge about 1800, we read:

For why was you passed a Fellow Craft?
For the sake of the letter G.
What does that letter G denote?
Geometry, or the fifth science, on which Masonry is founded.
What is Geometry?
Geometry is a science by which we are taught to find out the contents of bodies unmeasured by comparing them with those already measured.
What are the four principles of Geometry?
Magnitude and Extension, or a regular progression from a point to a line, a line to a superfice, and from that to a solid.
What is a point?
A small thing, the beginning of geometrical matter.
What is a line?
That point extended.
What is a superfice?
Length and breadth without determined thickness.
What is a solid?
Length and breadth with a determined thickness and forms a cube.

In this short catechism is summed up a very great deal of the essential original symbolism of masonry, which our early forebears identified with geometry. First it indicates a point going through a system of progressive degrees, and shows that the second degree of our order is devoted to the study of geometry, the science related to measurement, and so to building. The progression from a point is to a particular end—the formation of a solid. Not just any solid, but a cube. The cube is a body composed of six equal sides with all its angles right angles, a symbol of perfection. In its construction the important step is the incorporation of a third dimension, as the old lectures say, raised 'from a superficial flat to a lively perpendicular.' Here is an abbreviated story of three degrees.

It is possible that the use of a letter in this way as a representation of God is a reflection of the influence of Jewish tradition in masonic development. Jewish custom was not to pronounce the name of God which was represented by the Tetragrammaton, the four letter JHVH, but to use some other word, such as Adonai (Lord), instead, or to find ways of expressing the presence of God by some other representation. The use of the letter G, especially when surrounded by a glory suggesting the Shekinah, an indication by light of the presence of God, may well have come into masonry by copying a Jewish tradition. There is some evidence to suggest that up to the time of the union of Grand Lodges in 1813 the name indicated in the Tetragrammaton was particularly associated with the third degree; some of the papers relating to William Preston's lectures indicate that this was so, while the Tetragrammaton is often found on early third degree tracing boards. It is interesting to note that on a second degree tracing board designed by John Harris as late as 1845, there is an unusual use of the letter G and the Tetragrammaton. On this board, through the door of the middle chamber, the letter G may be seen in a triangle surrounded by a glory or Shekinah. Over the door to the middle chamber is a dormer, normally a feature of masonic illustrations of the Sanctum Sanctorum, and in the dormer, also enclosed in a Shekinah, is the Tetragrammaton. Harris is reputed to have been of Jewish origins. The board, with its companions for the other two degrees, was commissioned by the Emulation Lodge of Improvement and is in weekly use by them at Freemasons' Hall, London. This may be an indication that, in the old third degree, the object of a search was the discovery of this word, and that to emphasise this, the second degree gave only a representation.

In placing the G in a triangle and glory, Harris was doing what Hutchinson had done seventy years before, and Harris had given the same treatment to the Tetragrammaton. W. H. Rylands in *Notes on Some Masonic Symbols* gives a quotation which may indicate the origin of this treatment, and could be the reason for the practice:

. . . . in ecclesiastical art in the 16th century, the Deity was figured only by his name, inscribed within a geometrical figure. The triangle is the linear emblem of God and of the Divine Trinity. The name of God, or Jehovah, was inscribed in Hebrew letters within the triangle, and both the name and the figure were placed in the centre of a radiating circle, symbolic of eternity. (Didron, Christ. Iconog., Bohn pp. 231,232.)

Rylands goes on to show through the work of the sixteenth century architect, John Thorpe, that the triangle was considered in the building profession as a symbol of the Trinity. In general life the use of accepted symbols of this nature was much more common; in many cases, when masonry took such symbols into use, there was nothing unusual about the practice. Masonry has survived with these symbols incorporated, while the general practice has fallen into disuse and their general significance is often not remembered.

The Letter G and the Square

One of the more interesting suggestions for the original use of the letter G in a masonic connection arises in connection with the shape of the Square. In the Chapter on the working tools several writers are quoted on the true shape of the square when used in a masonic connection. There seems to be a good deal of opinion which says that a square with arms of uneven length was that used in early masonry, while there is no doubt that what is known as a 'gallows' square was at one time in popular use— ⌐ . J. S. M. Ward, in *An Interpretation of Our Masonic Symbols*, points out that this shape for the square is precisely the shape of the Greek letter *Gamma*, equivalent to G in the Roman alphabet, and, further, that in ecclesiastical script used in medieval Europe, this very gallows square shape was used to represent the letter G. (This refers to the capital letter only and not the small letter.) Ward also agrees with an opinion of Sir John Cockburn that the Square and the letter G in early lodges were depicted by the same shape. Cockburn is quoted as saying that it was the letter G which the early masons wished to depict, symbolising God, and so they used this gallows square shape to represent that letter. It could just as easily have been that the early masons wished to show the Square as the major moral instrument of the Craft and then found that it would also represent the letter G for Geometry. Whichever is the right way round, there could well be some justification for Ward's assertion that if a Lodge is to be absolutely correctly furnished according to the original tradition, that the symbol in the centre of the lodge, whether hung from the ceiling or placed in the pentangle on the floor, should take the form of a ⌐ —a gallows square.

One of the fullest examinations of this symbol is in *The Letter G*, by Harry Carr, in *Ars Quatuor Coronatorum*, Volume 76. Carr traces the earliest references to it as 1730 in Prichard's *Masonry Dissected*, which is also the first reference of any length to a three degree system rather than one of two degrees. In Prichard, the letter G is a symbol of the second degree and stands for Geometry. Later references have it as in the centre and there is ample confirmation of its being, by the 1740s, the symbol which converted the lodge to a fellow crafts' lodge, and that it was associated with a blazing star or glory as Hutchinson has it. In the satirical exposure-type paper on the 'Scald Miserables' first published in 1741, there is reference to the letter G as the item which converts a lodge into a fellow crafts' lodge.

When John Coustos was examined by the Inquisition in Portugal in 1743, in describing the lodge he said:

> The floor of the said Lodge has a design in white chalk wherein are formed several borders serving as ornament together with a blazing star with a 'G' in the middle, signifying the fifth science of Geometry, to which all Officers [? Craftsmen] and Apprentices should aspire.

The translation is from the actual Inquisition records and is that used by Dr Sidney Vatcher in his paper on John Coustos. The word 'officers' appears to have been consistently used in the translation back into English where we would use the word 'fellow-crafts' or 'craftsmen'. As Coustos had already lived in Lisbon for upwards of two years and previously to that time he had spent some time in France, he was referring to English practice in the 1730s. It has been suggested that he was confusing the practice in France at that time, although in this respect, it was likely to have been the same as in England. In any case, in rites which stem from the French masonry of that time and shortly after, the letter G, usually in a blazing star, is still generally found as the particular symbol of the second degree. Later in the century, William Preston also refers to the use of the letter G in a fellow-crafts' lodge, but places it in the centre of the *covering*—thereby suggesting that it was the practice of some to *suspend* the G, as long ago as the early 1800s.

Dr Wynn Westcott suggested that the origin of the G was the Hebrew letter *Gimel*, third of the Hebrew alphabet and so representing the figure three—for the Trinity and so its representation of God. Carr also mentions others who suggest the Hebrew letter, but some of these explanations seem a little far fetched.

Geometry

This stress on Geometry and the finding of God as the Grand Geometrician in the higher of the first two degrees marks the importance in the structure of speculative masonry given to Geometry by our ancient brethren. That same version of the Lectures given by Browne tells us:

> Geometry is the Origin of Mathematics, and the foundation of Architecture; comprehending the Doctrine of whatever is susceptible of Increasing or Diminishing; hence not only Point, Line, Superfice and Solid come within our Consideration, but also Time, Space, Velocity and Magnitude in general. By the further study of this Fifth Science, on which

Masonry is founded, we are led to contemplate on the inimitable works of the Supreme grand Geometrician of this vast terrestial Globe.

The earliest editions of William Preston's *Illustrations of Masonry* were published about the same time as Hutchinson was writing. Preston included in his book a *Vindication of Masonry* founded, Preston said, on a discourse composed by Charles Leslie and delivered by him at the consecration of the Vernon Kilwinning Lodge at Edinburgh in 1741. He includes the following, which has now been adopted almost as it was in the standard Lecture in the second degree:

Geometry, the first and noblest of sciences, is the basis on which the superstructure of Masonry is erected. By geometry, we may curiously trace Nature through her various windings, to her most concealed recesses. By it we may discover the power, the wisdom, and the goodness of the grand Artificer of the universe, and view with amazing delight the beautiful proportions which connect and grace this vast machine. By it we may discover how the planets move in their different orbs, and mathematically demonstrate their various revolutions. By it we may rationally account for the return of seasons, and the mixed variety of scenes which they display to the discerning eye. Numberless worlds are around us, all framed by the same Divine Artist, which roll through the vast expanse, and are all conducted by the same unerring law of Nature. How must we then improve? With what grand ideas must such knowledge fill our minds; and how worthy is it of the attention of all rational beings.

A survey of Nature, and the observation of its beautiful proportions first determined man to imitate the divine plan, and to study symmetry and order. This gave rise to societies, and birth to every useful art. The architect began to design, and the plans which he laid down, improved by experience and time, produced some of those excellent works which will be the admiration of future ages. Thus, from the commencement of the world, we may trace the foundation of Masonry. Ever since order began, and harmony displayed her charms, it has had a being. During many ages, and in many different countries, it has flourished. No art, no science preceded it. In the dark periods of antiquity, when literature was in a low state, and the rude manners of our forefathers withheld from them the knowledge we now so amply share, Masonry began to diffuse her influence. The mysteries of this science unveiled, arts instantly arose, civilisation took place, and the progress of knowledge and philosophy gradually dispelled the gloom of ignorance and barbarism. Government being settled, authority was given to laws, and the assemblies of the fraternity acquired the patronage of the great and the good, while the tenets of the profession were attended with general and unbounded utility.

W. L. Wilmshurst on Geometry:

Now Geometry was one of the 'seven noble arts and sciences' of ancient philosophy. It means literally the science of earth-measurement. But the 'earth' of the ancients did not mean, as it does to us, this physical planet. It meant the primordial substance, or undifferentiated soul-stuff out of which we human beings have been created, the 'mother-earth' from which we have all sprung and to which we must all undoubtedly return. Man was made, the Scriptures teach, out of the dust of the ground, that earth or fundamental substance of his being, which requires to be 'measured' in the sense of investigating and understanding its nature and properties. No competent builder erects a structure without first satisfying himself about the nature of the materials with which he proposes to build, and in the speculative and spiritual or 'royal' art of Masonry no Mason can properly build the temple of his own soul without first understanding the nature of the raw material he has to work upon.

Geometry, therefore, is synonymous with self-knowledge, the understanding of the basic substance of our being, its properties and potentialities. Over the ancient temples of initiation was inscribed the sentence 'Know thyself and thou shalt know the universe and God', a phrase which implies in the first place that the uninitiated man is without knowledge of himself, and in the second place that when he attains that knowledge he will realize himself to be no longer the separate distinctified individual he now supposes himself to be, but to be a microcosm or summary of all that is and to be identified with the Being of God.

Masonry is the science of the attainment of that supreme knowledge and is, therefore, rightly said to be founded on the principles of Geometry as thus defined.

The Masonic Jewels

Traditionally, there are six jewels in a masons lodge, three movable and three immovable. The square, level and plumb-rule are the three movable jewels and as they serve also as the working tools of the second degree—which has to do with geometry—they are considered in more detail under that heading. The immovable jewels are the tracing board and the rough and perfect ashlars, and are called 'immovable' because they lie open in the lodge 'for the brethren to moralize on'. They are all three related to a geometrical function as are the movable jewels and have arrived at their present positions and meanings after over two hundred years of development.

The tracing board, like its movable companion, the square, is essentially the Master's instrument. The lecture tells us that it is for the Master to lay lines and draw designs on, the better to enable the brethren to carry on the intended structure with regularity and propriety. It is on the tracing board that the Master sets out moral teachings for the instruction and guidance of his brethren in the matter of living. In these days the designs of the tracing boards related to the different degrees tend to be of a standard pattern and to reflect by symbols the moral teachings of the Craft. They developed in this way through the last quarter of the eighteenth century and the first quarter of the nineteenth. The English Grand Lodge certificate, still on a basic design first used in 1819, follows the layout of the first degree tracing board (except for the centre part left out to accommodate the necessary wording). This document shows a tracing board in the lodge—a draughtman's board, with pencil and ruler lying on it for the Master to use. It is believed that the name 'tracing board' is a corruption of the old Tressel or Tracel Board used in lodges in the late eighteenth century to display the masonic hieroglyphics, and in many lodges displayed on a tressel in the centre of the lodge. The lectures further compare the use of the tracing board by the Master in the instruction of his lodge, with the Volume of the Sacred Law as a means by which God may perform a similar function to mankind. It is regarded as the spiritual tracing

---

Explanation of the Frontispiece of the Book of Constitutions

The frontispiece to the *Book of Constitutions* of 1784 of the Moderns Grand Lodge. This is of particular interest in showing representations of Faith, Hope and Charity at that time, and without any connection with a ladder. But it is of interest also in demonstarating the use of symbolism in that part of the eighteenth century, for the Grand Lodge published this explanation of the symbols:

> The architectural part represents the inside of Free-masons' Hall. The uppermost figure is TRUTH, holding a mirrour, which reflects its rays on divers ornaments of the Hall, and also on the Globes and other Masonic Furniture and Implements of the Lodge. TRUTH is attended by the three Theological Virtues, FAITH, HOPE, and CHARITY: under these, the GENIUS of MASONRY, commissioned by TRUTH and her Attendants, is descending into the Hall, bearing a lighted Torch; she is decorated with some of the Masonic Emblems, and on her arm hangs a ribbon with a Medal pendant, with which she is to invest the GRAND MASTER, in token of the Divine approbation of a Building sacred to Charity and Benevolence.

Published as the Act directs —
By the SOCIETY of FREE MASONS —
their HALL in GREAT QUEEN STREET LINCOLNS INN FIELDS 178.

PLATE 2

The Frontispiece, dated 1786, for the Moderns Book of Constitutions.
This includes a number of symbols and, in particular, there may be noted
three female figures near the ceiling, representing Faith (with book,
Chalice and Cross), Hope (with Anchor) and Charity (tending children).
(For Grand Lodge explanation, see page 88)

PLATE 3

The north front of Somerset House, commenced in 1776, shows how the influence of the 'Augustan style' or neo-classical architecture continued into the later years of the eighteenth century with its accent on the use of columns in the classical orders.

PLATE 4

The Frontispiece of Stephen Jones's *Masonic Miscellany*, published in 1797. It is believed to have been designed by Lovejoy, a well known masonic illustrator, and is in the form of a Lodge Board covering the emblems and symbols of the first and second degrees.

PLATE 5

A dual Tracing Board designed for the Lodge of Unions, now No. 256 (and by whose permission it is reproduced), which bears the date, 1801, in its inscription. Although most of the emblems appear to relate to the first degree, the design is unusual, particularly in the inclusion of the forty-seventh proposition of Euclid. This was probably used as a 'Master's' Tracing Board.

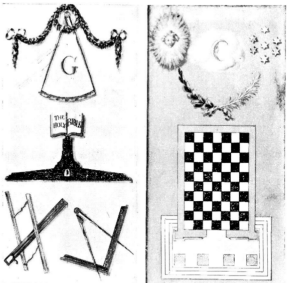

PLATES 6 and 7

These two 'Master's' Tracing Boards date from about 1800 and with the other examples of such boards and other illustrations, indicate the lack of uniformity in what were considered the more essential symbols at that time. The lower is reproduced by permission of the Britannic Lodge, whose property it is, while that above is the property of the United Grand Lodge of England. It is reproduced by permission of the Board of General Purposes.

PLATE 8

The first degree Tracing Board designed in 1845 by John Harris for the Emulation Lodge of Improvement. This shows the symbols which had, by the time the rearrangements at the union of Grand Lodges of 1813 had been completely absorbed, become associated exclusively with the first degree.

PLATE 9

The second degree Tracing Board designed in 1845 by John Harris for the Emulation Lodge of Improvement. The upper picture shows a staircase opening from a Temple entrance which is obviously not the main entrance with the two great pillars. This presumes that the words 'porchway or entrance on the south side' implies that there was a second entrance. The lower picture shows the main entrance (which was considered to be at the east of the building) with the two pillars. Inside the pillars can be seen a figure on the left, or south side. This is the position of the Junior Warden in pre-union manuscripts where the words appear to mean 'on the south side, inside the porchway or entrance'. Most studies of the Temple suggest that the main building had only one entrance.

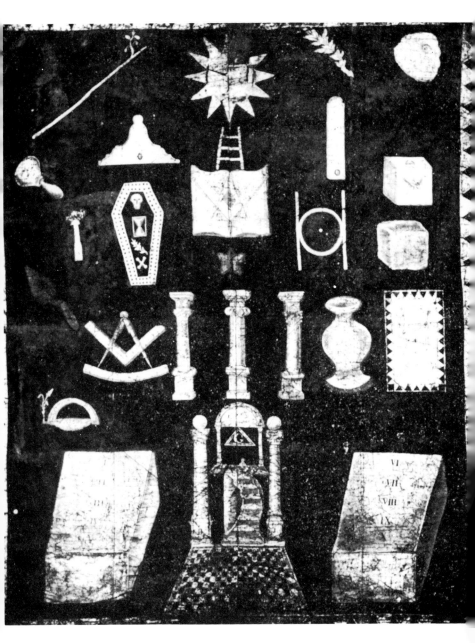

PLATE 10

A Lodge Cloth, used in the same way as a Tracing Board, which almost certainly belonged to Trafalgar Lodge No. 111 (Antients) which was formed in 1804 and met at Colchester and later at Brightlingsea. In addition to emblems and symbols now associated with all three degrees, there are others which have now fallen out of use—Aaron's Rod, the Pot of Manna, the Tables of the Law, and the Trowel (which has recently been re- introduced as the jewel of the Charity Steward). Reproduced by permission of the Lodge of Hope, No. 433, of Brightlingsea.

board of God wherein are laid down such Divine laws and moral plans, which, if followed, would bring us to an eternal mansion in the Heavens.

Dr Oliver summarised the content of the lectures of his time and adds his own thoughts:

> I will now call your attention to a Board with a few lines, angles, and perpendiculars designed upon its surface. This is the Tracing Board; and though it may appear rough and of little use, is yet an immoveable jewel, and contains a lesson of inestimable value. This board is for the Master to draw his plans on, for the direction of his workmen; but its mystic reference is to the great charter of our religious privileges, which, in all our open Lodges is displayed on the Master's Pedestal with its leaves unfolded as the visible standard of our Faith, subscribed with the hand of the divinity; the very ground and pillar of Truth.
>
> You have now before you an unhewn block of marble, rough as when taken from the quarry. This is another immoveable jewel, which points to the infant mind, rough and uncultivated as this stone; and as the marble can alone be brought into a definite and useful form by the skill and judicious management of the expert workman; so the mind can only be trained to the practice of virtue by the sedulous care, and insiduous instruction of parents, guardians, and teachers. Thus the ripening man becomes fitted for his station in society, and qualified to act his part with the approbation of his fellow men. These reflections lead us to contemplate this stone in another and a more perfect form. It has been under the chissel of the expert workman, and now assumes the shape of a true die square, polished according to art, which can only be tried by the nice application of the square and compass. The mind of man, after its previous cultivation, and progress through the chequered scenes of good and evil with which this life abounds is here represented. He has attained a good old age, and his time has been spent in acts of piety and devotion; the blessing of the fatherless is upon him, and he has caused the widow's heart to sing for joy. His soul therefore ripened for glory, may be aptly compared to this superb stone, for it can now only be tried by the square of God's holy word, and the compass of his own conscience.

The two ashlars are two stones of a cubic shape, the Rough Ashlar being, as its name implies, only roughly so and without any finish, while the Perfect Ashlar is, again as its name implies, a perfect, well finished and polished cube—the symbol of perfection. The Rough Ashlar represents the newly admitted candidate, the Entered Apprentice, and the object of masonry is, by the Master's instruction with the assistance of his Tracing Board, to make that Rough Ashlar into the perfect stone which the Perfect Ashlar represents. On the English

Grand Lodge certificate, the Rough Ashlar is shown with suitable tools lying on it, a maul and chisel, while the Perfect Ashlar has resting on it the compasses, representing conscience, that final test which the true man applies to his work. On most Tracing Boards, the Rough Ashlar is shown by the Corinthian column representing the Junior Warden and the Perfect Ashlar is shown by the Doric column which represents the Senior Warden. Traditionally, the Junior Warden is in charge of the apprentices, so that symbolically, the Rough Ashlar is shown as under his control, while the Senior Warden has charge of the Craftsmen. In many lodges this piece of symbolism is carried a stage farther by the placing of Ashlars in the lodge, either on the pedestal of, or otherwise near to the Warden concerned. Other lodges follow a different pattern by relating the Ashlars to the corners of the lodge where the Apprentice and Crafts-man are placed to receive a Charge on their being admitted to the degree.

The history of the Perfect Ashlar is a little confused, for an ashlar is among the earliest symbols found in masonic writings, although it is as a perpend ashlar it is first found, but sometimes spelt in unusual ways. A perpend ashlar is a dressed stone that extends through a wall from one side to the other, serving as a binding stone. This in itself provides a degree of symbolism, for binding together in friendship was an object of the Craft. Further, if the average building stone was likely to be cubic in shape, then the shape of a perpend ashlar would be an approximate double cube, a shape which has had some signi-ficance in masonry and in which some later writers see a special symbolic meaning.

Jacob's Ladder

The Union of Grand Lodges in England in 1813 caused a good deal of rethinking of masonic symbolism, none more than in connection with 'hieroglyphics' of masonry as displayed on what we now call tracing boards. This involved the final and complete separation of the symbols of the three degrees into three separate groups and so into three tracing boards. This is not to say that there had not been symbols especially regarded as the province of a particular degree before this, but there was some confusion in different places as to where they fitted in, as may appear from the development referred to later. There were, however, never any official designs of the tracing boards, although there were at least semi-official descriptions of the symbols which should make them up—and many of these had a history in masonry going back well before that time. The only official design which was published was that of the Grand Lodge certificate which first came into use in 1819, and which is based on the type of tracing board of the first degree which was being made at about that time. This famous 'pillars' certificate has had the centre of the usual tracing board design left out to allow for the wording. This centre part of the design usually shows a pedestal with a circle; on the pedestal stands the Volume of the Sacred Law 'supporting Jacob's ladder, the top of which reaches to the Heavens'. This ladder normally consists of three 'staves or rounds' and disappears at the top into cloud, or a glory of light, with the sun, moon and the seven stars placed around.

Dr Oliver in *Signs and Symbols* made comparisons with the mysteries in other parts of the world and expressed some surprise that masonic symbolism of the ladder was built round three principal staves whereas in all other parallel instances he finds the number used to be seven. He says, for example, of his examination of the Indian mysteries:

> The Ladder with seven steps was used in the Indian mysteries to designate the approach of the Soul to perfection. The steps were usually denominated *gates*. The meaning is undoubtedly the same; for it is observable, that Jacob, in reference to the lower *stave* of his Ladder, exclaimed 'this is the house of God, and the *gate* of heaven.' Here we find the notion of ascending to heaven by means of the practice of moral virtue, depicted by the Hebrew Patriarchs and by a remote idolatrous nation under the idea of a *Ladder;* which we may hence conclude was a Masonic symbol.

It is true of course that in some other aspects of masonry, a ladder of seven steps may be found. In all early masonic systems, somewhere there is found some attempt to show positive progress by rising above the ground and there is some confusion between the use of a ladder and the use of a staircase to illustrate this, as well as to the number and significance of the steps concerned. In the lecture forms current today, the three principal steps of Faith, Hope and Charity are merely described as principal steps out of many, with no specific number in total given. As numbers became associated with degrees, the number three was that for the apprentice, while the ladder also became more used as the path upwards connected with that degree. In the same book Dr Oliver summarised the masonic symbolism of the ladder:

Thus the dark clouds of divine wrath are dissipated, the heavens are opened; and we enjoy a ray of his glory in the *celestial covering of the Lodge*. And more than this; the same divine Being has taught us how to attain the summit of the same, by means which are emblematically depicted by a ladder consisting of three principal ROUNDS or STAVES, which point to the three Theological Virtues, FAITH, HOPE, and CHARITY. We are now to consider the origin and application of this Symbol, by which a communication is opened between the creature and his Creator, with the gracious design of restoring to man that supreme happiness which was forfeited by Adam's transgression.

The application of this emblem is said to be derived from the vision of Jacob. When the Patriarch, to avoid the wrath of his brother Esau, fled to Padanaram; benighted and asleep, with the earth for his bed, a stone for his pillow, and the cloudy canopy of heaven for his covering, he beheld a LADDER, whose foot was placed on the spot where he lay, and its summit lost in the subtile ether. On this Ladder, angels continually ascended and descended, to receive communications from the Most High, who visibly appeared above the uppermost round of the Ladder; and to disseminate their divine commissions over the face of the earth. Here God graciously condescended to enter into a specific covenant with the sleeping Patriarch; who was hence so impressed with the feelings of gratitude and devotion, that when he awoke, he pronounced this consecrated spot, 'the house of God, and the gate of heaven.' In ancient Masonry, the Ladder was figuratively said to rest on the Holy Bible, and to consist of three *principal* staves, although the general number was indefinite, pointing to Faith, Hope and Charity, as the fundamental virtues which exalt mankind from earth to heaven.

You have here a most extraordinary coincidence of custom with respect to the Masonic Ladder, existing in every region of the world, and all equally applicable to a gradual ascent to heaven by the practice of moral virtue. Amongst us this practice is founded on the strong basis of FAITH, which is the first step of the Ladder resting on the word of God. It produces a well grounded HOPE of sharing the promises recorded in that Sacred Volume; and this is the second step of the Masonic Ladder. The third or more perfect step is CHARITY, by which we attain the summit of the Ladder; metaphorically speaking, the dominion of bliss, and the mansion of pure and permanent delight.

The use of Jacob's ladder in this way in masonic symbolism seems to have been a product of the later years of the eighteenth century, for there is no mention in Prichard's exposure of 1730 nor in any of the early catechisms. The tressel boards at the end of the century have the device and the lectures have reference to Faith, Hope and Charity. In the earliest tressel board designs the virtues are depicted on staves of the ladder by their initial letters, F, H and C. Symbols depicting the virtues are first found on early English craft certificates, the forerunners of the present Grand Lodge certificate, and first issued in the second half of the eighteenth century. A paper on English Craft certificates by T. O. Haunch is in *Ars Quatuor Coronatorum*, volume 82 and several illustrations to represent the three theological virtues may be seen. On the certificate given to William Preston by the Lodge of Antiquity, No. 1, there are three architectural pillars each with a virtue represented on the top. That for Faith is a female figure bearing a cross, Hope another female figure with an anchor and Charity, a third female figure caring for children and relieving the poor and lame; there was no relationship with the ladder at this time, nor was there in a similar theme taken up by the Moderns Grand Lodge in a design in their *Book of Constitutions* of 1784. The use of the ladder came later, along with other symbols for the virtues, although the Christian religious connection is made plain. In this matter again, such symbolism was common practice at that time, particularly in an artistic or architectural context, and there was nothing special in its use in masonry.

With the coming of the Union of Grand Lodges and the resulting decision to make masonry in England non-denominational from a religious point of view, efforts were made when new tracing boards were designed to use symbols not associated with Christianity. There were no official designs and artists were left very much to their own devices so that although a Book was for a time used to represent Faith and the three female figures disappeared, later boards often returned to the Cross. Other devices also appeared. Josiah Bowring had designed boards from just before the time of the Union and made a practice of hanging a key from the ladder—representing 'that excellent key', and not as one of the virtues—while as representation of Heaven at the top of the ladder, some artists showed the Holy Grail being taken into Heaven by a hand, which, again, was the return to a Christian symbol. Later artists copied these without at times realising the symbolism and in some boards the Grail is made to represent Charity, for there is no other symbol for this, and the key appears as an additional stave.

The Point Within a Circle

Jacob's ladder rests on the Volume of the Sacred Law, which, in turn, was on a device, sometimes in the form of a pedestal, of two upright lines with a circle touching them and the Volume. The centre of the circle was accentuated. The point within a circle is found in early exposures but again, it is not until late in the eighteenth century that the full symbol is found. The two parallel lines represented in the times before the Union, the two Grand Parallels of masonry, the Saints John, the Baptist and the Evangelist. These were the patron Saints or protectors of Masons and the half yearly festivals were held on their two commemoration days, 24 June and 27 December, conveniently six months apart and at which period the installation meetings were traditionally held. William Preston picks up this point in his lectures and says:

> These two parallels in modern time were applied to exemplify the two St Johns as Patrons of the Order, whose festivities are celebrated near the solstices or the time when the sun in its zodiacal career touches these two parallels.

Before the degrees settled down to their present symbolism, this point within a circle was a symbol incorporated in all pictorial representations connected with masonry generally and was explained in the Lecture of the first degree along with other connected symbols. No doubt it was part of the decoration of a lodge room and it appears on present day first tracing boards and is dealt with in the first Lecture—much in the way that other matters which have altered in the ritual of the degrees have retained their place in the Lectures because of the way in which they were formulated.

In John Browne's *Master Key* of 1802 there is a series of questions and answers in the first Lecture leading up to the position of the point within a circle:

> Our Lodge being ornamented, furnished and jeweled, to whom do we generally dedicate it?
> To King Solomon.
> Why to King Solomon?
> Because he was the first Grand Master who brought Masonry into due form and under whose royal patronage many of our mysteries received their first sanction.
> As King Solomon was an Hebrew long before the Christian era, to whom do we now dedicate our Lodge?
> To Saint John the Baptist.
> Why to Saint John the Baptist?
> He was the harbinger or forerunner of our Saviour, who preached repentance in the wilderness and drew the first line of the Gospel through Christ.
> Had he any equal?
> He had; Saint John the Evangelist.

Wherein was he his equal?

He, coming after the former, finished by his zeal what the other began by his learning and drew a line parallel.

What is the first point in Masonry?

Left knee bare and bent.

Wherein is that the first point?

In a kneeling posture I was first taught to adore my Creator and on my left knee bare and bent I was initiated into Masonry.

There is a chief point.

To make each other happy and to communicate that happiness to others.

There is a principal point.

A point within a circle, in going round which it is said the Master and Brethren cannot materially err.

Explain that point within a circle.

In all regular, well-formed Free-masons' Lodges, there is a point within a circle, in going round which, it is said the Master and Brethren cannot materially err. The circle is bounded on the North and South by two perpendicular parallel lines, that on the North is said to represent Saint John the Baptist, and that on the South, Saint John the Evangelist. On the upper points of these lines and on the periphery of the circle, rests the Holy Bible, supporting Jacob's Ladder, which it is said reaches to the watery clouds of Heaven. It also contains the dictates of an Unerring, Omnipotent and All-wise Being, so that while we are as conversant therein, and obedient thereto, as either of the Saint Johns were, it will bring us to Him that will neither deceive nor be deceived by us. Therefore by keeping ourselves so circumscribed, it is impossible we can materially err.

Here we have a fair statement of much on which our masonry was founded many years ago, although many would reverse the qualities of the two Saints John which are mentioned in this excerpt. Quite obviously, arising in a Christian country, its religious basis, which comes through so strongly in this extract, was in the Christian faith. When, about 1816, freemasonry was made non-denominational, an attempt was made to alter all the specifically Christian references, this particular passage was considerably altered. The two Grand Parallels became Moses and King Solomon and the whole passage had to be considerably shortened as a result. The Bible became the Volume of the Sacred Law, not only in this passage, but throughout the whole of the Ritual. When the Lectures were considered, the Grand Master of the day, the Duke of Sussex, decreed that they should be based on the old lecture system such as we find in Browne's *Master Key* and so the point within a circle, ritualwise, became associated with the third degree, as it undoubtedly should in the revised sequence, but it continued in an abbreviated form in the first Lecture.

One of the syllabus books of William Preston's lectures belonged to Rev L. D. H. Cockburne who was Grand Chaplain 1817-26 and a member of the Lodge of Antiquity, Preston's Lodge, 1819-22. Inscribed in this book is a short draft of a section of a lecture dealing with the dedication of the Temple and part of it reads:

> How is this dedication designated in Lodges?
> By a point within a circle with two parallel pillars described as tangents to that circle.
> Why?
> As representing the Centre of the Universe, the Divine Architect, whose goodness we represent in the sun and for the benefits we derive from this great luminary.
> What does the circle represent?
> The Zodiac is here represented as the prescribed motion of the Sun's system to mark the limited nature of the most wonderful creatures we behold.
> What do the parallels represent?
> The tropics, to remind us of the Superior Being who has set bounds to all creatures and prescribed the limits of planetary systems.

Webb, the American writer who introduced so many of Preston's ideas to American masons in the 1790s and after, is reputed to have seen the point as an individual brother and the circle as representing the boundary line of his duty to God and man; John Fellows, who quotes Webb in his *The Mysteries of Freemasonry* (1871), says on his own account:

> The point in the centre represents the Supreme Being; the circle indicates the annual circuit of the sun; and the parallel lines mark out the solstices within which that circuit is limited. The mason, by subjecting himself to due bounds, in imitation of that glorious luminary, will not wander from the path of duty.

All seem to agree on the important lesson of constraint which is found in this device, which is now seldom actually seen in lodge decoration.

J. S. M. Ward sees a great deal in this masonic symbol, although he appears to have been unaware of much of the history of its development which I have given above. He wrote:

The two straight lines are usually described as the two St Johns, but are stated in our ritual to represent Moses and King Solomon. This, however, appears to be a mistake, for the two parallels undoubtedly represent the Summer and Winter solstices, which heathen festival in Christian days became identified with St John in Summer and St John in Winter; thus the other explanation is the more correct. As representing the Summer and Winter solstices they correspond to the two pillars, and stand for night and day, good and evil, male and female, and so forth. In short, those pairs of opposites which bound the whole circle of human existence. Hence when travelling round the circle we are compelled to touch both these poles and thereby gain through bitter experience that education of the soul which is the chief reason for our birth into this material world.

Freemasonry represents the quest of the soul after realisation of God, and at-one-ment with Him. It is the mystic quest of all ages, and true to the ancient symbolism it starts in the E, the place of light, and goes towards the W, the place of darkness and death; but in the particular symbol we are discussing now the N pillar stands for the place of darkness, a darkness more complete than that of death itself, the dread unknown which lies, 'twixt death and birth. We must envisage the Soul as starting in the E on the circumference of the c, passing down the sunny side of life, past the pillar of light in the South, through the sunset of the West, till it reaches the pillar of utter darkness typifying not only the darkness of the gr, but that greater spiritual darkness of utter disillusionment when the pilgrim finds that all man-made institutions fail him, and in the words of the greatest of all Masters he says, *Eli, Eli, lama Sabachthani*, 'My God, my God, why hast thou forsaken me?' But the pillar of the North only just touches the circle, and as the pilgrim completes the circumference he arrives at the dawn of the second birth, and finds the darkness is swallowed up in the glory of a Light which is far more resplendent than that which failed him, for at last the Quest is ended, and he can return whence he came. This is true alike of the journey of life in the flesh, and of the still more poignant journey of the Spirit. But how many pass the second pillar? Who knows? For this is the great tragedy.

Thus we perceive that the p within the c is an essential part of our ceremonial teaching, and the apparently casual reference to it in the tracing board of the first degree, and in the third degree itself, are meant to convey to those who are sufficiently evolved to appreciate it a most profound lesson. . . .

The compasses bridge the apparently unbridgeable chasm which separates the c from the circumference. If we were simply a digit, being whirled for ever around the circle of fate, our outlook would indeed be hopeless, but we are ourselves the compasses and the p which rests at the c is the Divine Spark within us, and therefore from that centre we can never err.

Rev J. T. Lawrence sees the point within a circle in relation to the individual mason:

There is that within him—the point within the circle—that rules and governs him. The circle is fixed as to its position by that point of the compass which is on the centre—where Master Masons meet. It is fixed as to its extent and area by that which radiates from the centre, which in other and familiar language we describe as the compass of the Freemason's attainments.

The point within the circle which indicates its centre has undergone much and various interpretation . . . . The fact that as an emblem the actual point within a circle has been used by astronomers in all ages to designate the sun gives us a clue to the direction in which to make historical research.

And not only at Stonehenge, but many other parts of the country the Druidical remains to be found there show that their sacred places were circular, with the sacrificial stone in the centre.

We are less concerned with antiquarian than with spiritual and moral investigation, and beyond telling us that it is a point from which no Master Mason can err, the traditions and legends of Freemasonry are silent.

Now from the centre regarded as a fixed point, held in position by one leg of the compass, an infinite number of circles can be described. They are all similar and similarly situated and all symmetrical, but no two of them are of the same size. Their size depends upon where the other leg of the compass is placed.

May we not moralize upon this fact by claiming that the fixed centre from which the brother cannot materially err is that whereon his faith and hopes are fixed? Starting from that, all his ambition and attainments and acquirements are matters of temperament and opportunity. But, large or small, the area he sweeps out as he describes the circle of life always has the same centre. The law of centrifugal force would cause him to fly away from that centre, but the compass restrains the operation of that law and keeps him within due bounds and maintains his relation not alone with the centre, but with all other circles that may be described around it—in other words, with all mankind.

Dr Oliver also had views, some of which are, in accordance with his constant practice, culled from the lectures:

The point within a circle occupies a conspicuous situation on the Tracing Board of an Entered Apprentice. And deservedly; for it embodies a series of useful lessons, which, if reduced to practice in our commerce with the world, cannot fail to make us wiser and better. This significant emblem takes its origin from the garden of Eden, which was circular—the trees of life and knowledge being placed in the centre, symbolical of the divine Omnipresence, the centre being everywhere, and the circumference nowhere.* The perpendicular parallel lines represented by these two trees, signified *justice* and *mercy*, which were practically exemplified at the unhappy fall of our first parents.

The primitive explanation of this symbol did not differ very widely from the elucidation still used in the lectures of Masonry. The circle referred to *eternity*, and to the point to *time;* for the purpose of shewing that time was only a point compared with eternity, and equidistant from all parts of its infinitely extended circumference; because eternity occupied the same indefinite space before the creation of our system, as it will do when it is reduced to its primitive nothing. The application of the circle and perpendicular parallel lines amongst us, refers to the duty of circumscribing our wishes and actions within such prudent limits as to escape the severity of God's *justice* untempered by *mercy.* To speak in the technical language of the old lectures, the point represents an individual brother; and the circle, the boundary line of his duty to God and man; beyond which he is enjoined never to suffer his passions, prejudices, or interests to betray him.—The circle is supported by two perpendicular parallel lines, representing the two St Johns, who were perfect parallels in masonry. On the vertex rests the Book of the Holy Law, which points out the whole duty of Man and supports the theological Ladder, the top of which reaches to the heavens. In going round this circle, we must necessarily touch on these two lines, as well as on the sacred volume; and while a Mason keeps himself thus circumscribed, it is impossible that he can materially err.

Dr Oliver refers to other symbols, some commonly found in lodges and others in general use in former times but only occasionally seen today:

The *Coffin, Skull, and Cross Bones* are emblems of mortality, and cry out with a voice almost more than mortal, *prepare to meet thy God.* The *Hour-glass* is an emblem of human life. We cannot without astonishment behold the little particles which are contained in this machine, pass away almost imperceptibly, and yet, to our surprize, in the short space of an hour all are exhausted. Thus wastes human life. At the end of man's short hour, death strikes the blow, and hurries him off the stage to his long and darksome resting place.
The *Scythe* is an emblem of time, which cuts the brittle thread of life and launches us into eternity. What havoc does the Scythe of Time make

---

* *Dr Oliver's interpretation of Genesis 2:9, is that the Garden was Circular.*

among the human race! If by chance we escape the numerous evils incident to childhood and youth, and arrive in perfect health and strength at the years of vigorous manhood; yet decrepid old age will soon follow, and we must be cut down by the all-devouring scythe of time, and be gathered into the land where our fathers are gone before us. The *Beehive* is an emblem of industry, and recommends the practice of that virtue to all created beings, from the highest seraph in heaven to the lowest reptile in the dust. It teaches us that as we came into the world rational and intelligent beings, so we should ever be industrious ones; never sitting down contented while our fellow creatures around us are in want, when it is in our power to relieve them without inconvenience to ourselves.

5
DARKNESS AND LIGHT

THERE ARE, in the ceremonies and lectures of Craft masonry, many references to Light and Darkness. These references not only relate to illumination as a distinction from a state of darkness, but also to light as a source of illumination. Bible quotations relating to different aspects of these ideas recur from the earliest days of speculative masonic writing and the distinction between these extremes as well as light as a source have a big place in the symbolism of the Order.

The two obvious examples which will immediately spring to mind are the *personal* darkness symbolically imposed on the candidate for the purpose of Initiation and the later restoration to material light in a ceremonial manner, and the *general* darkness associated with the ceremony of Raising. The old lectures give three reasons for this imposed darkness, the first being the severely practical one that the form and nature of the lodge room itself and the dress of the members would not be made known to the candidate until he had taken an oath of secrecy. While this was a reasonable safeguard, it was not really a completely necessary precaution; the symbolism of the lodge room is not apparent by merely looking at it, and there was no real masonic secret contained in mere sight of lodge room or clothing—such things are certainly not regarded today as secret, although their hidden meaning is not so readily made apparent. The reason that 'my heart might conceive before my eyes should discover' falls very much into the same category and seems merely to form a nice turn of phrase with no especial significance, for while some appreciation of first steps in masonry might make some impression on the mind, the fact that the candidate was deprived of light had very little to do with it; it is more likely that three reasons sounded better than two. The real symbolism is in the third reason—'as I was received into masonry in a state of darkness, it was to remind me to keep all the world so unless they came by the light in the same legal manner I was then about to do.' This was the symbol—something intended to recall a fact by association; the deliberately inflicted darkness was meant to indicate at this point, secrecy. The word 'light' was used in this old phrase taken from John Browne's

Master Key, and, in this instance, implied knowledge—knowledge of masonry and of the secrets connected with it, for this was the immediate light which the candidate was about to receive. The restoration to light in a ceremonial form—for there seems always to have been some special point made of this particular act—was a restoration to illumination, in much the same way as a man might enter a lighted room from a dark passage. The creation of light as given in *Genesis*, Chapter 1 is often referred to in masonic documents and *Sit lux, et lux fuit* is often found in headings and decorations of masonic documents and even buildings, merely representing the third verse of that Chapter of *Genesis*. When English masonry was essentially Christian in religious outlook, the first Chapter of *St John's Gospel* was considered to be a suitable place for the Bible to be open, partly because of its reference to light. With these Biblical references before them, the masons of those times no doubt also thought of the experience of the Apostles at Pentecost recorded in the first four verses of *Acts of the Apostles*, Chapter 2.

> And there appeared unto them cloven tongues like as of fire, and it sat upon each of them.
>
> And they were all filled with the Holy Ghost, and began to speak with other tongues, as the Spirit gave them utterance.

This was an experience which gave an immediate transformation and was symbolised by the physical appearance of sources of light. But it was not intended that the restoration of the candidate to light, even in a ceremonial manner, was meant to symbolise his immediate transformation merely by taking an oath of secrecy. No, he was restored to general light in the same way as the man entering a lighted room, and the light here, first of all, was a symbol of opportunity. The candidate is made aware of the light of masonry and now has the opportunity to discover what it has to offer. And the first things that he is invited to discover are specific sources of light, the three great lights. The brethren of the eighteenth century were divided in their views as to what were the three great lights. Those of the original Grand Lodge of 1717 believed them to be three sources of light situated in the east, south and west. *The Wilkinson Manuscript*, provisionally dated around 1727, is the earliest to call these the three great lights in as many words, although in many of the manuscripts dated well before this and back into the previous century there is reference to the lights of the lodge in something like this sense. Prichard's well known *Masonry Dissected* of 1730 has reference to three great windows as lights in these three directions, and for good measure refers also to three candles. All these references are from material well before the time when any consideration could have been given to the formation of the Antients Grand Lodge in 1751, and so it is reasonable to say that the symbolism of three great lights in masonry, so far as the Moderns or original Grand Lodge was concerned, referred to sources of light in the east, south and west. These were variously to represent the sun at its different points through its apparent daily travel when it gave light to enable masons to work, and the sun, moon and Master of the Lodge as separate sources of light. It was the purpose of the sun and moon, those two grand luminaries of nature and gifts of God, to provide physical light at their due season to enable the speculative mason to study his lodge and his Craft. Even in darkness, the lodge and Craft were still there, but it required this God-given light to enable physical awareness of their existence. Even if seen, they would not be fully understood without their moral tendencies and teachings being pointed out and explained; for this purpose the Master was the essential source of light; it was he who employed and instructed his brethren in masonry; it really was his peculiar province to communicate light and instruction to the brethren of his lodge, and it was quite fair to compare him in this relation with those great physical luminaries.

In the development of the practices of the Antients Grand Lodge in the second half of the eighteenth century, and possibly with some Irish influence, these three grand luminaries, the sun, moon and master had become lesser lights and the great lights of Antient Masonry were the Bible, Square and Compasses; not physical sources at all, but emblematical, spiritual or symbolic sources of light or inspiration in the conduct of life by pointing out together the duty of man, and especially the speculative mason, to God, to his neighbour, and to himself. It was by the help of those other lights again that masons were able to see and obtain instruction in this concentrated field of study which contained within the symbolic meaning of the three great, though emblematical, lights everything of masonry and of life. When the amalgamation of the two Grand Lodges came in 1813 and a revision to produce a common ritual was required, it will be seen that the revised ritual form followed the symbolism of the former Antients Grand Lodge in this particular feature. It is interesting to note that in the revision of the lecture forms after the Union of Grand Lodges, that which has proved the most acceptable and has survived still contains some of the basis of the old Moderns pattern by referring to the V S L, Square and

Compasses, not as the three great lights, but as the essential 'furniture' of the lodge.

To the candidate his restoration to material light symbolises the light of opportunity and of knowledge, so that his previous state of darkness, in addition to recalling to him in recollection the need for secrecy, also symbolises the darkness of ignorance from which his restoration represents the opportunity for release. Although this release is to general light, this light has been available to all others in the room with the exception of the candidate, so that it is a matter made personal to him, a release from a personal rather than a general darkness. It is interesting to note in the practice of the Antients Grand Lodge, that in coming forward for his passing, the candidate was 'half veiled'. The reason given for this was 'because the light of Masonry was only in part revealed unto me', so indicating that the light given to the candidate was a knowledge of masonry, but not all immediately absorbed.

The old lectures tend to identify different aspects of the lodge with darkness and light. With what we call the three lesser lights tracing the due course of the sun from its rising in the east, through its meridian splendour in the south to its setting in the west, it follows that the north must be a place of darkness, for we place no light there. Indeed the old lecture confirms this:

> The sun going below our horizon to the North, that quarter appears to us as a state of darkness by reason the sun casts no rays from thence to this our hemisphere.

Following on from this, the south being the area of the sun's greatest altitude, it would be expected that this was the area of light. This is not so in the view of the earlier speculative masons:

> Why do you leave the West to go to the East?
> The East being a place of light and the West a place of darkness, I prefer light to darkness.

It is easy to follow the reasoning; the west is the place in which the sun sets and disappears and so heralds the onset of darkness, while it is in the east we look for the sunrise, the beginning of a new day with all it may have to offer, so that this light in the east represents Hope and perhaps Faith in the future.

A later writer has seen in the juxtaposition of these two areas of light and darkness, the east and north, some speculative thought on the placing of the candidate in the north-east part of the lodge. At this point the candidate is at a critical stage in his Initiation—as indeed he is, for first the questions at this point test the correctness of part of his preparation, or he must go through the ceremony again, and second, there is a true test of his character in his voluntary reaction to the questions put, for he should not normally be prompted by precise replies. The north-east corner represents an area of choice, between the darkness of the north on his right and remaining in his ignorance, or the dawning light of the east on his left, promising increasing light and knowledge—and probably cares and responsibilities with it—and the expected answers to the questions will, after a suitable homily, bring him into the east for further progress.

It is probable that the great symbolism of darkness and light in relation to the Raising did not make its appearance generally into the ceremony until early in the nineteenth century, for neither set of old lectures has any reference to general darkness and in the works of William Preston, a possible alternative source, there is no early copy of his third lecture. In the lectures of immediate post-Union times, however:

On your admission into the Lodge, did you observe anything different from its usual appearance?

I did; all was darkness, save a glimmering light in the East.

To what does that darkness allude?

The darkness of death.

Am I then to understand that death is the peculiar subject of this degree?

It is indeed.

The symbolism of the dark general state of the lodge is explained in those few words. But there is yet hope; there is a glimmering light in the east and we know from letters which have survived from that time that much discussion went on in the settling of the ceremony as to what light should be permitted. At first there was a shaded light, then a faction put forward the idea of a lantern in the form of a star, but this savoured too much of a direct Christian reference at a time when the new rulers were seeking to make masonry non-denominational in a religious sense, particularly as there were several Jewish lodges already in existence. So, as the Master was present in the lodge, his light remained, as the spiritual and moral teaching which he gave would still be with a brother at the time of death although those grand luminaries, the sun and moon, would no longer be of use to him. By the help of this teaching, he would triumph over death and succeed to life eternal, symbolised not only by the Raising itself, but by the restoration of general light to the lodge. This is the symbolism and message of this great ceremony.

The subject of light has naturally interested a great many of the speculative writers, who have given it many representations. Thomas Dunckerley wished to be 'enlightened' with wisdom and understanding, and most when dealing with it in a general illuminatory sense, have 'Masonic light' in mind as enlightenment and knowledge. Dr George Oliver wrote very deeply on the subject of light in masonry in his *Theocratic Philosophy of Freemasonry* published in 1840 and ranged so widely over the subject of general light as well as special light or sources of light, that this long extract seems worthy of study:

[It was] the opinion of Eugubinus and others, that Light was the supreme empyrean or local habitation of the Deity, which always shone with surpassing splendour; because the Eternal himself was believed to be the source and origin of Light. In all his communications with man, Light has been his constant attendant; or, in the felicitous language of David, 'he clothed himself with Light as with a garment.'

The Holy Book which constitutes the furniture of the Pedestal, is full of testimonies to this effect. God is termed by the prophet Isaiah, the Light of Israel. Daniel says, the Light dwelleth with him; and Habakkuk compares his brightness to the Light. Simeon calls him a Light to lighten the Gentiles. The glory of that Light appeared to Saul at his conversion, and to Peter at his miraculous deliverance from prison. St John affirms that God is Light; and in another place, that he is the true Light.

On this view of the subject, primitive Freemasonry may be referred to as the Light of Wisdom, which the Almighty Architect of the Universe possessed 'in the beginning of his way before his works of old'. This Wisdom or Light, is indeed 'the breath of the power of God;' a pure influence flowing from the eternal source of Light; compassing the whole circuit of heaven, and forming the architrave of pure and holy religion. It is to be observed that Solomon, our Grand Master, speaking masonically, generally used the word Wisdom as a substitute for Light.

In all the divine manifestations which have been vouchsafed to man, it was necessary to accommodate the grossness of his nature, by the use of a visible and material Light. But it must be understood that this was only a symbol, or a mild emanation of the glorious Light which illuminates the celestial regions. This Light, or Freemasonry, so to term it, was peculiarly intellectual. A Light adapted to the spiritual faculties the Light of God's word and spirit. It was enunciated with equal perspicuity by the Jewish prophets. Thus Isaiah says, that in those blessed mansions, 'the sun shall be no more their Light by day, neither for brightness shall the moon give light; but the Lord shall be an everlasting Light.' It is evident, therefore, that the Light of heaven is supernal and intellectual; and that a gross material Light will be unnecessary to its glorified inhabitants; of whose complete illumination we are at present unable to form any just or rational opinion. It has been correctly termed 'a glorious lustre, filling all heaven—an abyss of Light, in which the imagination is lost.'

This luminous principle is represented in our Lodges by the *First Great Light*, and symbolised by *Three Lesser Lights;* which being material, point out palpably to the senses, a reference to the operation of Light on the mind. The subject can be treated only as the Almighty himself has condescended to treat it, in pity to the weakness and incapacity of his creatures, viz. by a reference to material fire and Light, under which his personal appearance has been manifested amongst men.

These preliminary ideas naturally direct our attention to the divine SHEKINAH, or blaze of Light which usually accompanied the divine appearance on earth. It consisted of a visible splendour, or pure emanation of the deity, and has been termed *splendor gloriæ Dei*, as St Paul described the glory of Moses' countenance when he returned from the mount.

This supernal Light protected Abraham in the fiery furnace of the Chaldees; as it did subsequently Shadrach, Mesech, and Abednego, in that of Nebuchadnezzar; shewing that while the divinity assumed the appearance of 'a wall of fire' for the protection of his people; he was 'a consuming fire' for the destruction of their enemies.—Abraham enjoyed the advantage of frequent revelations of Light from on high; and the same Shekinah destroyed the cities of the plain. It was a gracious manifestation of Light that the Almighty vouchsafed to Jacob, when benighted and weary on his journey to Padanarum, he saw the vision of that wonderful Ladder, with Seraphim ascending and descending, which was intended to increase his Faith, encourage his Hope, and animate his Charity; while the Great Architect of the Universe, in a flood of Light at its summit, gave him those cheering promises which were so amply fulfilled in his posterity.

Moses, at the Burning Bush was favoured with the inspiration of Light, and received that holy and incommunicable name, which still constitutes the awful Secret of Speculative Masonry. The Shekinah, manifested on this important occasion, was a very significant symbol. The Bush burned with fire but was not consumed; and Israel was subjected to the fiery oppression of Egypt, and was not destroyed; although possessing no greater power of resistance against Pharaoh and his people, than the feeble bush to prevent the encroachments of the devouring element. The truth is, God was in the midst of both; and therefore fire and persecution were equally powerless. Moses was here instructed to approach the majesty of God with his feet bare, and his face covered; and it was not till the deliverance of Israel from bondage that the Light shone permanently amongst them.

The preparations for this remarkable Deliverance were solemn and imposing; and the difference between the Darkness of idolatry and the Light of Truth; or in other words, between the Spurious and the true Freemasonry, was specially manifested for the instruction of the Israelites, as well as the punishment of the Egyptians. A thick and tangible darkness was upon the latter for three days. But the Israelites had Light in their dwellings. They were illuminated by the true Shekinah, or Light of Heaven; which was a mystery to the Egyptians equally incomprehensible with the preternatural darkness in which they themselves were shrouded. The Light shone in darkness, but the darkness comprehended it not.

From this time the Light took the form of a pillar of Cloud and of Fire, which in the day time was bright, and perhaps transparent; and at night was like a fierce fire of ample dimensions to enlighten a camp of twelve miles square. It may be objected that the heat of such a fire would have consumed the tents, the tabernacle, and every thing within its focus. But this was no natural or elemental fire, for it existed without fuel; and, like the fire at the Burning Bush, its consuming properties were restrained, although it retained sufficient light for the most distant tribes. In a word, it was the cloudy Pillar, illuminated by the Shekinah of God. This divine Pillar took its station amongst the people, and formed the sublime object of Jewish Freemasonry. It continued with them during all the fluctuations of their history, till their renunciation of the true, and abandonment to the abominations induced the Almighty to withdraw the Light of his presence, and give up their city and temple to the rage and fury of an idolatrous people.

Nothing could have been assumed to point out in a more clear and explicit manner the essential difference between Light and Darkness, than the divine Shekinah at the period when Israel passed through the Red Sea. It was a Light and a guide to them, but a darkness and a terror to their unhappy pursuers; who were annihilated by the junction of the waters, when Moses lifted up his rod as a signal that the power which restrained them had been withdrawn.

It was the Shekinah of God that appeared in clouds and fire on the holy mountain when the Law was delivered to Moses. The mountain was clothed in darkness, and nothing but the smoke or cloud was visible to the people; while the legislator at the summit was favoured with a view of the Shekinah as a lambent flame of Light, out of which Jehovah conversed with him on the religious and political government of the people whom he had redeemed, with signs and wonders, from the power of the Egyptians. ... [The Israelites] were unable to endure the lustre proceeding from the reflected brightness of the Shekinah; a striking evidence that their minds were not sufficiently enlightened to bear the revelation of the mysterious system which was typified by the Law. Moses therefore drew a veil over his face as a token that 'their minds were blinded;' and that though the true Light was shadowed forth, gloriously indeed, in the Jewish religion, it would not be fully developed till the veil was removed by the appearance of the Messiah, or Light personified. These emanations of the deity form constituent parts of the system of Speculative Masonry, as it is practised at the present day.

This dissertation on the subject of light in relation to speculative masonry serves especially to introduce in some detail the subject of the Shekinah, that symbol of the presence of God among the ancient Jews which was manifest by a special source of light. This symbol, as Dr Oliver says, was an essential part of speculative masonry and its symbolism. From the earliest times masons' lodges of a speculative nature were dedicated to the worship of God, for, as has already been stated, our forebears were essentially formally religious men first of all. It was not therefore unreasonable for them to find some symbol to represent to them God's presence among them in the lodge, and this they did by using the symbolism of the old Jewish religion and placing a representation of the Shekinah. Unfortunately in many lodges today this old symbolism has disappeared, and it seems likely that the more practical of our rulers at the time of the Union of the two old Grand lodges did a great deal to help this disappearance.

In the present day version of the masonic lectures, a section deals with the ornaments, furniture and jewels of the lodge. The ornaments are the mosaic pavement, which is the flooring of the lodge, the blazing star, or glory, in the centre, and the indented or tessellated border around the flooring. In many lodge rooms carpets or tiled floors are still found to this design, usually with a pentangle or five pointed star in the middle of the squared flooring and with some form of border around. In some cases the star in the middle is enclosed in irradiated lines or some other form to represent a special brightness. Reference to John Browne's *Master Key* reveals the following explanation of the blazing star, for the ornaments were the same in the pre-Union Moderns lodges as those described in the post-Union lectures:

The Blazing Star, the Glory in the Centre, reminds us of that awful period, when the Almighty delivered the two tables of stone containing the ten commandments, to his faithful servant, Moses, on Mount Sinai, when the Rays of His Divine Glory shone so bright, with such refulgent splendour and unparallelled lustre, that none could behold it without fear or trembling.
It also reminds us of the Omnipresence of the Almighty, overshadowing us with His Divine Love and dispensing His blessings amongst us; and

by being placed in the Centre, it ought also further to remind us that, wherever or however assembled, God the Overseeing Eye of Providence, is always in the midst of us, overseeing all our actions and observing the secret intents and movements of our hearts.

Beside this particular reference in the old lectures, several references may be found to the Presence and to the Shekinah. Our brethren of the 1700s certainly believed in this piece of symbolism; the use of a Glory or an irradiation still survives today in two of the officers' Jewels. That of the Chaplain is described as 'A book on a triangle, surmounting a glory'—and in symbolism, the triangle is often found as an emblem to represent God; the other is that of the Grand Master—'The compasses extended to 45°, with the segment of a circle at the points and a gold plate included, on which is to be represented an eye within a triangle, both irradiated'. It is hardly necessary to give a reminder that the emblem, the All-seeing Eye, is also a symbolic representation of God.

William Preston also refers to the blazing star as one of the internal ornaments and sees in it 'a lively emblem of the omnipresence of the Deity who superintends with love and beneficence the various works He has created which is exemplified by our beholding in that figure infinite goodness overshadowing the whole system and darting, as it were, from His beneficent bounty, beams of love and mercy to the beings of every species formed by Him.'

The Three Great Lights

As already stated, the Bible, square and compasses in the former Moderns Grand Lodge represented the furniture of the lodge up to the time of the Union of Grand Lodges, and this is reflected in the lectures in use in some of the lodges under that Grand Lodge:

What is the Furniture of a Mason's Lodge?
  The Bible, Compasses and Square.
Their uses?
  The Bible is to rule and govern our Faith and on it we obligate our new-made brethren; so is the Compass and Square when united, that of our lives and actions.
From whom are they derived and to whom do they belong?
  The Bible is derived from God to man in general, the Compasses to the Grand Master in particular, and the Square to the whole Craft.
Why is the Bible derived from God to man in general?
  Because the Almighty has been pleased to reveal more of His divine

will in that Book than he has by any other way, either by the light of reason or rhetoric with all its powers.

Why the Compasses to the Grand Master in particular?

The Compasses being the chief instrument made use of in all plans and designs in Geometry, they are appropriated to the Grand Master as a mark of his distinction, he being the chief ruler of the whole Craft and under whose royal patronage our Grand laws are so judicially inforced and strictly and universally obeyed by the Craft in general.

Why the Square to the whole Craft?

All the Craft being obligated within the Square are consequently bound to act upon it.

The working of the rival Grand Lodge of the Antients apparently referred to the Bible, Square and Compasses as the three great lights of freemasonry from the time of their appearing as a separately organised Grand Lodge in the 1750s, for exposures of the 1760s give this interpretation. In this they were different from the much earlier writings of a period before the Antients Grand Lodge arose, and so from the practice of the Moderns, although one earlier manuscript from Scotland has the Antients' practice.

Whatever differences our brethren of those days had, they were united in what these emblems meant—the guide and rule of our Faith, and inculcation of our duty to God; the others united to rule and govern our lives and actions, to inculcate our duty to our neighbours and ourselves and to manifest to the world our merit as masons. We see in the times before the Union of the two Grand Lodges that both of them were basically Christian in their workings, and refer only to the Bible.

The Sacred Law

With the making of our masonic working undenominational in a religious sense in 1816, masons were charged to study the Sacred Law, and to consider it as the unerring standard of truth and justice, to regulate their life and actions by its Divine precepts. William Preston's *Illustrations*, in the next edition after this date, has a footnote about Sacred Law—'In England, the Bible; but in countries where that book is unknown, whatever is understood to contain the will or law of God.' As I have already said earlier, this First Great Light of masonry is, while the essential of all the degrees, especially relevent in the first, for a belief in God is a vital qualification and a greater knowledge of Him and His Will and Works, through this Book, the essential study of the apprentice before passing on, through Moral Truth and Virtue. In the course of the Moderns eighteenth century Lectures, the Sacred Law was referred to as:

> .... may justly be deemed the spiritual Tracing Board of the great Architect of the Universe, in which are laid down such Divine laws and moral plans, that were we conversant therein, and adherent thereto, would bring us to an ethereal Mansion, not made with hands, eternal in the Heavens.

The 1816 version of William Preston's third lecture has this note:

> The sacred law is the guide of our conduct. This, in every degree, we inculcate. To God, our neighbour and ourselves are the duties in the code contained and he who regulates his conduct by these duties is best esteemed among masons. To view the Supreme Being as the Father of the Universe and the source whence all blessings flow is the prime tenet of our profession. Hence we are taught to supplicate His protection in every disaster, and with reverence to impress His Name upon our tablet as a marked symbol of our veneration. The interest of our neighbour we consider to be inseparable from our own, and always render unto him those friendly offices which we in the same situation should expect to receive. Hence in social union we live, all nations are our friends, and every climate is our home. The blessings of life we enjoy in peace and tranquillity, and while we use, we never abuse, the bounties of providence.

This combines the three duties in the Bible, and is probably a carry-over from an earlier version. In a later version the reference to the furniture of the lodge is found in the first lecture and the wording follows more closely to present day use and the three duties are spread over the three items.

In more recent times, the Rev John T. Lawrence in *Sidelights on Freemasonry* has written in a chapter on the Sacred Law:

> The Bible should have no stauncher defenders than Freemasons. The tendency seems to be among many people to apologise for belief in the Bible, to give it a place as a classic in the language, and to deny its claim to be anything more. But we, by our very obligations, regard it as the expression of a Divine voice, and therefore, let us see exactly what the claims of the Bible are, not only upon our sentiment and sense of reverence, but upon our common sense. The word Biblia is plural, and that which we possess, bound up in one volume, is not one book, nor

a score—in fact, if the number of authors be considered they would run into many scores.

The whole of the literature of the ancient times was of the kind we should call sacred. That is to say, it never occurred to any writer to put on permanent record anything that did not connect the history of the race with its religion. ·And this feature was not only Jewish, for the records of all other races that we have had handed down show that all history was referred to Divine intervention, until, at all events, the time of Herodotus, who was the first purely political historian.

Now the Bible has this fourfold claim on our regard: its antiquity, its history, its adaptability, and its inspiration.

Its antiquity. This by itself would not make a strong claim. Many institutions attain an old age because it has not been worth anyone's while to pull them down. But still, whatever value antiquity may give, our Bible has it. Not a word in it is less than 1800 years old. It is the work of writers who have written hundreds of years apart, but all with the same intention—God's revelation of Himself to man. There is no other book in the world that even pretends to give a sober connected account of prehistoric events, and nothing in it is grander than its opening sentence. It does not presume to suggest that people are to derive their knowledge of God from its record on that page. It assumes God's existence, and begins, 'In the beginning God created—'.

But what has been its history? There are other ancient and dignified works in existence, the works of classic writers, full of noble thoughts, which, however grand they are, have survived only by reason of the anxious care of scholars of all ages. And even with that they are out of common reach, the languages in which they are written are dead, and they are only to be found dust-covered on the top shelves of libraries, known to none but the student whose business is to read them, and but little read outside the University classroom. But our Bible! what an eventful history it has had! Yet it has survived it, unchanged. It has not made the slightest concession either to persecution or intolerance, and but little to scholarship, but it stands like some rock, immovable, around which the billows have raged for centuries, from every quarter of the compass. To prince and peasant, to gentle and simple, to wise and ignorant alike, the Bible has handed down through the centuries the unchanged message of man's downfall, and its consequences, his relations with God, and his only hope of salvation.

Let us now speak of its adaptability. Other great works have been written for the few. But the Bible is for all. It has been translated into nearly every language. The fascination of its stories attracts the very infant, its very suggestions are attracting the attention of the most profound scholars, and it contains mysteries into which angel and archangel might vainly peer. It suits all tastes, whether it be its history, its law, its poetry, its literary style, its moral lessons, or its wordly wisdom, and it suits all times.

It must never be forgotten that the Bible does not pretend to be a scientific handbook. If it did we should want a fresh edition every few years, because we have not yet got to the end of scientific investigation even in the twentieth century. And it is quite possible that the too–confident critic of today, will be laughed at as much, even in ten years time, as he laughs at the Bible to-day. But if the descriptions of the Bible had been written to satisfy the learned men of to-day, they would not have been understood, even a century ago, and certainly they would be out of date a century hence.

The truth is that the Bible is in parts far beyond any human intellect. Wherever human intellect stops exhausted, there God begins, and the only difference between the scholar and the unlearned is that one has waded a few inches farther into the infinite ocean than the other. The problems of our destiny are such that we want a rock to stand upon, not a shifting quicksand. We want to be guided by a light that will always burn brightly. The Bible provides us with both. Therefore let us hold on to our Bible, which, for ages past, and for countless generations has given us a foundation for the present, a light for the valley of the shadow of death, hope for the illimitable future.

Let us come lastly to its inspiration. And let us ask what the word means. Does it mean that the pen of the writer was subject to some supernatural agency, and that he wrote *literatim et verbatim*, beyond his own control? Or does it mean the Holy Spirit of God sweeping the strings of the soul, like the wind making music amongst the forest branches?

And did the inspiration cease when the last words were added to the Bible? Every word of truth is inspired. The writer remembers a missionary making a speech on a platform. His grammar was faulty and some of his references were inaccurate, but one result of that speech was that two young men who heard him wanted to go out as missionaries, and they did so, and certainly that man's speech must have been inspired. If the words of the preacher, or the hymn writer, or the newspaper man, have the effect of making men think about eternal things who have never done so before, who shall deny their inspiration?

The Square and Compasses

From the earliest times of masonic writing these two instruments are referred to together, and more than just the Square alone do they symbolise masonry. Throughout the world they are used as the one completely understood emblem to represent something that has a masonic connection. The old lectures of masonry refer to them 'when united', and by their separate uses in our masonic philosophy, they teach us our duty to both our neighbour and ourselves. Naturally much has been written of them, and Rev J. T. Lawrence says:

Although the Square always comes before the Compasses, it has to be remembered that the Square cannot be described without the aid of the Compasses. They are necessary even to construct a right angle. Here we learn that rectitude of conduct cannot come other than from a self controlled life.

J. S. M. Ward sees a much more spiritual symbolism:

On the VSL the Square is united with the Compasses. By itself the Square represents matter, and hence our bodies. The ends being over the Compasses, which represent the spirit, imply that the man in the state of spiritual development represented by an EA is mainly animal. As yet the body is not under the active and complete control of the spirit. To such a man it is a waste of time to talk of high spiritual truths, he must first of all be trained in sound morals, be taught to use his body with respect and curb his animal appetites. It is for this reason that the EA is merely told that Freemasonry is a system of morality, veiled in allegory, etc. This sentence is often misunderstood by those who in symbolism have reached the third degree, but in reality are still in the Entered Apprentice stage of spiritual development. Such men say glibly that Freemasonry is nothing more than a system of teaching sound morals.
A limited code is unfolded to the EA, and in practice that code is enlarged as he advances from degree to degree, and even the code of the third degree is not meant to be exhaustive, but simply a bare minimum, and implies that until a man has lived up to this bare minimum he is not fit for deeper spiritual teaching.
So the Square in the first degree warns the candidate that he must devote most of his time to learning to control the body. In the second it implies that he is now fit to learn a little more about spiritual truths, while in the third is symbolised a man who, so far as he can, consistently obeys the voice of the spirit and not the animal side of his nature.

W. L. Wilmshurst sees a special significance in the various positions of the Square and Compasses:

In the concealment of the lower points of the Compasses beneath the Square lies a most instructive lesson. Thereby is implied that man's immortal and powerful spirit is at present overlain and prevented from full function by the contrary tendencies of his mortal material body. [In Masonry] this position must become reversed. If man is to be perfected and rise to the full height and possibilities of his being, his spiritual principle must not remain subordinated to the flesh but gain ascendancy over them. This the Mason is taught to achieve for himself and in proportion as he subdues his lower nature he will liberate the powers and faculties of his immortal spirit and rise to mastership over all that is fleshly and material in himself.

The Position of the Great Lights

In private lodges in the English Constitution the general rule is for the three great lights to be placed on the Master's pedestal and when the lodge is open the Square and Compasses are placed on the Volume of the Sacred Law. In Grand Lodge and in Provincial and District Grand Lodges this does not necessarily apply and, certainly in Grand Lodge, the great lights are on a separate pedestal in front of that of the Grand Master (although it has been suggested that this has a practical application in making more room for the Grand Master's papers). In a number of private lodges, the custom is for the pedestal in front of the Master to be at some distance from him towards the centre of the lodge and for the great lights to be on this pedestal. This practice is a continuation from times before 1813 in England, when the great lights in the lodges under the Antients Grand Lodge were displayed on an altar in the centre of the lodge room, or near to that point, while the Moderns' lodges used a pedestal in front of the Master. In Moderns lodges, obligations were taken by the candidate being brought up to the Master's pedestal, while in Antients lodges the Master left his place and went to the candidate.

This difference in practice has also given two methods for the actual opening of the Volume of the Sacred Law—either placed so as to be able to be read by the Master, or by a candidate opposite the Master. The symbolism of the open Volume, so far as the Moderns were concerned was that the Master's duty was to instruct his brethren, and to instruct them in those tenets contained in the Bible. To do this the Bible must be placed so that he could read it and it would be in that position the whole time that the lodge was open. If a ceremony requiring an obligation was worked, then the candidate went to the pedestal and placed his hand on the Bible. It was not in the lodge just for the taking of obligations, it was always there as God's word and for the Master to instruct from, so that the fact that the Volume was upside down to the candidate was of no significance. In the case of the first obligation in an Antients lodge, the Bible was not left on the pedestal for this, it was taken by the Master to the candidate, resting on his left hand and with his right hand on it.

Circumstances were different here for the Bible was not in its position for the Master to instruct from, it was being put to a specific separate use. It was, therefore, customary for it to be placed on the candidate's hand so that he could read from it.

In the re-arrangement after 1813, although all obligations were to be taken with the Volume remaining on the pedestal, the question of which way the Volume should be placed depended on the previous allegiance of the lodge concerned. If it was from the Antients, the Book would face away from the Master; if from the Moderns, it would face towards him. There is no absolute standard working in the English constitution and there can be some latitude in matters of this nature, and as different workings have developed, some follow one practice and some the other. One thing has been decreed, by a Grand Director of Ceremonies, that the position for the Square and Compasses is with the Square at the bottom of the page, whichever way the Book faces.

The Lesser Lights

The nature of the lesser lights and their position in the lodge has been dealt with in the description of the lodge itself. From very early catechisms the lights refer to the positions of the sun, both as a reminder of fleeting time and an orderly day, and as material light to be used for reading the Scriptures. The name of lesser lights was a late appearance in England in connection with lectures associated with the Antients lodges; references in the early catechisms and in later lectures associated with the Moderns to these lights are as the great lights of masonry (the Bible, Square and Compasses being the furniture of the lodge). They appear to have been associated from early times with the sun, moon and Master, it being the Master's duty to give the light of instruction from the Book and by the moral example of the Square and Compasses.

6

THE CEREMONIES

THE WHOLE of Masonry is based on progress, and that progress is made in two senses. In the first place, there is the ultimate goal of the progress, the reaching out and constant coming nearer: nearer to what?—to the ultimate perfection, perhaps unattainable in this life, but to come as near to that goal as may be possible. The proliferation of masonic degrees in the eighteenth century was perhaps caused by the realisation that perfection is unattainable and that, however well a man's progress is maintained, there always remains something more to be done, something more to be achieved. Masonry had been based on religious beliefs, so far as England, its original home, was concerned; those beliefs would be of a Christian, and even of an established Church, character, regarding the Bible as the Holy Book. Masonry used Bible stories in its ceremonies and instruction, so that, when degrees of a new character were formed, or more likely 'hived off', each could take for its theme one more aspect of Bible history or teaching. Thus, while life lasted, the keen mason could never become complacent but must continue to strive.

During the early years, before this proliferation, and afterwards too for the many who were content with the Craft degrees alone, the masonic goal was the perfection of the third degree, symbolised by the old mason as that perfectly regular structure, the cube. This thought is still expressed in masonic teaching by the consideration given to the rough and perfect ashlars. These are treated as the immovable jewels of the lodge and are nowadays explained in the first degree. But the inference is still there; the rough ashlar represents the entered apprentice, while the perfect stone, of a true die or square— that is a cube that is exact in all its proportions—represents the mason in the decline of years after a regular, well spent life in acts of piety and virtue.

This perfection of the cube, symbolically applied to the individual mason, is wrought by a progression through three degrees. The third of these is seen by some of the old lectures as worked in a lodge symbolically shaped like a cube—for that was the shape of the Holy of Holies in King Solomon's Temple, as set out in the Bible. The dimensions are summarised in one of the old lectures in the part relating to the third degree:

How long was it? — Sixty cubits.

How broad? — Twenty cubits.

How high? — Thirty cubits, but twenty cubits in length of the west end was only twenty cubits high.

What was that place called?
The Sanctum Sanctorum or Holy of Holies.

The entrance porch was in the east, leading into a main structure whose plan had the shape of a double square, and at the further end, the west, was a room twenty cubits in length, in height and in breadth, forming a cube. Thus the three degrees may be regarded as a progress from outside the porch, through the various parts of the Temple, towards that cube of perfection at the furthest end.

The *Encyclopaedia Judaica* (Keter, Jerusalem, 1971) collates the Biblical references and adds further notes. It states that the original Canaanite Temples of this period and before usually had but one Hall; the Temple erected by King Solomon was unusual in that, in addition to its main Hall, it had structures on each end. This meant that it had three separate rooms, (1) the Porch or Hall, *'ulam*, (2) the main room for divine service, *hekhal*, and (3) the Holy of Holies, *devir*. The layout thus given stresses the threefold nature of the construction and the progression from Porch to Holy of Holies. The dimensions vary slightly from those in the lectures, but the cubic shape of the Holy of Holies is also stressed.

The second aspect of progress is in relation to the events which happen during this journey towards perfection. This may seem very close to the theme of *Pilgrim's Progress*, but that book is a product of the earlier part of the times when speculative masonry was developing, This may have been the fashion of those times, or John Bunyan (1628-88) may, by his writings, have influenced the development as so many later writers did. There are symbolic happenings on the way through the degrees enabling lessons to be drawn which, if learnt, will bring the mason nearer to the perfection for which he strives. This aspect is much more clear in ceremonies of the eighteenth century than in those of the present day. Of course, each separate degree may well have an intermediate object of its own, each bringing the mason along part of the road he has to travel. On this development of the ceremonies, William Hutchinson wrote:

There is no doubt that our ceremonies and mysteries were derived from the rites, ceremonies, and institutions of the antients, and some of them from the remotest ages. Our morality is deduced from the maxims of the Grecian philosophers, and perfected by the christian revelation. The institutors of this society had their eyes on the progression of religion, and they symbolized it, as well in the first stage, as in the advancement of masons. The knowledge of the God of Nature forms the first estate of our profession; the worship of the Deity under the jewish law, is described in the second stage of masonry; and the christian dispensation is distinguished in the last and highest order.

It is extremely difficult, with any degree of certainty, to trace the exact origin of our symbols, or from whence our ceremonies or mysteries were particularly derived.

Hutchinson was writing of the ceremonies of his own times which, in England, were later adjusted for the purpose of compromise and uniformity to the basis in use today, but he shows that this progression was there, and not by accident.

In the course of the old ceremonies the candidates were paraded round the lodge, sometimes on the outside of the assembled company, for there are many references to meeting with obstruction 'at the back of' the Master or the Wardens, and sometimes on the inside. This developed into part of the ritual progression procedure, for the progression was always in a clockwise direction—which brought the candidate from the dark of the north, through the east and via the south, back to the west.* The number of perambulations—or, more properly, circumambulations—was varied from degree to degree and was in a progression, either of increasing or decreasing numbers. This was combined with the element of test or proof included in the ceremonies, and enabled the assembly not only to witness the probation, but also to recognise the candidate as the man for whom it is the intention to conduct the ceremony. There is an echo of this in the Master's address to the brethren before the candidate's perambulation, '. . to show that he is the candidate . . ', or as the old lectures puts it, 'that all the Brethren present might see that I was the candidate proposed . . '.

It is possible that the intermediate objects of the earlier degrees had to change with the times and with the development of masonry, particularly as this development took place under two quite separate Grand Lodges. It was also affected by the deliberate re-thinking which went on in England in connection with the ceremonies as a

---

*Masonry developed in the northern hemisphere and the sun's apparent movement was taken into masonry with reference to that hemisphere.

result of the amalgamation of the two former Grand Lodges in 1813.
A version of the old lectures from the early 1800s gives a view of the
degrees:

> How many different degrees are there in Masonry?
>
> Three, which are generally received under different appellations, the
> privileges of each are distinct, and particular means are adopted to
> preserve those privileges to the just and meritorious. Honour and
> probity are recommendations to the first class in which the practice of
> virtue is enforced and the duty of morality inculcated, while the mind is
> prepared for social converse and a regular progress in the principles of
> knowledge and philosophy.
>
> Diligence, assiduity and application are qualifications for the second
> class, in which an accurate elucidation of science, both in theory and
> practice is given, human reason is cultivated by a due exertion of our
> rational and intellectual powers, nice and difficult theories are explained,
> fresh discoveries are produced, and those already known are beautifully
> embellished.
>
> The third class is confined to the selected few whom truth and fidelity
> have distinguished, whom years and experience have improved, and
> whom merit and abilities have entitled to preferment; with them the
> ancient landmarks of the order are preserved, and from them we may
> learn and practice those necessary and instructive lessons, which at
> once dignify the art and qualify its possessors to convince the unin-
> structed of its excellence and utility. This is the established mode of our
> government when we act in conformity to our rules; hence true friend-
> ship is cultivated between different ranks and degrees of men, hospitality
> is promoted, industry is rewarded, and engenuity encouraged.

This passage is an adaptation by the compiler of this version of the
lectures from William Preston's *Illustrations of Masonry* and illustrates the sort of borrowing which took place in this development so
that such passages found their way into the work of lodges. A
borrowing of a different type is shown in the following passage taken
from the writings of Doctor Oliver. He has borrowed the basic idea
of the separate meaning of degrees from the passage from William
Hutchinson already quoted, although Oliver was writing of the
ceremonies after the re-arrangements made on the union of the two
former Grand Lodges:

> The very first step taken by a candidate on entering a Mason's Lodge,
> teaches him the pernicious tendency of deism and infidelity; and
> shows him that the foundation on which Masonry rests, is the belief and
> acknowledgement of a Supreme Being, the Creator and Governor of the

world; accompanied by a confession that in Him alone a sure confidence can be safely placed to protect his steps in all the dangers and difficulties he may be called on to encounter in his progress through the mazes of good and evil with which this world abounds; assured that if his faith be firmly grounded in that Supreme Being, he can certainly have nothing to fear. In connection with this faith, the First Degree of Masonry teaches him that his actions must be squared by the precepts contained in the Holy Bible, the constant study of which is strongly recommended. It goes on to enforce the practice of the three duties of morality,—to God, his neighbour, and himself. It reminds him of the value of time, by an emblem which points out the division of the day into twenty-four equal parts; and the absolute necessity of regularly appropriating certain portions of it to the purposes of labour, rest, and the worship of his Maker, is forcibly impressed upon his mind. It teaches him the Three Theological, and the Four Cardinal virtues; connected with which, it points out to him the necessity of cultivating Brotherly Love, the capestone, the glory and the cement of the Institution; it incites him to the duty of relieving the necessities of others with the superfluities of his own substance; and in all places, and on all occasions, to adhere strictly to truth, as one great and effectual means of pleasing God. These are all emanations of the faith which the Candidate professes at his first admission. We have Three Luminaries in our Lodges;—and what do they point out? They refer to the three precepts of Micah the prophet; that, as Masons we ought to do justly in every transaction of life; to love mercy, and to walk humbly with our God. We are clothed in white, as emblematical of the innocence and integrity which ought always to distinguish a Free and Accepted Mason. Our Jewels have all a moral tendency; and there is not a figure, letter, or character in Masonry but points out some moral or theological duty.

If we pass on to the Second Degree, the first object that strikes us is the symbol of an eternal and self-existent Deity, who will reward or punish us everlastingly, according to our works. In this degree we are solemnly reminded that the All-Seeing Eye of Providence observes our actions, and notes every improper word or thought to produce against us at the day of Judgment. The Star of this Degree points to that supernatural appearance in the heavens which directed the wise men of the East to the place where the Incarnate God was prepared to receive the rich tokens of their adoration.

When the veil of the Third Degree is raised, we are presented with a series of historical facts and ceremonies which illustrate many passages in the Jewish scriptures, and refer to the fundamental truths of our holy religion. It is truly called a sublime degree, for it contains the essence of Purity and Light.

This Degree has a reference to the Christian dispensation, when the day of salvation is more fully revealed; atonement is made for sin; and the

Resurrection from the dead plainly communicated and confirmed by the resurrection of Christ from the grave.

The Basis of the Degrees

To masons at the time of the development of the degrees, the first and second degrees, taken together, formed a natural progress which was understood because of its similarity to the method of trade organisation. The common practice was the binding of an apprentice and after a definite time, his qualifying as a craftsman or journeyman, although it was not many years before the masonic sequence, and, presumably, the reasons for it, were affected by other influences in the Craft and it became common for both degrees to be taken on the same evening. This passed the initiate to the basic status of craftsman, as understood in all trades, and it was in this grade that the tradesman remained unless he became an employer and so took a separate and deliberate step of a more responsible nature. In that case he became a Master, something to which all tradesmen need not aspire in the same way that an apprentice would seek to qualify as a craftsman. The third degree in masonry, that of a Master Mason, was similarly looked on and its serious aspect was something not to be undertaken lightly. Only from this class could the Master of the lodge be selected and the higher posts in the Craft were open only to those who were of the third degree. William Preston emphasises the status of this degree:

Here the ancient landmarks of the society are preserved, and the expert and ingenious craftsman is qualified to discharge every duty in the craft with honour and reputation. To the knowledge of this degree few indeed arrive, but it is an infallible truth, that he who merits the privileges of a master-mason, here meets with his just reward; a reward which amply compensates for all his past labour and assiduity. By employing his abilities in the pursuit of useful knowledge, he demonstrates his wisdom, and is justly entitled to respect and veneration. From this class our rulers must be selected; as it is from those who are capable of giving instruction, we can only expect to receive it.

Even for some time after the re-arrangements after 1813 there was a distinction between those appointments which were open to fellowcrafts and those which were restricted to Master Masons, while fewer still were open *only* to those who had passed the lodge chair. For many years up to the early 1800s separate Masters' lodges were summoned for conferring the third degree, and it was some time later that the present practice of expecting every initiate to progress automatically through the other two degrees came into use.

The First Degree

The symbolism of the first degree starts with the preparation. In this, and during the later ceremony, there is a strong accent on 'left' and this was explained in the old lectures as implying that the left side of the body in the normal person is the weaker side, and so it is associated with the making of an entered apprentice as that is the most superficial degree in masonry. The question of deprivation of metal has been dealt with in another chapter, and it implies not only a state of poverty from which a moral may be drawn, but also indicates that the privileges of masonry cannot be bought and that the introduction of metals into a lodge symbolically based on King Solomon's Temple could cause it to be polluted. The removal of shoes is generally held to imply that the lodge, to masons, is holy ground dedicated to the worship and service of God and is based on the common practice of many religions the world over of removing the shoes before entering a place of worship. Some of the old lectures, and the Scripture references often found in them, give another symbolism based on the quotation of the Book of *Ruth*, Chapter 4, verse 7:

> Now this was the manner in former time in Israel concerning redeeming and concerning changing, for to confirm all things; a man plucked off his shoe and gave it to his neighbour; and this was a testimony in Israel.

The act of surrendering a shoe was therefore regarded as symbolic of confirming the intention to abide by the undertakings given in the course of the ceremony, a pledge of good faith in addition to any other pledge and in addition to any other symbolism seen in the act.

The use of a c t also had a number of symbolic explanations. In some old ritual documents, the Bible reference, *I Kings*, Chapter 20, verse 22 is specified:

> So they girded sackcloth on their loins and put ropes on their heads and came to the king of Israel and said, Thy servant Ben Hadad saith, I pray thee let me live. And he said, Is he yet alive, he is my brother.

From this is drawn the use of the c t as a symbol of submission. (The reference to sackcloth on the loins is also often quoted as a justification for the use of the apron as a badge.) In the ceremonies of the

Antients Grand Lodge, it was in some places the custom to use the c t in all three degrees, it being bound twice or three times in the other degrees. The reason given for this practice was that with each succeeding obligation, the candidate was not once, but twice or thrice bound, and the use of the c t in this way was as a symbol of bondage. Other explanations of breaking out, which would enable the candidate to be recognised and brought back, or that of a rope being worn by a trader in an unfriendly country as a symbol of what would happen if he were caught spying, seem somewhat outlandish as symbols, and that of a token of submission, apart from the practical explanation of the Master in the course of the ceremony, seems the most reasonable.

One version of the old lectures has:

The state of darkness or obscurity of the first degree strongly figures out the darkness of chaos before man's creation, or the night into which his forefathers were plunged by the fall consequent upon his original transgression. It is also forcibly emblematic of the darkness of the womb antecedent to man's natural birth, the pain inflicted on his entrance aptly represents his pangs and both sensations of his entrance into the lodge of this chequered life like a benighted traveller found in a dreary and hopeless desert. His indifferent condition suggests to him the forlorn and helpless situation of man in a state of nature, teaches him the value of mutual good offices and directs him to extend that relief afterwards to others, which he then so much wants himself—by comforting the afflicted, feeding the hungry, and covering the naked with a garment. He is brought to the light of the world and the light of knowledge by the help of others, his investiture is strongly significant of the first clothing of the human race and marks out the modest purpose of primeval dress. His tools are the rough implements of uninstructed genius and the rude emblems of the simplest moral truths, pointing out the hard labour which human industry must undergo when unassisted by the cunning devices of educated art.

The matter of darkness and light in masonry is examined in a separate chapter, as is that of the special lights within the lodge. Once inside, the whole ceremony is symbolic of a series of tests, of probation that the candidate is worthy. In some other constitutions, where the form of ceremony has developed differently, these probations and tests are of a much more spectacular nature and provide the opportunity for many more homilies than the normal ceremony under the English constitution. But the symbolism of test and probation is still there, a belief in God, a humble and halting posture, poor and penniless, and in a state of darkness, all proved to the assembled company in addition to the declaration of a proper approach to masonry. Only after these tests does the real ceremony get under way and, after due entrustment and investment, some instruction is given in masonry. This instruction used to be more extensive two hundred years ago and even the re-arranged system was designed to have the full explanation of the symbolism of the Lodge Board given to the candidate. On some aspects of the ceremony Dr Oliver had some views:

> *Genuflection*, was used in the infancy of the world, as an act of devout homage to God; for it is in reality a just expression of humility and reverence from a created mortal to the Great Author of his existence. Pliny says, that 'in the knees of man there is reposed a certain religious reverence, observed even in all the nations of the world. For humble suppliants creep and crouch to the knees of their superiors; their knees they touch, to their knees they reach forth their hands; their knees they worship and adore as religiously as the very altars of the gods.'
> In the system of christianity, this custom is universally prevalent in obedience to the repeated injunctions of Christ and his Apostles. Here it is described as a proper and approved act of devotion; and one of the Fathers of the Church has conferred a still higher character upon it. He says, 'when we bow the knee, it represents our fall in Adam; and when we rise, having received the benefit of prayer addressed to the throne of grace, it is a type of our restoration in Christ by the grace of God, through whom we are able to lift up our hearts to heaven.' The candidate for Masonry is directed to bend his knee with a similar reference. He is in a state of intellectual darkness, as far as regards the science into which he is about to receive initiation. His mind unenlightened with the bright rays of Masonic knowledge, bends before the *divine illuminator*, in the humble hope that his understanding may be opened and his mental faculties improved by the process of initiation, commenced with a devout supplication to, and a firm reliance on, that Great Being whose favour alone can convey protection and assistance in every difficulty and danger he may be called on to sustain, as a trial of his patience, fortitude, and zeal.

It is customary to refer to the ceremonies of masonry as arranged round the building of King Solomon's Temple. The lodge itself is a representation of that Temple, as is shown in the chapters dealing with it. From the early 1700s it was the custom for the Master to be placed in the east in the lodge and for both Wardens to be seated in the west, each Warden representing one of the great pillars at the porch of King Solomon's Temple. Thus, the entry of the candidate in the west was between those pillars, and his entry into masonry was symbolic of his start on a journey through the Temple. Development in the second half of the eighteenth century was towards placing the Wardens in the south and west so that the entrance of the candidate in all lodges under the English constitution after 1813 (in theory, after 1810) was no longer a symbolic entrance into the Temple through the pillars. In the re-arranged ceremony, the concentration of the instruction of the candidate in the first degree is not particularly concerned with the Temple or its building. With the transfer to the second degree of the symbolism of the two pillars at the porch, some different interpretation came to be put on some aspects of the ceremony of initiation. Only in a general sense not connected with its construction is the candidate brought into knowledge of the Temple and its environs. His apprenticeship will be spent in those environs of the Temple and not in the building itself. His first sight is of three great lights and he quickly finds his attention taken by the greatest of those three. He is given a short explanation of some symbolical aspects of the square, for this instrument which typifies masonry could hardly be left out; the compasses are virtually hidden and are given but a passing mention. It is the Holy Word which is essentially the great light which has a special reference to this degree, for it is of the moral truth and virtue explained in that Book which will be the major study of his apprenticeship. He learns of Faith and Hope, and especially of Charity, those three staves of the ladder by which he may climb upwards; of Wisdom, Strength and Beauty and their meaning as the columns which support the lodge; of the extent of a masons' lodge and of its flooring and ornaments. The tools to which he is introduced are more concerned with preparation rather than building itself, and his sole introduction to construction is in connection with a foundation stone. But, having made closer acquaintance with God's Word and the attributes of the Craft and its members, he may become qualified to enter the actual building.

The Second Degree

When the stabilisation of the position of the Wardens in the lodge, settling them finally in the west and south, meant some change in the symbolism of the first degree, William Preston became concerned about the symbolic structure of the second degree. His lecture system shows a second degree layout with the Junior Warden moved back to his place in the west, beside the Senior Warden, so that the candidate could now symbolically enter the Temple between the Wardens as representing the two great pillars and then proceed up a staircase to arrive in the middle chamber of the Temple. This practice ceased in England on the reconstruction of the degree ceremonies after the Union of the two former Grand Lodges in 1813. The whole of the second degree is part of the general progress of the candidate, in this instance from outside the Temple proper, still by the route Preston's method suggested, to a central place. Here is discovered something which the candidate has, unknowingly, been seeking—the manifestation of God as the Grand Geometrician. Thus, with the initial discovery of Him and a greater acquaintance with His works in the outer environs of the Temple and now this added knowledge on gaining entry into it, there must be a greater appreciation of His omnipotence as the Creator and Controller of the universe.

The stress in the first degree is on things of the 'left', and in the second the accent is on the 'right', emphasising the old connection between these two degrees as complementary to each other. In older times the right side was considered superior to the left in matters of strength and so the right symbolised the higher degree. The Square, the second of the great lights of masonry, is the special symbol of this degree, for the whole of it is based on the use of the Square. Even the threefold sign of this degree is a combination of many squares, and it is possible to conceive that this sign is an attempt to form the letter G, standing for Geometry, the special study of the degree and in which the Square is of paramount importance. The significance of this letter and of Geometry in relation to masonry, as well as that of the Square, are discussed in other chapters, but it is in this degree that the candidate is introduced to the use of these principles and instruments in the construction of the Temple.

The development of this degree through the years has meant that, in some ways, its symbolism has become somewhat mixed. This is bound to happen in circumstances of independent development in several places, followed by reconstitution, probably based on a measure of compromise, and affected by later changes dictated for other reasons. For all this, the second degree has a special significance of its own and shows the candidate as a craftsman at the midway point. It is a restful degree, one of peace and tranquillity and with some sense of achievement. In his progress through the lodge from the west to the east, he has reached the centre of the lodge, half way between the Senior Warden and the Master, where, in former times, the letter G was displayed in this degree. In the centre of the chequered carpet there was in many lodges a five pointed star in which this letter was placed when the lodge was opened in this degree—and this tended to emphasize that the number five appeared to have a special association with this degree. Although several numbers of masonic significance appear in it, the five appears most of all (is it the hypotenuse of the right angled triangle?) so as to stress that number as particularly related to Craftsmen.

If the centre point of a standard lodge layout is taken, and, using it as a centre, an arc of a circle is described with a radius equal to half the length of the lodge (i.e. the distance from this centre point to either the Master's or Senior Warden's pedestal), that arc on the south side of the lodge should properly pass through the Junior Warden's pedestal. Euclid tells us that if two lines are drawn from the ends of a diameter of a circle—say from the Master's and Senior Warden's pedestals—to meet at any point on the circumference of that circle— say the Junior Warden's pedestal—the angle contained by those two lines is one of ninety degrees, a right angle or square angle. This makes the true layout of the lodge as set by the positions of principal officers into a right angled triangle with the Junior Warden sitting at the right angle. This appears at some time to have been a deliberate change, probably for this reason and, so far as the second degree is concerned, who better than the Junior Warden, sitting at the point where this very angle is made, to tell us in the opening that he will be proved by the square, which is an angle of ninety degrees? The arc of a circle which we have described is that between east and west via south, the course of the sun's daily travel, and all the members sitting round this arc are at the point of a square angle to the centre line of the lodge.

The hieroglyphics or tracing board of this degree has now settled down to the detail of the Temple on the way to the middle chamber, with particular reference to the two great pillars at the entrance and to the winding staircase leading to the middle chamber. In some ritual workings confusion occasionally arises as to the juxtaposition of these two features where the ritual includes words such as:

. . . . the F.Cs. were paid their wages in specie, which they went to receive in the middle chamber of the Temple. They got there by the porchway or entrance on the south side. After our ancient brethren had entered the porch, they arrived at the foot of the winding staircase which led to the middle chamber.

It is not completely clear from this version whether 'on the south side' refers to (a) a separate entrance on the south side of the Temple, whereas the main entrance with the two great pillars was at the east, or (b) the south side of the porch at the main entrance after the porch was entered. Tracing board designs have never been official and those responsible for them have often been left to apply their own interpretation and some have two separate pictures of two entrances indicating that they have read the passage according to the meaning in (a). In the old lectures and in the Bible there is some help as to where our forebears got their basic information and how they interpreted it. They had no doubt the meaning in (b) was what they intended. A winding staircase to them was usually a very narrow, tight turn contained in the thickness of the wall (many can still be seen in old buildings), and this one opened off the porch as soon as the two great pillars were passed. *I Kings*, Chapter 6, verse 8 says:

> The door for the middle chamber was in the right side of the house and they went up with winding stairs into the middle chamber, and out of the middle into the third.

The old lectures in one version give:

> After our ancient brethren had passed those two great pillars, where did they next arrive?
> At the foot of a winding staircase.

In Preston's system, the craftsmen, after passing the columns at the porch arrived at the entrance or foot of the winding staircase leading to the middle chamber. A further quotation from a different old lecture version confirms this and also relates the right side mentioned in the Biblical quotation with the south:

> You told me you got to the middle chamber of the Temple through a winding staircase; pray how did you get to that winding staircase?
> Through the porch.
> Did you see anything remarkable when you came to the porch?
> Yes, two great hollow brass pillars, one on the right hand of the porch and one on the left.
> What does the right hand signify?
> The South.
> What does the left hand signify?
> The North.
> Why so?
> Because the Hebrews express the East by before; the West by behind; the North by the left hand; and the South by the right hand; according to the position of a man who has his face to the sun rising.

Thus, the masons of the eighteenth century intended that the winding staircase should be found after passing through the pillars, on the left of one entering (that is on the south side—to the right of one looking out). Many tracing boards which have two pictures show in the main picture an impression of a staircase or the entrance to one just through the pillars on the south side. It must have caused those who wanted to give a clearer indication, some difficulty in making an illustration of a true winding staircase with the appropriate entrance at the top. The second picture seems then to be a stylised representation of a true winding staircase, although some lodges attempt to copy the steps as shown in this second picture.

There is little doubt that our forebears saw, in the passage from *I Kings*, the third chamber as the progression on later to the third degree. W. L. Wilmshurst saw significance in the staircase in the second degree. He considered that, symbolically, progress in a moral sense must be upward and so this going up the stairs to the middle chamber and so on to the third represented a special moral progress. The number of steps in the staircase, for which there is no Biblical mandate, have been ingeniously used by those who through the years have edited the story of the hieroglyphics of a fellow crafts' 'Lodge' to bring out some matters of significance in what Dr Oliver calls, Moral Geometry.

In a system where almost all initiates automatically go on to take the other two Craft degrees, the passing seems to have lost a lot of its original significance. In the two degree system which existed up to probably the late 1720s, the second step in masonry in England was that of 'Fellow Craft or Master' and as the latter might have tended to become the prerogative of Masters of lodges, an intermediate degree began to take shape, hived off from that of initiation, for it is clear that the secrets of both these degrees as they appear later in that century were given in the first degree in the 1720s. It may be that the five points of fellowship, which are of extemely ancient use, are so called because they originally were found in the higher of a two degree system, but retained their name when that degree became a third step and known as the Masters' degree. In later times the second step did not have the same significance as a making, nor, when everyone took it, the solemnity of the third which made the candidate equal in rank to the majority of the lodge. But it is a necessary degree and should have a particular meaning in its part in the masonic progress for all thinking masons. It represents achievement, it refers to reward for labour—a necessary preparation for the next step. It demonstrates that those who have come thus far through preparation by apprenticeship and greater knowledge by entering the Temple may, because of their square conduct, level steps and upright intentions, meet their fellows with head held high and accept their just due without scruple or diffidence. A sense of belonging and a job well done.

W. L. Wilmshurst summarises his view of the symbolism of the second degree:

> The work of the Second Degree is ... a purely philosophical work, involving deep psychological self-analysis, experience of unusual phenomena, as the psychic faculties of the soul begin to unfold themselves, and the apprehension of abstract Truth (formerly described as mathematics). This work is altogether beyond the mental horizon and the capacity of the average modern Mason, though in the Mysteries of antiquity the *Mathesis* (or mental discipline) was an outstanding feature and produced the intellectual giants of Greek philosophy. Hence it is that today the degree is found dull, unpicturesque and unattractive, since psychic experience and intellectual principles cannot be made spectacular and dramatic.
>
> The ritual runs that our ancient brethren of this Degree met in the porchway of King Solomon's Temple. This is a way of saying that natural philosophy is the porchway to the attainment of Divine Wisdom; that the study of man leads to knowledge of God, by revealing to man the ultimate divinity at the base of human nature. This study or self analysis of human nature Plato called Geometry; earth-measuring; the probing, sounding and determining the limits, proportions and potentialities of our personal organism in its physical and psychical aspects. The ordinary natural consciousness is directed outwards; perceives only outward objects; thinks only of an outward Deity separate and away from us. It can accordingly cognize only shadows, images and illusions. The science of the Mysteries directs that that process must be reversed. It says: 'Just as you have symbolically shut and close-tyled the door of your Lodge against all outsiders, so you must shut out all perception of outward images, all desire for external things and material welfare, and turn your consciousness and aspirations wholly inward. For the Vital and Immortal Principle— the Kingdom of Heaven—is *within* you; it is not to be found outside you.'

The Third Degree

From the earliest times, even in the early days of the eighteenth century when there was but a two degree system of masonry, this higher degree had a special significance, and under the earliest Constitutions it could only be conferred in Grand Lodge itself.

This situation was quite quickly changed, followed closely by a division of the lower degree into two and so giving a three step system more in keeping with the odd-number concept—or perhaps, superstition—of the masons of the time. But the Masters' degree, as Preston averred towards the end of the century, was still something special and achieved by the relative few. This was certainly the practice in the original 1717 or Moderns Grand Lodge, although as time passed the full progression may have been more easily obtained in the rival, Antients, Grand Lodge. One of the reasons for this may have been the proliferation of additional degrees which tended to be worked in the normal lodge among the Antients, and not as separate organisations. The Antients also regarded the Royal Arch degree as the real kernel of their masonry. The Moderns would have nothing official to do with degrees other than the three basic Craft ceremonies, even refusing officially to recognise the Royal Arch which was separately organised for Moderns under a Grand Chapter. If the Antients looked for a normal progression through all the degrees they practiced, then, however important it might be, the candidate for the Royal Arch and other additional degrees must have taken all three Craft degrees first.

There is some evidence that, at first in the very early days, the degree was intended for rulers in the Craft—requiring some qualification—rather than for anyone just interested. For a large part of the eighteenth century, lodges which were called just for the conferment of the third degree were termed 'Masters' Lodges' and were often held in addition to regular meetings. In these circumstances, only Master Masons were summoned.

In this degree it is the third of the great lights which occupies the attention. The Compass, or Compasses, is concerned with circles and when the great lights are called to the candidate's attention it is to demonstrate that he has now reached a point where this instrument is freed for his use, in order that he may render a circle complete. In the earlier degrees the sun was shown going round part of a circle, and a central point had been discovered. But now this central point may be used to describe a full circle to demonstrate the due bounds our masonic duties promised in the first degree on first acquaintance with those great lights. Restraint and definition are the twin messages it gives and these are related in the complete teaching of the third degree, for the mason must recognise his duties, his responsibilities, for what they are and then exercise a proper restraint on himself in seeing them carried out. This centre, the unknown object of the search in the middle chamber in the second degree, is now shown to be, not an end in itself as the second degree may have seemed to indicate, but a stage on the longer road and a starting point for the next stage. In defining a centre point the second degree has prepared the candidate who now has a defined point on which to place the static leg of the compasses he may now use. A circle, a complete figure enclosed by one continuous line, is a complex and mystical figure requiring more intensive study than the more simple triangular and square figures of earlier times, and so is progress shown. The candidate in this degree becomes aware that God is the very centre of the lodge; it is built round Him and with Him as the starting point, the bounds of our lives, duties and actions may be more readily drawn. In the opening of a master masons' lodge, reference is made to the circle and its centre and how by bounds thus set, a master mason may be kept from error. The circle has ever been a symbol of eternity, for the line comprising it has no beginning or end; this reminder of eternity is the lesson also of the allegory which comprises the work of the third degree.

The pattern and symbolism of this ceremony is different from those through which the candidate has already passed. This was stressed in earlier times by a combined tracing board doing duty for the first two degrees, but a separate board of hieroglyphics came into use quite early for the third degree. At the reconstruction of the ceremonies after 1813 some proof of being properly qualified was inserted in this degree; it is doubtful if this was in the actual ceremonial work in earlier forms. A circumambulation and an advance towards the east in some form were probably the only similarities in late eighteenth century raisings to the other ceremonies. This was a degree which related to the third dimension. With the attainment of it the candidate was able to appreciate a solid body and make a clear advance towards perfection—the stone of true die or square, the cube.

The theme of the degree is one that, according to many of the speculative writers through the years, is found in many religions and in the form of an allegory or legend, in the old Mysteries. The message is plain, that true fidelity to one's principles can only be shown by being prepared to make the supreme sacrifice, if that be necessary, and thus can true immortality be obtained. W. L. Wilmshurst says:

> Hence the third degree is that of mystical death, of which bodily death is taken as figurative, just as bodily birth is taken in the first degree as figurative of entrance upon the path of regeneration. In all the Mystery-systems of the past will be found this degree of mystical death as an

outstanding and essential feature prior to the final stage of perfection or regeneration.

The Combination of the Three

Before the allegory of the third degree is explained to the candidate his attention is called to a retrospect of those degrees through which he has already passed, intended to give him an appreciation of the interdependence of the three. To the mason who has given little thought to these words or to the connection itself, the only relative dependency and connection may well seem to be merely that the rules prevent you from taking the later degrees before going through the former. He might appreciate the very slight explanation of the two previous degrees then given him, but it is very slight. In the course of the ceremony, unless the appropriate emphasis is carefully given, there may be no depth of meaning. But this connection and dependency is there. W. L. Wilmshurst sees it in this way:

> The entire symbol is but one comprehensive glyph or pictorial diagram of the condition of a candidate aspiring to Master Mason's rank. As high priest of his own personal temple he must have his own bodily nature and its varied desires under foot. He must have developed strength of will and character to 'walk upon' this chequer-work and withstand its appeals. He must also be able to ascend the winding staircase of his inner nature, to educate and habituate his mentality to higher conscious states and so establish it there that he will be unaffected by seductive or affrighting perceptions that there may meet him. By the cultivation of this 'strength' and the ability to 'establish' himself upon the loftier conscious levels he co-ordinates the two pillars at the porchway of his inmost sanctuary—namely, the physical and psychical supports of his organism—and acquires the 'stability' involved in regeneration and requisite to him before passing on to 'that last and greatest trial' which awaits him. 'In strength will I establish My house that it may stand firm'. Man's perfected organism is what is meant by 'My house'. It was the same organism and the same stability that the Christian Master spoke of in saying 'Upon this rock will I build my church and the gates of the underworld shall not prevail against it.'
> During all the discipline and labour involved in attaining this stability there has shone light on the path from the first moment that his Apprentice's vision was opened to larger truth; light from the science and philosophy of the Order itself which his proving his 'porchway' to the ultimate sanctuary within; light from friendly helpers and instructors; above all, light from the sun in his own 'heavens', streaming through the 'dormer-window' of his illumined intelligence and slowly but surely guiding his feet into the way of peace.

But now the last and greatest trial of his fortitude and fidelity, one imposing upon him a still more serious obligation and endurance, awaits him in the total withdrawal of this kindly light. Hitherto, although guided by that light, he has progressed in virtue of his own natural powers and efforts. Now the time has come when those props have to be removed, when all reliance upon natural abilities, self-will and the normal rational understanding, must be surrendered and the aspirant must abandon himself utterly to the transformative action of his Vital and Immortal Principle alone, passively suffering it to complete the work in entire independence of his lesser faculties. He must 'lose his life to save it'; he must surrender all that he has hitherto felt to be his life in order to find life of an altogether higher order.

Each mason should regard himself, individually, before joining masonry as a point in space and time. A point, as the lecture tells us, is the beginning of geometrical matter and the first degree establishes the extension of that point into a line. A line is the shortest distance between two points and may be regarded as symbolising friendship. The second degree teaches the use of several of those lines in one plane to enclose a superficial area—a society or lodge or family. In the old lecture on the third degree, the question is asked:

From what to what was you raised?
From a superfice flat to a lively perpendicular; from the square to the compass; from a fellow-craft to a just and upright Master Mason.

Thus is completed a perfect whole with the introduction of the third dimension.

7

MASONIC CLOTHING

You have made good work, you and your apron men.

This is from William Shakespeare, *Coriolanus*, Act 4, Scene vi.; surely such should be the accolade of every Master of a lodge.

THE CLOTHING in lodge worn by masons under the English Constitution follows a basic design settled by the Board of Works and approved by the United Grand Lodge of England early in 1814. The need for uniformity in use had been created by the Union of the two former Grand Lodges in December 1813, and the decision covered the size, shape, decoration and colours of aprons, collars and jewels of office. There has of course been some development since that date, but without much substantial change, and there has been need on occasion to provide for additional clothing or jewels, particularly when additional offices have been created. This was not the start of distinctive masonic clothing for wearing in lodge; the principle goes back into the mists of antiquity, both in connection with providing a distinctive badge for masons, and for providing recognisable differences for rank or office, for, as the lecture tells us: 'distinctions among men are necessary to preserve subordination'. In other words, there has got to be a management—'Such is the nature of our Constitution, that as some must of necessity, rule and teach, so others must of course, learn, submit and obey.' The necessity for some form of due subordination must have had some influence, for these were times when political and social unrest were beginning to make themselves felt in England. These times were before true democracy in public affairs—still in the same reign which had witnessed the revolt of the American Colonies on the score of 'No taxation without representation.' Among the early drafts for part of the obligation in the second degree put forward in 1814 and actually taken into use in some places although it was afterwards abandoned, there occur the following words:

.... as a Craftsman I will continue to pay due obedience to a Master Mason whilst from an Entered Apprentice I will preserve ...

In the society of those days, the important thing was for a man to know his place and to know how to keep his place. It was in these conditions that much of our procedure and usage of today was first formulated. Hence there is distinction of masonic rank on the badge.

John Ladd published four lectures in 1770 under the title of *The Science of Free-Masonry Explained.* He acknowledged that he had compiled these lectures from the works of earlier writers, so that the following passage may represent the speculative thinking of the middle eighteenth century:

> It is not a white, red or yellow apron, a gaudy ribbon, with an impending, trifling jewel, or anything superficially striking, that entitles a brother to be called a good mason; nor is he who can answer by rotation, and ready fluency, the catechetical questions, commonly called the working of a lodge, that merits the title of a perfect mason, but at the same time, whatever appears meritoriously respectable for the honour and emulation of the craft, is highly commendable, and ought properly to be aspired after.

The Apron

This basic badge of the speculative mason was an obvious choice in a moral society arising from one which used such clothing in its normal operation. Our forebears, religious men, sought justification in Holy Writ and found it in *Genesis*, Chapter 3. This, and the mention in *Numbers*, are not the only mentions of an apron, for there are many references to the wearing of an ephod, particularly by Hebrew priests. As many writers have informed us, the ephod of the priests was an apron type garment of linen.

The apron is an unusual badge for a society, but has ever been worn in the craft with pride and has occasioned as much speculative thought and writing as any of the masonic symbols. Prior to 1814 there was no standard design in England, the apron usually consisting of a complete lambskin worn in a convenient manner, and, in the years just prior to the union of 1813, often decorated at the whim of the wearer with masonic symbols and hieroglyphics. The only distinction officially laid down was the incorporation of a colour, usually by lining, dark blue being used for Grand Officers and red for Grand Stewards. The lambskin has always been white and from 1814 remained plain white for the apprentice, although now with a definite shape. Some lodges make a practice of having the apprentice wear his apron with the flap up, the fellow craft having the flap turned down; in the English Constitution this distinction is unnecessary and was not intended—two rosettes decorate the fellow craft's apron and provide all the distinction that is required. In some Constitutions there is no difference in design between the apron of the apprentice and that of the fellow craft and this method of wearing the flap is the only distinguishing mark.

The reference in an earlier Chapter to *Numbers*, Chapter 15, on the decoration of aprons, indicated a particular symbolism in the wearing of an apron—that of a reminder to follow the command-ments of God. Many speculative writers have sought to justify a 'flap up' position for the apprentice by pointing to the moral lessons to be drawn from this and indicate particularly, first, the flap up indicates an entrance without completeness while the flap down for the fellow indicates complete acceptance and absorption; and, second, the significance from ancient philosophy of the apron, with its square shape, representing material things, while the flap, a triangle, represents the spiritual, so that the 'flap-up' position indicates the required supremacy of the spirit in an entered apprentice. We say that our badge is one of innocence, but our brethren of former days really saw this as of moral significance. William Hutchinson before 1770 wrote of the white apron:

Masons, as one of their first principles, profess INNOCENCE:- they put on white apparel, as an emblem of that character, which bespeaks purity of soul, guiltlessness, and being harmless.

We have the following passage in the Biographia Ecclesiastica:- 'The antients were also wont to put a white garment on the person baptized, to denote his having put off the lusts of the flesh, and his being cleansed from his former sins, and that he had obliged himself to maintain a life of unspotted innocency. Accordingly the baptized are both by the apostle and the Greek fathers frequently stiled, the ENLIGHTENED, because they professed to be the children of light, and engaged them-selves never to return again to the works of darkness. This white garment used to be delivered to them with this solemn charge, "Receive the white and undefiled garment, and produce it without spot before the tribunal of our Lord Jesus Christ, that you may obtain eternal life. Amen." They were wont to wear these white garments for the space of a week after they were baptized, and then put them off and laid them up in the church, that they might be kept as witness against them, if they should violate the baptismal covenant.'

While the apron with which we are clothed indicates a disposition of INNOCENCE, and belies not the wearer's heart, let the ignorant deride and scoff on: superior to the ridicule and malice of the wicked, we will enfold ourselves in the garb of our own virtue; and safe in self-approving conscience, stand unmoved amidst the persecutions of adversity.

The raiment which truly implies the innocence of the heart, is a badge more honourable than ever was devised by kings;—the Roman Eagle, with all the orders of knighthood, are inferior:—they may be prostituted by the caprice of princes; but innocence is innate, and cannot be adopted.

To be a true Mason, is to possess this principle; or the apparel that he wears is an infamy to the apostate, and only shows him forth to shame and contempt.

In considering this passage, it must be borne in mind that it was written as part of a lecture to masons over two hundred years ago when conditions may have made the references to derision and persecution more realistic. But the origins of our present address on the badge are apparent in this, as well as a symbolism of comparison of initiation with adult baptism on conversion long ago, and a consequent re-assumption of innocence in the sense of freedom from sin.

Dr Oliver, in a lecture published in *Signs and Symbols* in 1837, speculates in a different manner over the meaning of the apron:

A primary ceremony of the First Degree is, the investiture of *the Apron*, an unequivocal symbol, which accompanies every step of your progress. And lest any misunderstanding should give an improper bias to the mind respecting its moral application, the candidate is told that it is an emblem of innocence, of high antiquity and unequalled honour.

The great design of the Apron is to point out a figurative division of the human body into two distinct parts; separating the noble portion which contains the head and the heart, as the seat of reason and the affections, from the more base and corporeal parts, which are merely intended to perform the carnal functions of nature; and while the spiritual man stands erect and open to the view, the natural man is veiled in obscurity, that no impediment may interrupt the speculative avocations and pursuits of Masonry. The Freemason thus clothed is a striking emblem of truth, innocence, and integrity; for the parts only which are the conservators of these virtues are supposed to be in operation, while exploring the hidden mysteries of the science, in the tiled recesses of the Lodge.

Oliver then goes on to show twelve different instances in the Bible of either ceremonial use of the ephod or the girding up of loins, with which he sees a connection. He stresses the message to Christian converts of old 'to gird up the loins of their mind, to be sober, and hope to the end; and to stand firm in the faith, having their loins girt

about with Truth.' Oliver further goes through other uses of aprons
he found in old Mysteries and, ever being a borrower, includes a
paraphrase of part of the lecture of William Hutchinson quoted
above; he also finishes with an invocation:

> To you, Brethren, who are clothed in this exalted badge, I need not
> recommend a systematic adherence to the virtues which it represents.
> At your initiation you were taught that innocence of conduct and
> purity of heart, were expected to be your peculiar characteristics from
> the moment of your investiture with the Apron. Is it necessary
> for me to add that Masonry expects from you an obedience to her
> precepts, if you are ambitious to share in her peculiar benefits?

In another lecture Oliver endeavours to show a reason for the colours
used as lining and borders to the aprons. The dark blue and the red
had long been established as for Grand Officers and Stewards, but
prior to 1814, other aprons were plain white, so that the adoption of
the sky-blue border for master masons and installed masters was a
deliberate act of 1814. Oliver had already been a mason for over ten
years at that time (he was master of a lodge in 1815), so that he may
have had direct information. In any case he points out that the three
colours follow those of the veils of the Temple, blue, purple and
scarlet:

> Or rather azure, purple, and crimson. The original word for the former
> is Teheleth, which is translated *hyacinthum*, in reference to the precious
> stone called by that name; which, like the sapphire, was anciently
> believed, according to the testimony of Oleaster, Tostatus Lyranus, and
> other learned men, to be the colour of a clear serene sky. The second
> is Argaman, which signifies purple ; being derived from Ragam, or
> prince, who was distinguished by his purple robes; and the latter
> Tolaghath shani. The first word means a worm, as Psalm xxii. 6. and
> has been translated by the word *coccinum*, from *cocus*, which means
> either scarlet or crimson; and shani is derived from shanals, to double.
> Hence the phrase means the crimson colour twice dyed.

W. L. Wilmshurst comments how each successive change of status of
a Mason, brings with it a change of apron; he sees this as still the
image of self, but relates it to all creatures being in different progressive positions on the same path, when we see a lodge with those
present wearing a variety of aprons. He points out that no-one shall
enter Heaven without a 'wedding garment' and so no mason may
enter a lodge without this distinctive badge of qualification, thus
proclaiming his friendship and amity. He asks that we all imagine

ourselves clothed with it at all times, to inspire us in our daily lives.

The writer on the apron in *Leaves from Georgia Masonry* speculates on the square and triangular shape which he finds there.

Pulling up the bib and pulling down the skirt you see a triangle with the point upward and a square. The square in this aspect of the Apron symbolizes matter, physical matter, the earth and the appetites and passions which belong to the physical body. The square in its various aspects and forms has many other meanings which you will learn when you are entitled to know them. The equilateral triangle with the point uppermost, symbolizes God in existence, while the right angle triangle, such as this is, with the point uppermost, signifies God in action and also the works of God and as man is considered to be among His greatest works it signifies the soul of man which is a spark from God. This is sometimes represented by a flame, the flame representing the triple nature of man, the fire, the light and the heat, representing the soul, the spirit and the body—three in one—and the point being upward as in a flame, indicates aspiration.

There is another meaning of the Apron. The square is used to symbolize the receiving faculties, and the triangle the giving powers. In this Apron you see your life history in that heretofore you have received far more than you have given. Masonry has long ago discovered that happiness consists in giving not less than we receive. Heretofore you have received more benefits than you have conferred, but by this symbol you are told that you cannot keep this up. You must confer at least as much as you receive.

This Apron you may remove when you leave the lodge room, but symbolically it will ever be tied about you, and to your dying day you can never remove the obligation which this garment symbolizes. If you disgrace it by dishonesty, stain it by impurity or by any of those things which are immoral, you will be inexpressibly base, for you will violate your own most sacred promise and also—and now since you know it, it will be a deliberate violation—of the fundamental laws of nature and of God.

The Installed Master's Apron and the Past Master's Jewel

On the apron of a brother who has been installed in the chair of a lodge, there are placed, instead of rosettes, devices which have come, for some reason to be known as 'levels'. J. S. M. Ward in *An Interpretation of our Masonic Symbols* declares that they cannot be levels and sees them as three tau crosses and models of the architect's T-square. As the master of the lodge is in the position of the architect he sees this decoration as appropriate. A glance at the *Book of Constitutions* in which there is a description of the apron to be worn by masters and past masters of lodges, would have told him that the device is 'perpendicular lines upon horizontal lines, thereby forming three several sets of two right angles.' This description has continued unchanged since the device was first introduced in 1814 and seems to reflect the fashion at about that time in masonic history of especial reverence for the ability to raise a perpendicular. (The same description appears in the *Constitutions* of the Grand Lodge of Scotland with the addition,' in imitation of a rude level', which is no doubt the reason the devices are so called). It is from the same period that the regular steps date and these, if carefully made from the standing position described in documents of the period, give precisely the same effect. This ability to create right angles has long been considered as a special masonic secret and there is a school of thought which believes that this ability, requiring three separate measurements, was the secret lost through the death of H A and that development in the last quarter of the eighteenth century changed matters to what we now have. With the confusion in the same period over the status of master mason and master of the lodge—before there was as much in installation as there now is in England—the re-affirmation of the ability to form a right angle as the status symbol of an installed master seems very proper.

In the same book Ward refers to the device of the 47th proposition of Euclid, which, in England, is the jewel which distinguishes a past master. This is peculiar to the English Constitution and to some other Constitutions which owe their formations to England; it is not found in many of the older obediences. This proposition also has particular reference to a right angle, in relation to a triangle, and is among the oldest formal devices connected with the English Grand Lodge—it appeared on the frontispiece of the 1723 *Book of Constitutions*, which also commented on pages 20-1, 'But his scholar, the greater Pythagoras, prov'd the Author of the 47th Proposition of Euclid's first Book, which, if duly observ'd, is the Foundation of all masonry, sacred, civil and military.' The connection with Pythagoras was sufficient to make it acceptable as a masonic emblem, while there are several instances of those concerned with the changes of 1814 and later going back to Anderson's Constitutions for inspiration. In this connection Ward says:

> In mediæval days one of the most valuable building secrets was how to plot out the ground plan of a building, and the key to it was the

correct use of the right-angled triangle. How to construct and then to use this right-angled triangle was a jealously guarded secret of the master builder, and though when we know how to do it we can see it is simplicity itself, to the more ignorant craftsman it must have remained a complete mystery. In the Operative Lodges which still exist the members are informed that the secret which the villains wished to discover was this, which in those days was concealed in the use of three rods, one three cubits long, one four cubits long, and one five cubits. These rods were the insignia of office of the three Grand Masters, and when placed together in the form of a right-angled triangle at the centre of a piece of ground on which the building was to be raised, the three Masters could plot out a building.

Again here is confusion between what was considered master mason work and the device of an installed master, pointing to the late development of installation as a full rite. Ward also mentions that in the Scottish Constitution, the past master wears a letter G as part of his jewel. In old tracing boards of the third degree in England the letter G is also found—and it has a different explanation from that on the second degree board. The old lectures tell us that it is a reference to those specially able stone workers known at the building of the Temple as Ghiblim, men from the town of Gebal or Ghebal and sometimes translated as 'stone-squarers'—again a reference to the speciality of being able to work in squares. This G in old English practice is an essential part of the third degree, but the letter disappears from third degree tracing boards after the union of 1813, despite the fact that the Ghiblim are mentioned in the 1723 *Constitutions*.

Collars

J. S. M. Ward had speculative thoughts on the officers' collars also:

The collar is a yoke or collar similar to that worn by horses, and implies 'service'. 'Take my yoke upon you' might well be said by the Master as he invests each officer. Essentially it teaches us the dignity of service, and clearly shows that it is a high honour to be allowed to serve our fellow men. . . . . . There are numerous references to the bestowal of a 'collar of honour' in the Bible, and also in Babylonian and other Eastern records, and in practically every case these 'collars' were bestowed for the valuable service rendered. Thus we see that the collar, historically as well as symbolically, denotes the reward of service.

8

THE WORKING TOOLS

Lo, where our silent emblems breathe
Their sacred influence o'er the soul,
In mystic order ranged: while round the whole
A starry zone the sister virtues wreathe.
Ye, who by compass, square, and line,
Those hidden truths can well divine,
To all besides unknown.

WALLER RODWELL WRIGHT (1775—1826)

IN THE great majority of lodges under the English Constitution there are three working tools allocated in a speculative sense to each of the three Craft degrees—giving a total of nine in all. This arrangement, obviously a very neat one, only dates from about 1816 and was incorporated as part of the revised system of ritual of the three degrees made as a result of the Union of the two former English Grand Lodges at the end of 1813. Prior to this time there does not seem to have been much common practice, although it is apparent that the former Antients Grand Lodge used a moral explanation of working tools in the first and second degrees. Those of the first degree were 'the twenty-four inch gauge, square, and common gavel or setting maul'; those of the second degree were 'the plumb, square, and setting maul'. There is little variety in these, although the germ is there very early in the second half of the eighteenth century. It is really quite natural that the square, the great emblem of masonry, should be a tool of both degrees, while the same applies to the 'common gavel or setting maul', with its special use by the master for calling to order.

Although Dr Anderson's *Constitutions* for the original Grand Lodge have in the 1738 edition a reference to the hammer and trowel being the tools requisite for a freemason, the one to separate and the other to join, there is no reference in any early manuscripts traceable as definitely Moderns *ritual* practice, to any explanation of working tools as such. There is the standard reference to the square, level and plumb rule as the movable jewels of the lodge and to the square and compasses in relation to the Bible. It is however quite clear, as will appear from quotations later on, that a great deal of speculative thought was directed to the ordinary tools of masonry.

In the second edition of his *Illustrations of Masonry* published in 1775, William Preston included some notes on the ceremony of consecrating a new lodge and the consequent installation of the first Master; he indicated that a similar sort of ceremony ought to be observed at subsequent installations. The warrant was delivered over to the first Master:

> after which the Holy Bible, the square and compass, the book of constitutions, the minute book, the hiram, the movable jewels, and all the insignia of the different officers are separately presented to him, and the necessary charges suitable to each, are properly delivered.

The hiram was the name given the hammer, mallet or gavel used by the Master as a symbol of authority and to maintain order in the lodge. In the edition published in 1792 certain additional items appear for the first time—the rule and line, the mallet, the trowel and the chisel. He adds:

> For the accommodation of those brethren, whose distance from the metropolis may deprive them of gaining the necessary instruction in this important rite, we shall here insert a few moral observations on the instruments of Masonry, thus presented to the Master of a lodge at installation.

He then proceeds to give short moral explanations on the rule, line, trowel, plumb, square, compasses, chisel and mallet in that order. His wording and the appearance of these new instruments in 1792 suggests that this was something new in formal *ritual* matters, arising towards the end of the 1780s. In a manuscript lecture believed to date from the late 1790s and to come from Lancashire, something very similar appears, in circumstances which make it look like an addition to an older lecture. Because this contains even more than Preston, it is reproduced below:

> As the various implements of our profession are emblematical of our conduct in life, and are intended to imprint on the memory wise and serious truths which every Mason ought well to understand and constantly bear in his mind an explanation of them is requisite in this Lecture:— What does the Rule direct?
> The Rule directs that we should punctually observe our duty; press

forward in the path of virtue, and neither turning to the Right nor
to the Left, in all our actions have eternity in view.
What does the Line teach us?
The Line teaches, the criterion of moral rectitude, to avoid dissimulation in conversation and action, and to direct our steps to the
path which leads to immortality.
What does the Trowel teach us?
The Trowel teaches, that nothing can be united without proper
cement and that the perfection of a building must depend on the
proper disposition of that cement, so Charity, the bond of perfection
and social union, must link separate minds and separate interests,
that, like the radii of a circle which extend from the centre to every
part of the circumference, the principle of universal benevolence may
be diffused to every member of the community.
What does the Plumb admonish us?
The Plumb admonishes, to walk upright in our station, to hold the
scale of justice in equal poise, to observe the just medium between
intemperence and pleasure and to make our passions and prejudices
coincide with the line of our duty.
What does the Square teach us?
The Square teaches, to regulate our actions by rule and line, and
to harmonise our conduct by the principles of morality and virtue.
What do the Compasses teach us?
The Compasses teach, to limit our duty in every station that, rising
to eminence by merit, we may live, respected and die, regretted.
What does the Level represent?
Birth, Masonry and Death.
What does the Level demonstrate to us?
The Level demonstrates, that we are descended from the same
stock, partake of the same nature, and share the same hope; and
though distinctions among men are necessary to preserve subordination, yet that no eminence of station should make us forget that we are
brethren, and that he who is placed on the lowest spoke of fortune's
wheel, may be entitled to our regard; because a time will come, and
the wisest knows not how soon, when all distinctions, but that of
goodness, shall cease, and death, the grand leveller of human greatness,
reduce us to the same state.
What does the Chisel demonstrate?
The Chisel demonstrates the advantages of discipline and education.
The mind, like the diamond, in its original state is unpolished, but
as the effects of the Chisel on the external coat soon presents to
view the latent beauties of the diamond, so education discovers the
latent virtues of the mind, and draws them forth to range the large
field of matter and space, to display the summit of human knowledge,
our duty to God, and to Man.

What does the Mallet teach us?

The Mallet teaches, to lop off excrescences and smooth surfaces, to correct irregularities and reduce man to a proper level, so that, by quiet deportment, he may, in the school of discipline, learn to be content. What the Mallet is to the workman, enlightened reason is to the passions; it curbs ambition, it depresses envy, it moderates anger, and encourages good dispositions.

What do the Crane and Pulley teach?

They teach that human strength, without genius and judgment, can do but little, and that genius and judgment will effect that which strength alone cannot.

What does the Trassel Board teach us?

The Trassel Board teaches that as the workman executes the designs of the Master, so we should faithfully copy in our life and conversation those excellent rules of conduct which are laid down for us in the Holy Scriptures, which will infallibly secure to us permanent felicity in the realms of endless bliss.

The last two are not included by Preston. They both still appear in the lodge, the crane and pulley being associated with the lewis, or cramp, used to lift stones 'to certain heights with little encumbrance, and to fix them on their proper bases', the whole signifying Strength. The Trassel Board, or tracing board, represented a draughtsman's board on which, as the description implies, the master laid out the plans for the workmen to follow. The tracing board is now one of the three immovable jewels of the lodge, and, as the rough and perfect ashlars are associated with the junior and senior wardens in most lodges, so is the tracing board essentially the master's implement. In old renderings of the third degree, it was to draw the designs for the next day that Hiram Abiff went every day at high twelve, before paying his daily adoration, and he left these designs on the tracing board. Unfortunately, in the change over at the time of the Union of Grand Lodges, or probably just after, confusion arose over the master's tracing board (which would in older times be displayed on tressels, and might have on it representations of masonic symbols or hieroglyphics of a moral nature), and the new form of separate lodge boards for each degree, now known as tracing boards, so that the passage in the modern lecture forms, regarding the immovable jewels, that 'the tracing board is for the Master to lay lines and draw designs on, the better to enable the brethren to carry on the intended structure . . . ' is rendered quite unintelligible, in a symbolic sense, by the indentification of the tracing board as the modern name given to the lodge board. On

English Grand Lodge certificates (designed in the present form in 1819), the draughtsman's tracing board is quite clear, with pencil and rule resting on it for the Master to use.

Apart from the crane and pulley and the trassel board, the remainder are those included by Preston, and the wording of them is virtually precisely the same, although it is a matter for conjecture as to which came first, and who copied from whom. One thing is quite clear, that in this formal moralising of the tools, seeming to date its development from the 1780s, much is still used in masonry today; it is equally apparent that those who settled what should be included in the new arrangement in 1816, decided to omit certain of the earlier symbolism and to re-arrange a good deal of what was to be left. Firstly, it was decided to keep the number of tools for each degree at the special masonic number three. Secondly, and this has added a good deal to the confusion of lodge work and symbolism, some of the instruments were to have more than one reference in the lodge. The square, that special symbol of the free and accepted mason, remained as one of the great, though emblematical, lights; also as one of the movable jewels—that worn by the *Master* for the year; and was also retained, as the Antients had used it, as a working tool in the second degree, although it was dropped from the first. With it, as working tools for the second degree, were put the level and plumb rule, which also retained their status as movable jewels. The second degree, after the Union, became identified much more closely with the actual moralising of building, so that this was a happy thought—for these three jewels or tools, taken together, enable a construction to be proved square in all three planes of the building.

The square then disappeared from the tools of the first degree as the Antients had them, but the twenty-four inch gauge, which was not included at all in the Preston list, was retained; this left no room for the, very similar, rule, which was dropped. The expression 'masonic line and rule' is still used, but both implements have vanished; the meaning implied can be seen by taking the moral explanations of the two instruments in the above quotation. Some of the attributes of the discarded rule and line were applied to the plumb. Perhaps it was confusion in earlier references which caused the line to be abandoned, for although in some instances, being stretched as the shortest distance between two points—as when stretched between the corners to give a straight line for the apprentices to lay the stones for the wall—it provided a moral reference to directness and straightness of conduct, one version of the old lectures looked at it as a hanging line with a plumb bob. After expanding to some degree on the attributes in the version already quoted, it goes on:

> it points out to us the direct but narrow path that leads to a glorious immortality and that sincerity in our profession will be our only passport thither; this Line, like Jacob's ladder, connects Heaven and Earth together, and by laying hold of it we climb up to that place where we shall change this short line of time for the never ending circle of eternity.

Reference to the modern 'long' working tools of the second degree (or the explanation of the movable jewels in the lecture, which has the same wording) will show the 'turning neither to the right nor to the left . . .etc' of the rule is now applied to the plumb rule. It is easy to see where the compilers of 1816 looked for their inspiration.

The common gavel (or setting maul) was retained as well in the first degree (although dropped from the second) under one name only; also combining the former separately named hiram, assuming a dual purpose; and the hammer, which was in use in some places, was dropped. The mallet also disappeared as a separately named implement, some of its moral attributes being absorbed by the gavel. The chisel was added to the first degree to make up for the square. Again, some serious thought was given to this matter, for the gauge and the gavel represented beginners' work, and education is an equally obvious primary need.

So far as can be ascertained, it had not previously been the custom for moral tools to be applied in the third degree. Prior to the Union, the third degree was intended to be of an entirely different character from the other two, which were regarded as complementary to each other, whereas, after the Union, it quickly became the rule to regard all three as separate steps in a progression intended for all who wished. The skirrett appears for the first time as a tool in 1816; it does seem to have taken on some of the characteristics of the line of earlier times, which had been discarded, but most of its moral tendencies were new to speculative masonry; the pencil also was new in this way. It was but natural to allot the compasses to this degree. This instrument continued with a dual purpose, being one of the three great lights, but it had always had a special identification with the third degree—in which its *full* character and use is brought to the candidate's attention.

The trowel found no place as a working tool in the immediate post-union arrangements, although a use is found in some places as the distinguishing jewel of the tyler or of the inner-guard, who started as an inner tyler. It is not clear what significance it might have in this connection. William Preston included the implement among those which should be presented to a new master at his installation; this is found from the 1792 edition of his *Illustrations of Masonry* and also in the 1816 version of his third lecture. The wording is similar to that found above. William Meeson, writing nearly thirty years earlier than Preston's first inclusion of the trowel, 'moralises' it in a different way:

He that expects the kind assistance of others should by all means endeavour to deserve it, by contributing all in his power to the happiness of all men.

He should put his hand to the TROWEL of *peace* and *beneficence*, and not lay it by so long as he is able to join one *stone* to the *building*. Beneficence, or *active goodness*, is the perfection of that good-will we owe to all mankind; not excepting those who differ from us either in rank, persuasion, or otherwise.

And tho' prejudice or partiality may prevail with some weak minds, stiffly to refuse doing good to those who cannot think or do as they do; yet let them remember, that the Almighty Being has laid this injunction upon us, and therefore we should not withhold our hand when it is in our power to do good. But if prejudice must cavil, know then, that if we differ more from the infinitely great perfections of the Deity, than we possibly can from one another, it will thence follow, that if we refuse to do good when it is in our power to do it, and because they differ from us; then the Almighty Being, for the same reason may withhold his hand from us: the fatal consequence of which I leave you to consider. 'As we have therefore opportunity, let us do good to all men.'

Let us endeavour to reform the wicked and impenitent; and heartily desire the Almighty to turn their hearts.

Let us assist the King in his lawful government, by paying his rightful dues, and obeying his commands.

Let us honour and reverence the ministers of the sacred word, and help to maintain them according to our abilities. Let us faithfully discharge every duty we owe to our parents, wives, children, brethren, etc.

To every one let us speak the truth, and fulfil every engagement.

Pay a suitable deference to superior merit; and give honour to persons of quality.

Let knowledge, comfort, counsel, advice, reproof, etc. be dispensed where necessary.

Let the poor and indigent be assisted: and if you can conveniently, endeavour a reconciliation betwixt those at variance, etc.

These and a great many more particulars regarding the great duty of doing good, are largely insisted on by more worthy hands: and if I was inclined to expatiate, my prescribed limits will not permit.

But that there may be no mistakes for want of particulars, let the

PLUMB LINE be applied, and you will have the true upright of this duty, 'Do good to them that hate you.'

The advantages arising from a conscientious discharge of this duty, are great and many, it relieveth us from the remorse which always attends the unwelcome reflections of having wilfully lost the opportunities of doing good. And when we communicate happiness to another, and with a good heart, that happiness is directly returned back to us, to increase that we had before. But what infinitely outweigheth all other considerations, is, that we shall by so doing, 'be the children of the Highest;' and be received as such when it shall be said, 'Come ye blessed of my Father, inherit the kingdom prepared for you from the foundation of the world.'

In the twentieth century the trowel reappeared as a working tool in some places using charity and beneficence as its symbolism and with some of Preston's words. With the recent creation of a new lodge officer called the Charity Steward the trowel has been adopted as his jewel because of its long use as a symbol of charity and beneficence.

The re-arrangements in connection with these tools probably gave English masonry a much more orderly and logical set-up, but with a good deal of the original symbolism in disarray. Is it to be wondered that a very great deal of the speculative writing of later times was on the subject of these tools? The dual nature of some of them produces even more speculative comment, but they have been treated as working tools essentially for the collection of later speculation, except for consideration of the square and compasses when taken *together* as two of the great lights. In earlier years the square and level had also been especially related, as representing equality and fair dealing with all in the lodge. Most of the old lectures, from whatever source, contain the comment that masons meet and part on one or other of these two implements, although, strangely enough, all lectures did not agree on which to meet or part. Rudyard Kipling, in *The Mother Lodge* immortalised the sentiments:

We met upon the Level, an' we parted on the Square,
An' I was Junior Deacon in my Mother-Lodge, out there!

William Meeson was a master mason of Birmingham and belonged to a lodge under the Moderns Grand Lodge. Whether his speculative thoughts were entirely his own or whether they reflected those generally felt at the time, we may never know, but he did commit them to print. They could have influenced those responsible for the arrangements made following the union of Grand Lodges forty years after he published his *An Introduction to Free Masonry* in 1775. His

book is divided into parts and the first part is devoted to the needs of
'the Apprentice only.' In this part he concentrates on the main
symbol, the square, but the other three tools he suggests as those best
suited to the needs of the apprentice are the chisel and gavel, and the
rule—using the last as a measure with much the same thoughts in
mind as those included in the standard moral implications used today.
The following are extracted from the first part:

THE GAVEL AND CHISEL

The laws both sacred and human (when they are consonant) tend to
make men happy, by refraining from the sly incroachments as well as
the growing power of vice. The examples and precepts of great and
worthy men, and the several most *sacred* OBLIGATIONS, all tend to
this very same purpose; out of all which I shall recommend only one
method, (not indeed as the best of all others or that even anything
conducive to this purpose should be neglected, but as it best comports
with my present purpose) by which we may attempt to trim off these
irregularly luxuriant passions of the mind.
Let then him that is fully resolved to part with every vicious habit,
and every evil thought, directly and without delay, put his hand to the
work; and with the keen CHISEL of *Reproof*, and true GAVEL of *Sincere
Penance*, force them off: and at this work let me advise you to be both
ingenious and industrious, nor give it over until you have formed
yourself into a perfect SQUARE; and this rather by your own hands, than
the skill or labour of others.
Would men be persuaded to make the experiment, by inflicting some
small punishment on themselves, by self denial, mortification, &c. I am
almost persuaded the utility of this method would then appear. For we
are apt, too soon apt to forget our failings, and often attempt to bury
them in eternal oblivion: which great piece of imprudence often re-
iterated, may insensibly lull the soul into a fatal lethargy.
A little *Penance* then, when we find ourselves imposed on by false
deluding passions, is very necessary, as it strongly impresseth on the
mind the ill consequence of our great depravity, and puts us in a better
disposition to guard against it.
The possibility of putting this useful method in execution is in every
one's power, if they are fully resolved to do it. For the passions, whether
good or bad, are only different affections of one and the same principle,
which principle is the soul: now, since there is such an infinite variety of
things pleasing to this principle, it will therefore follow, that we cannot
fail (if we have a will to do it) to keep back some one gratification or
other, or inforce by way of punishment, some useful duty, when we are
sensible of any *irregularity*.
And tho' to cut off a right hand, or pull out a right eye, should afford

no pleasure in the operation, yet that will follow as a necessary consequence: for, when every irregularity is removed from us, what then can remain, but that which is *uniform*, pleasing and delightful.

This being premised, it will be no very hard thing, even for an apprentice to handle the GAVEL, the CHISEL, and the SQUARE, with dexterity and judgement.

For whatever is preferred before the greatest of duties, love to the Supreme Being, will of consequence be projected beyond it, and therefore of necessity must be cut off.

Again, whatever is preferred before that great duty of Equity we owe to all men, and as performed in uprightness and sincerity to the first great duty, love to the Deity, is of consequence projected beyond it, and therefore of necessity must be cut off, in order that the SQUARE may fit just and easy each way. When this is done, the *Stone*, or *Rough Ashlar*, is completely finished: and the GAVEL and CHISEL may be laid aside till the SQUARE discovers some other irregularity.

THE RULE

Time is a most precious jewel to him who maketh a good use of it; but to the careless and indolent, a mere nullity—to such an one the precious moments are as days, and his days as years; his employment is troublesome, and his life a burthen: in a word, a moving statue is a comparison too low for that worthless soul who cannot find time to do good to others, nor be beneficial to himself.

For he who squandereth away his time seemeth to be in or near to a state of non-existence: for though his eating and drinking, &c. may sufficiently prove that he is an animal substance, yet, where are the manly actions? where are those truly great and noble emotions of soul, that dignify him Human? where is that great light which ought to be put on a stand, and by which the world may plainly see that he is a good Mason and a true Christian? certainly these amiable dispositions and acquirements fly the presence of the indolently inactive, and leave him unfit to govern himself, or to give light to others. Let then such insignificant lumber be banished from the face of the earth, or the character *worthless* be stamped on his forehead, and be for ever deprived of the benefit of every social enjoyment.

But the good Mason will see to it, that his time be well improved, that the stone be well SQUARED, and that the building go forward with courage.

Let the several parts of our work be measured out only by the RULE of one Day; allowing to every part of our work its just and proper quantity of length and breadth: for he that taketh care of his measure is more likely to bring his work to perfection, than he who neglects it; notwithstanding he may still be doing something towards it.

Our grand master Solomon tells us, that 'to every thing there is a season; and a *time* to every purpose under heaven.' *There is a time to serve the great Author of our being; a time to work at our necessary calling; a time to do good to others; and a time to rest:* the well adjusting of which is both useful and necessary. For he that keepeth a good measure is the more sure to work in truth and regularity; while that which is done carelessly and without measure, is imperfect and disgusting. How delightful then, as well as profitable, must it be, to parcel out well that little *Time* we have, and to adopt each part thereof, to great and manly purposes.

The well doing our duty, and discharging that great and important trust committed to us, is certainly the most pleasing satisfaction that can possibly enter the breast of a rational being. The deceitful charms of opulence, and greatness, and power, even that of kingdoms and empires, compared with this inward satisfaction, are as a twinkling vapour to the sun, or an atom to the universe. The good mason *secure* in this, needs not fear the upbraidings of others, nor that which is infinitely worse, the merciless cruelty of a relenting conscience. On the contrary, he enjoyeth the fruits of his industry with a calmness and serenity of mind here and in eternity, a happiness which shall never end.

Even when the new compilers of 1816 had settled what were to be the working tools of an entered apprentice, it seems probable that there were two opinions as to their precise moral significance. In the more generally used version of today, the twenty-four inch gauge is divided into three parts, for prayer, labour and refreshment, and service. In the Antients lodges, from which this tool derives, 'part are assigned to work, part to serve God and assist a brother, and part in sleep and refreshment.' In some old documents, there is some doubt whether the day should be divided into three periods or four. Although some writers have traced this division into three to the practice of St Augustine, it is probable that the cult of four divisions arose before the time when the number three had acquired such significance in connection with the first degree. William Preston refers to the division into three:

Because the three employments allowed to those three divisions are equally essential to the happiness of man and distinguish him from the brute creation, for man must support himself by the produce of his manual industry. But then, he equally wants rest and comfort to continue his work and, as a rational being, he is also bound to employ his mental faculties in the contemplation of nature and pay due worship to his Omnipotent Maker.

The Antients regarded the gavel as the monitor of conscience, while the mallet in the quotation above serves to lop off excrescences and to smooth. These combine the standard use of today, but the alternative moral explanation which came out of the 1816 period through the Stability Lodge of Instruction is worth comparision for its different sentiments:

> From the twenty-four inch gauge we derive a daily lesson of admonition and instruction, for being divided into twenty-four parts it reminds us of the division of the natural day into twenty-four hours, and directs us to apportion them to their proper objects, namely, prayer, labour, refreshment and sleep. From the gavel we learn that skill without exertion is of little avail; that labour is the lot of man; that the heart may conceive and the head devise in vain if the hand be not prompt to execute the design. From the chisel we learn that perseverence is necessary to establish perfection; that the rude material can receive its fine polish but from repeated efforts alone; that nothing short of indefatigable application can induce the habit of virtue, enlighten the mind, and render the soul pure. From the whole we deduce this moral, that knowledge grounded in accuracy, aided by labour, and promoted by perseverence, will finally overcome all difficulties, raise ignorance from despair, and establish happiness in the paths of science.

Dr Oliver, in collecting the thoughts of earlier writers with his own, writes:

> the Twenty-four Inch Rule, whose apparent use is merely to measure lines and distances; amongst Masons, refers more particularly to the twenty-four hours of the day, and points out the necessity of a regular distribution of Time, one portion of which must be applied to labour, another to rest and refreshment, and a third to prayer and meditation. Thus that excellent monarch and Grand Master of Masons, Alfred the Great, made a regular and judicious appropriation of his hours, after he had vanquished all his enemies, and sat in peace on the throne of his hereditary dominions. It is indeed of primary consequence to ascertain the progress of time. Time does not appear to move. Look at the hour index of your watch. It stands still; you cannot see the process by which time is divided; and yet hour after hour passes on; the index still moves round, and is as actually advancing as if it were visible to your eye. In like manner the Sun in the firmament measures days, and weeks, and months, and years; and yet, how attentively soever it is observed, you have not the least visible perception of its course. It rises in the east, and you behold it in the purple morn; it attains its meridian in the south, still imperceptibly to the human eye, and you know that half the day is gone. It moves majestically towards the end of its daily course, and when setting in the west, you perceive that you are another day nearer to that event which must ultimately close all your connections with this world,

and introduce you to another where the division of time will cease, and an endless eternity be open to your view. Let this consideration be the spur and incentive to virtuous pursuits, that your admission into eternity may be glorious, and full of peace and joy unspeakable.

The Square

Although it is the second in mention of the three great lights which the old Moderns Grand Lodge called the Furniture of the Lodge, the word 'square' has become a by-word for honest dealing and sincerity of purpose. It is one of the principles adopted generally into the language from a masonic source, and it is, of all others, *the* symbol of the Craft itself. This is as it should be, for the old lectures tell us that, although the Sacred Volume is derived from God to man in general, the square belongs to the whole Craft. It so belongs because the attitude when being obligated is based on squares and especially on *the* square, within which the body is erect. So, being obligated within it, the whole Craft are bound to act upon it.

As the Sacred Volume is essentially the great light with special reference to the initiate, so is the square that which has a special reference to the fellowcraft's degree. The craftsman is concerned with practical building, and not just building anyhow, but in a proper manner. This implement is essential to him in proving the structure and the materials. The rude matter is the character and actions of each individual mason, and the building which should be truly square is the structure of his life, built on a foundation laid earlier in the proceedings.

The square makes other appearances than as one of the great lights. It is the jewel of the master—the most important office in the lodge—and is worn by him symbolically to show that it is by the square conduct of the master that the lodge is justly ruled. It appears as one of the working tools of the craftsman, all three of which are concerned with practical building. In addition to its practical functions it symbolically teaches the regulation of lives and actions and due regard to our duty to our neighbour. It is used as a test on admission in the second degree, and of this use Preston says:

> The square being allowed to be the chief test of merit intimates that his conformity to its rules could only have entitled him to share further in the privileges of the Order.

A square from the mason's point of view, consists of an instrument made up of two arms enclosing a right angle where the arms join.

It may be used to measure squareness, and so to try, and adjust, rectangular corners of buildings and assist in bringing rude matter into due form. As Meeson wrote in the 1770s, 'This Square, if well applied, will perfectly show where the Gavel and Chisel should be employed and how far their use is necessary.' He also went on:

> But that we may make no mistake in the application of the Square, it will be necessary to shew the nature of its construction, and then its use will be easy.
>
> The Square then is the theory of universal duty and consisteth of two right lines, forming an angle of perfect sincerity, or 90 degrees; the longest side is the sum of the lengths of the several duties we owe to the Supreme Being; the other is made up of the lengths of the several duties we owe to all men. And every man should be agreeable to this Square when perfectly finished.
>
> For if it be allowed that no duty we owe to the Supreme Being should be omitted, and that we ought to be equally forward to the performance of every one; it will thence follow, that this great duty, geometrically considered, may be as a right line. Again, if love to the Supreme Being be an animating principle; and if the love we owe to all men, (when in its greatest perfection) flows directly (sincerely or right forward) from this principle; it will thence follow, that our whole duty, geometrically considered, may be as a rectangular plane; and therefore ought perfectly to coincide with the perfect Square of theoretical duties.
>
> It was asserted by Aristotle, 'That he who bears the shocks of fortune valiantly, and demeans himself uprightly, is truly good, and of a Square posture without reproof.'
>
> Now he that would smooth himself into such a perfect Square Posture, should often try himself by the *perfect* Square of *Justice* and *Equity*. For, *Thou shalt love the Lord thy God with all thy heart, with all thy mind, with all thy soul, and with all thy strength; and thy neighbour as thyself: by doing to all men as we would they should do to us.'*

Most of the squares supplied for lodge use today tend to have arms of equal length, but it is quite clear from what Meeson writes that the square he was writing of—and presumably this was the accepted square in masonry in his day—was one with arms *not* of equal length. Nor was there likely to be any latitude in the proportions of the two arms, for these were bound to be in the proportion of 3:4, so that the missing side, to make up a right angled triangle, would measure 5 units and conform to the 47th proposition of Euclid I. Sydney T. Klein develops this point in papers published in *Ars Quatuor Coronatorum* for 1897 (*The Great Symbol*) and 1910

(*Magister Mathesios*). Klein tends very much towards the occult in his approach to symbolism, but he was at pains to point out:

that symbols signs and SS of our Fraternity were based upon what I called 'the knowledge of the ⌐ ', and it is natural, therefore, to expect the arrangement of the Lodge to be in accordance with the same principle. Now our oldest manuscripts maintain that at the head of all the liberal Sciences stands 'geometry, which is Masonry', and that emanation from the First Grand Lodge, called Anderson's *Constitutions* (1st edition, 1723, 2nd edition, 1738), gives evidence as to what was then looked upon as the most important part of that 'head of all the sciences', for it specially names Euclid, Book I, Prop 47.

It is clear that for Klein, writing from a different point of view and based on research and theory, arrived at a conclusion which accords with Meeson's description. When it first became the practice for the jewel of a Past Master to be based on the forty-seventh proposition of Euclid, that is around about 1820, it is interesting to note that the type of Square first used, and this continued into the 1830s, was what is known as the 'gallows' type, as portrayed by Klein and described by Meeson.

Later writers also refer to the square. Rev J. T. Lawrence, in *The Perfect Ashlar*, cites most of the ritual uses mentioned above and also the many times in the course of a ceremony that movement and attitude have reference to the square. He also states that, from the operative point of view, the importance of the square is derived from the fact that it is one of the three regular figures whose angle is an exact submultiple of 360 degrees, the other two being the triangle and the hexagon. The exact form of the square we use also concerns Lawrence and he writes:

What, first of all, should be the exact form of the square? The term 'square' is something of a misnomer, as the symbol in question is but the two adjacent sides of a square. Let that pass, however. In many foreign lodges, and especially in lodges working under the Grand Orient of France, we find one limb shorter than the other, thus making it into a carpenter's square, which it is not. Marking it off in divisions to represent inches is somewhat unnecessary, as it thereby becomes a measuring instrument, which it is not. The stonemason's square is intended only as a test of rectangularity. The engraving sometimes found on the two limbs does not much matter, but the two ends should not be trimmed off with ornamental finials. The symbolism is very ancient.

Brother Dr J. P. Bell [sometime] Deputy Provincial Grand Master of North and East Yorkshire, recovered a very curious relic in the form of an old brass square containing the inscription:

> *I will striue to liue with love and care,*
> *Upon the leuel by the sqvare.*

This was found under the foundation of an ancient bridge near Limerick, in 1830, and the date on the square is 1517, and it proves, if proof were necessary, that the teaching of our old operative brethren was identical with the speculative application of the working tools of the modern Craft. This is more than can be said for a good deal of Masonic symbolism. The well-worn, though somewhat ungrammatical phrase, 'We apply these tools to our morals', has led to some remarkable absurdities being perpetuated, as in fact, there is simply no limit to fancy in this respect. The square as found in the Craft is really what the Greeks called a

Γνώμον (gnomon), and it has been suggested very ingeniously that the 'sacred symbol' found in the centre of the lodge is really the initial letter of this word. If it be so, it helps to preserve the unity of our lodge symbolism.

Now, the gnomon was a square of two unequal limbs, the usual ratio of the lengths being 3:4; and Pythagoras, having joined them, and found the joining line to be exactly 5, combined this result with the arithmetical formula $3^2+4^2=5^2$ the result being the forty-seventh proposition of Euclid I. The method of proof which adorns the Past Master's jewel is said to be due to Euclid himself.

J. S. M. Ward also puts forward the view that the letter G was originally depicted in medieval lodges by a square of the 'gallows' type with unequal arms and similar in shape to the Gamma or G of the Greek alphabet. This symbol also stood for Justice, one of the great characteristics of God. Ward believed that it is this Gamma shape which should be placed in the centre of the building, combining both the square itself and the representation of Geometry. He goes on:

> Symbols have meanings within meanings, growing as it were out of each other, and it is at times difficult for those who are just commencing to study symbology to avoid becoming a little befogged by this fact. For example, in general the Square represents matter . . . . but at the same time we should bear in mind that, as symbolising the letter G it also stands for God. This appears to be contradictory, but in reality is not, since matter is also divine, and like the spirit, indestructible, as modern scientists know. Matter may change its form a hundred times, but it is not thereby destroyed, and so we may truly say that matter is only one form of the outward manifestation of God in this world.
> The Square therefore teaches us that God created matter out of his

own substance, and this being so it is also divine and eternal, though in form, transient.

Moreover, if we think carefully we shall perceive that this is the only possible solution of the problem of how anything can be created out of nothing. If we believe that God has existed from all eternity, this difficulty vanishes. Nothing can be created out of nothing, but since God has existed from all eternity He clearly can create out of Himself anything, for He merely changes its form, and what we call matter is that part of Him which we can perceive, while in the body, by means of our five senses. Thus the Square in itself is not only the emblem of matter but shows us how matter comes forth from God and is 'created.' The Square also represents morality in general, and more especially justice. In ancient Egypt the Gods are depicted as sitting on squares when acting as judges, whereas at other times the square in their thrones is missing. In architecture the Square is used to prove a stone true, an angle of a building correct, and it must not be forgotten that if each course is not square at the corners, the building will be liable to collapse. Similarly, the man who does not square his life and conduct by what he knows to be just and right will ultimately come to grief spiritually, however well he may appear to prosper in material things.

The Square of the Master symbolises that in the Lodge he is a judge and must act justly, but it means more than this, for the Master typifies the spirit in man and also God the Creator. The characteristic of Jehovah which is stressed by the Old Testament was his justice. He was the Just Judge of all, both great and small. Jehovah could be relied on to deal justly with every man—a stern but impartial judge, and the creative aspect of God or, if we like so to call it, the Law of Nature, is just but stern, and those who transgress His laws suffer heavily, even in this body. The Master's Square therefore typifies Divine Justice, and coupled with other emblems of his office mark him as symbolising the creative aspect of God and the Divine Spark in man. To the good man his own conscience is the sternest as well as the most impartial judge. Other men may judge his faults lightly, but the spiritually minded man shows himself small mercy and knows how worthless are the petty excuses which may serve to blind the outside world.

Thus we see that the Square in itself represents God, then matter, which is a manifestation of God. It likewise stands for His essential attribute justice, and hence is the test of right conduct. As the letter G, it is to be found in the centre of the building. We may indeed say that in a sense Freemasonry is built upon the basis of the Square.

On the question of the shape of the square, it is often pointed out that, in the arms of the original Grand Lodge of 1717 (copied from those of the Masons' Company and incorporated in those of the United Grand Lodge to-day), the compasses are shown extended on a chevron. This chevron is a device which looks exactly like a square with arms of equal length and, as the square and compasses together represent the symbol of masonry to many people, the change from the square of unequal arms to one of equal arms has been considered as copying that included on the coat-of-arms. This seems to have come about in the 1820s, shortly after the union of the Grand Lodges, which was followed by the adoption of a new coat-of-arms incorporating those of the two former Grand Lodges, so that matter was in consideration at about the same time.

I am informed by an official of the College of Arms that the chevron is not intended to represent a square at all. It may be found on the arms of about a quarter of the livery companies of the City of London, not necessarily restricted to those which have any connection with building. It is probable that it *arose* from a building connection and it is most likely that it represents a gable roof form. It is not therefore even necessary that the angle enclosed is a right angle, although such an angle is often a convenience in design. It is equally possible that it is often found as a device in arms as it forms a convenient method for the designer to divide a shield into three more or less equal parts, where a cross would give inconveniently small areas in dividing the shield into four.

William Hutchinson wrote of the square in the 1770s:

> To try the works of every mason, the SQUARE is presented, as the probation of his life,—proving, whether his manners are regular and uniform;—for masons should be of one principle and one rank, without the distinctions of pride and pageantry: intimating, that from high to low, the minds of masons should be inclined to good works, above which no man stands exalted by his fortune.

while Doctor Oliver's collection includes:

> When I hold up the Square, what virtues are presented to your view! As an appendage to an operative mason, it is indeed used merely to try and adjust all irregular angles, and to assist in bringing rude matter into due form. But as a speculative mason's jewel, it teaches morality and justice; it shows the beauty of order and sobriety, and displays the advantages arising from a mutual communication of benefits. In a word, we are instructed by this instrument, to act upon the square with all mankind, by doing to others, as in similar circumstances we would have them do to us.

Doctor Oliver also quotes from a Reverend Mason of the eighteenth century regarding all three of the second degree working tools, which in that century were the movable jewels of the lodge:

By these he learns to reduce rude matter into due form, and rude manners into the more polished shape of moral and religious rectitude; becoming thereby a more harmonious corner-stone of symmetry in the structure of human society, until he is made a glorified corner-stone in the temple of God, made without hands, eternal in the heavens. In the lodge he learns to apply the square of justice to all his actions; the level of humanity and benevolence to all his brother men; and by the plumb-line of fortitude to support himself through all the dangers and difficulties of this our fallen, feeble state.

Since 1816 the three movable jewels have been regarded as the working tools of the second degree, so that the level and plumb rule combine with the square in this connection also. As the quotation from the Reverend Mason indicates, it was a plumb line rather than plumb rule which was the tool indicated in the eighteenth century. The use of the word, level, does not of itself indicate the form which this implement takes. Rev J. T. Lawrence begs 'leave to doubt whether the device with which the Senior Warden is invested is really a level or not.' He has in mind that a modern level is based on the use of a bubble, and in his speculative thoughts on the level as an implement in masonry he says:

... it depends on the fact that the definition of a true level is that of the surface of a fluid when at rest. It is only at rest in the absence of any external disturbing force, or when such forces are exactly balanced. We might, then, regard the level as bidding us to strive to attain a disposition from which all disturbing forces are absent, or are kept in perfect subjection. A peaceful and unruffled disposition is one to be envied, and it cannot be attained so long as our passions are apt to run away with us. We have to weigh carefully every impulse, so as not to be easily swayed first on one side and then on the other. Of course this is an ideal and a counsel of perfection, but if Freemasonry did not present us with ideals, and, what is more, with constantly receding ideals, we should soon tire of it.

The bubble level was invented and developed in the seventeenth century and it was hardly before 1700 that it started to come into general use. Even then it is doubtful whether it would replace very quickly the form of implement which had previously been in use for this purpose, so that at the time of the development of masonic symbolism, the level which would be in the minds of most concerned would be that which had literally been in use for thousands of years. In ancient Egyptian times the level consisted of an isosceles A-shaped piece with a plumb bob hung from its apex. In land surveying this A-level was used to get a horizontal sight line by placing the level on a board and raising or lowering the end of the board by means of wedges until the plumb line coincided with a mark on the crosspiece. This principle continued in use until the bubble level finally superseded it, but the device we call a level in masonry is based on this design and perpetuates the old idea. That which we call a plumb rule is similarly dependent on the use of a plumb bob.

William Meeson in his publication of 1775, considered these implements:

But leaving this sort of men to the quiet adoration of their own invented idol, let us who have assumed the name of Masons 'press forwards towards the mark for the prize of the high calling.' Let us also be as 'examples of the believers, in speech, in conversation, in love, in spirit, in fidelity, in purity.' Yet with such an humble deportment as will always keep us from that assuming arrogance, that would in conceit only, place us above our own LEVEL.

And as we are to set others a good example, so let us emulate and endeavour after the greater attainments of others: striving with all our might to overcome the corruptions of our nature; and to come up to the true LEVEL of *prudence*, *virtue*, and *piety*, along with the most exalted patterns of purity and perfection.

These will cause us to be esteemed by the truly generous and impartial, who love that which is good, whether it be in a *mason* or any other *name*. It is possible that some such as these may value themselves on the SQUARE; but let me ask, how do they look unless they stand *upright* in the building? thus you plainly see the unfitness and absurdity of placing any trust or confidence in the weak supports of dissimulation and imposture. On the contrary, he that would be accounted a MAN, and worthy of trust, let him pursue the great qualifying virtue *sincerity*, or let him not hypocritically assume that sacred title; neither let him think himself *upright*, because he is *sincere* in a few particulars, for this would be a vain deception: *Sincerity* is an universal duty; neither can that man be said to be so, who cannot stand the test of the true PLUMB LINE of *gospel sincerity*.

And he that is truly SQUARE, well *polished*, and thus *uprightly* fixed, is well qualified, and fit to be a member of the most honourable society that ever existed.

He that trusteth such an one with any possible engagement, is freed from all trouble and anxiety about the performance of it. For his words are the breathings of his very heart; he promiseth and is faithful to his trust, and is an utter stranger to things of a double meaning.

And as he endeavoureth at all times to give satisfaction to others, so he is sure, as a reward for his *constancy*, to be admitted a member in that most amiable society where every individual is perfectly SQUARE, perfectly *polished*, and perfectly *upright*.

Lawrence had further thoughts on the principle of equality which the level demonstrates:

The word equality has in every age possessed a strange fascination, and like the two others of the trinity, liberty and fraternity, has been responsible for unnumbered crimes. Equality of circumstance is an absolute impossibility even between a man and his fellow. And it would be disastrous to the best interests of the human race if it were. On the earth some have five talents, some two, and some but one.

Equality of regard approaches more nearly that which lies within practical radius. Whether like the Archangel Gabriel we serve God and humanity with two white wings, or like the toiling artisan with two black hands, we can command the highest respect and regard of our fellows and the equal approbation of the Most High. And here we approach what is really the masonic teaching of the level. Every one in the lodge is equally concerned in the erection of the stately edifice whereof the corner-stone was laid in the north-east: the architect who with the pencil draws plans, the workman in the yard who with the gavel and chisel shapes the stones, the superior workmen who deposit the stones in their respective places, the officers who marshal the workers and see that they receive their wages. Is not every one of these the equal of every other so long as he does his duty?

We cannot conceive a better definition of equality than an entire absence of scruple and diffidence. A sense of superiority on the one hand or of inferiority on the other makes for diffidence. A sense of unworthiness or of duty ill-performed causes scruple. But the man who has acted up to and expressed the best there is in him is the equal of his fellows in the very highest and most unassailable sense.

The level step is in the first instance that which is planted firmly on the ground, which is neither timid nor furtive nor self-conscious, and it betokens the man who has a firm assurance of rectitude—in other words, it comes of square conduct. A steadiness of progression is also implied in the terminology. It means that capacity and intention and execution are all on the same level. Whatever be a man's capacity, it generally acquires the same level as his execution. The man who consciously falls below his powers cannot again command them when he will, and sinks to a lower level. And the man whose intentions are always beyond his powers may be of a higher order, but none the less he may turn out to be an incompetent workman, wasting the master's time and material.

Again to show that all work even in the English Constitution is by no means standard in the matter of moralising the tools, the following is the method of explaining the significance of the second degree tools in the All Souls Lodge No. 170. After the section quoted, they finish with most of the normal 'long working tools' description:

> The Square is an instrument used in architecture, which enables the architect to form and fashion his work, symbolically teaching us to form and fashion our lives. It is an emblem of morality and points out that most important obligation, to do unto others as we would they should do unto us, and to act on the square with all mankind.
> The Level is an instrument used in architecture to make the building plane and even and serves as a reminder that we are all equally destined to act our part in this great theatre of life: that we are all alike subject to sickness, infirmity and disease: that we are all equally under the control of the Great Parent of us all: that we are all destined to die, to be level with the earth, to corrupt, to be forgotten. Art or accident may vary our condition and station, yet, taking life all through, we shall find a more equal participation of good and evil than is generally imagined. In the edifice of freemasonry equality is the chief corner-stone and every Brother at his initiation enters the Lodge not in splendour of dress or pride of heart, but in the garb of humility and with a mind of lowliness.
> The Plumb-rule is an instrument used in architecture by which the building is raised in a perpendicular direction and is figurative of an upright and unblamable course of life and typifies care against any deviation from our upright line of conduct.

Leaves from Georgia Masonry have a comment on these three symbols which form the movable jewels and working tools:

> The Master's square does not merely represent the infinite justice of God, nor is it merely a symbol of the cross, which is itself the greatest of all symbols, nor does it merely represent virtue. It is itself a symbol of the 47th problem of Euclid. That figure, the squares inscribed upon the three sides of a right-angled triangle, symbolizes another truth; that although the works of God cannot be harmonized or understood in this life, that when we are raised to a higher plane—symbolized by squaring the sides—we will find that there is a definite harmony and proportion in all that God permits to be done on this earth.
> Also, you will note that things which always keep on the same level never progress, but die; for Nature shows you that to live you must move upward. But when you apply the square of right conduct to the dead level of mere animal existence, then is formed the plumb, the living perpendicular, emblem of life and upward growth, immortality. And it needs but faith to make this combination work out for you a far more

exceeding and eternal weight of glory. Note also, that virtue, right living, is represented by an angle of ninety degrees, while love, brotherly love, unselfish love, the level, is twice as much. Remember, too, that 'love is the fulfilling of the law'.

The Third Degree Tools

Because there were no tools specifically connected with the old third degree working in either Grand Lodge, we find that two of the working tools allotted to this degree in 1816 have little or no prior symbolism and also that usage in their explanation is fairly uniform. The skirret, or skirret line, assumes some of the qualities of the straight line and does point out to us straightness of conduct, while the pencil is an instrument which probably defies speculative comment beyond that contained in the usual explanation.

The Compasses

This instrument, often referred to in old documents as 'the compass', is that which, while being one of the great lights of masonry in a general sense, has a special reference to the third degree. It is only in this degree that it is fully exposed, thus enabling the master mason to use it to complete his experience, and it is in this degree that it also re-appears as one of the working tools. It reminds us to limit our desires in every station of life, that, rising to eminence by merit, we may live respected and die regretted. It also reminds us of God's impartial justice. Thus it is the representative of self control and as the square shows us our duty to our neighbour, so the compasses show us our duty to ourselves. The old lectures also tell us that, being the chief instrument made use of in the formation of architectural plans and designs, it is peculiarly appropriated to the Grand Master as an emblem of his dignity, and indeed, the jewel of the office of Grand Master incorporates the compasses. Only his Deputy and Assistant, and the Provincial and District Grand Masters and Grand Inspectors—who are his local deputies—have the compasses as part of their jewel, thus emphasising this appropriation of the compasses. Dr Oliver wrote of this instrument:

> The obvious use of *the Compasses* is for the formation of plans and designs from which all noble works of art are completed in their just and elegant proportions. In Masonry however they have a reference to something more than this. They admonish us to walk righteously and soberly amongst our brethren; to avoid every degree of intemperance

which may degrade the man into the brute, and to render to everyone his due, tribute to whom tribute is due, fear to whom fear, honour to whom honour.

The Spirit of Masonry of William Hutchinson gives some idea of the Compass as an instrument for the Master.

> But as the frailty of human nature wageth war with truth, and man's infirmities struggle with his virtues; to aid the conduct of every mason, the master holdeth the COMPASS, limiting the distance, progress and circumference of the work: he dictateth the manners, he giveth the direction of the design, and delineateth each portion and part of the labour; assigning to each his province and his order. And such is his mastership, that each part, when asunder, seemeth irregular and without form; yet when put together, like the building of the TEMPLE at JERUSALEM, is connected and framed in true symmetry, beauty, and order.
>
> The moral implication of which is, that the MASTER in his lodge sits dictating those salutary laws, for the regulation thereof, as his prudence directs; assigning to each brother his proper province; limiting the rashness of some, and circumscribing the imprudence of others; restraining all licentiousness and drunkenness; discord and malice, envy and reproach: and promoting brotherly love, morality, charity, benevolence, cordiality, and innocent mirth; that the assembly of the brethren may be with order, harmony and love.

William Meeson includes the compasses in the four tools he moralises in connection with the degree of 'Master or Journey-man', the second degree to him. The third part of his book was on the subject of Moral Geometry and for 'the Master only'—presumably the master of the lodge as the master mason, for there is a suggestion that in earlier times the third degree was restricted to the master and wardens of lodges. This probably also included those qualifying for these offices although it seems likely that, by the time Meeson's book was published, this practice had virtually ceased. His moral geometry contains no tools as such, but for the master or journeyman he recommended the Compasses for Moderation, the Plumb Line for Sincerity, the Trowel for Beneficence and the Level for Example and Emulation. Of the compasses he writes:

> As the husbanding well of our time is the only way to acquire a competence suitable to our station here; and as this competence well managed may conduce towards our everlasting happiness, it will thence follow, that we should always maintain frugality, and keep within the COMPASS of *Moderation*.

Excess in anything is always attended with some inconvenience, and very frequently with inevitable ruin. For excessive sensual pleasures often cause exquisite pain, lasting sickness, and certain death; and too great profusion in expences, entail poverty, shame and contempt: But *Moderation*, as far as any thing can do it, secureth us against all these evils.

But the ill effects (consequences) of intemperance will fully appear, (even to a demonstration) from the following considerations.

The functions (powers or offices) of the body, are, (1.) *The* VITAL; which are, the circulation of the blood, the actions of the brain, and respiration. (2.) *The* NATURAL, which are, digestion, nutrition, growth, generation, evacuation of the excrements, and the secretions. (3.) *The* ANIMAL, which are the motions of the body; the free and ready exercise of which constitutes what is called Health.

But the free exercise of the functions cannot exist without a due tone or tensity of the fibres of the solids requisite to a free circulation and excretion of the several fluids. While these are well balanced to each other, the body enjoys the most desirable serenity, ease, pleasure, and chearfulness of mind. But this ballance when destroyed, even in the least, some disposition or other will follow.

Now these mentioned above, (as far as art can do it) are kept in good order by a due and proper use of what are called the six non naturals, viz. air, meats and drinks, sleeping and watching, motion and rest, the passions of the mind, the retentions and excretions. But if we do not observe a due quantity in these, the even balance of the solids and fluids will be destroyed, the functions impaired, and in proportion to these, illness and death will follow.

But since the censorious world is too apt to condemn the brotherhood, as being intemperate in drinking and sitting up late hours, I shall consider so much of the non naturals as regards them only; by shewing the ill effects of intemperance in watching and drinking, and this by way of persuasion, not to give umbrage to others in such things; and also for their own good, to avoid every the least appearance of intemperance. But to proceed;

Intemperate or immoderate watching dissipates the spirits, weakens the fibres, and exhausts the fluid parts of the blood; whence great disorders may arise, concomitants to a sluggish inactivity. And most certainly, weakness of the fibres and a tenacious blood produce obstructions, which tend to various diseases, as inflammations, fevers, dropsies, &c.

But the immoderate drinking strong drink or spirits is by far more pernicious, as it tends to produce dropsies, atrophies, consumption of the lungs, hectics, the jaundice, anorexy, and languor of the whole body; also pains in the head, the apoplexy, epilepsy, palsy, &c. whence all the ill consequences of such intemperance are fully manifest.

I shall add only a word or two more on this head, (by way of comfort to the valetudinarian drinkers, if such there be amongst us) and that from a worthy doctor.

'It often happens (says he) to hard drinkers, that the glands of the liver which separates the bile from the blood, are sometimes so hardened or stopped as to resist the strongest deobstruents; whence the motion of the blood in the liver is so impeded, and to such a degree, as forces it into the gastric arteries (which go or branch off from the hepatic) that it breaks into the stomach. And from hence it is that such unfortunates are subject to vomit blood, which in this case is a very fatal symptom, and such as does not admit of a cure.'

That profusion in expences (as mentioned before) entaileth poverty, shame, and contempt, needeth but little proof; for if you allow that it tends to these, it is then only supposing profusion as in a flowing state and the other (of course) will follow.

You see then the great necessity of keeping within the COMPASS of MODERATION; which yet will further appear, if we consider it as the great and sure road to opulence and power, and which has the very great advantages, knowledge and greatness of soul annexed to it. If you would be convinced of this, try the experiment; keep within COMPASS, frequent the company of the great, assume an air of importance, and then you have a stock of knowledge irresistable. For what blockhead dares or can wrest an argument from you? is he impertinent, dares he insist on't? tell him he knows nothing of the matter; this, together with a good surly front, will secure to you the character of a knowing man.

Now for greatness of soul;

Are you by trade, acquaintance, or otherwise tacked to the company of the trivial? then promise and never perform; and if you please to shove them quite off, desertion on your part, and a few dry looks will do it completely.

For be assured, if you would look truly big, that you are not then to waste nor squander away your time with the little low-lived impertinents, but with those whose souls are of more noble extraction.

But where now, brothers! pardon my raving; I had almost forgot that I was talking to masons, whose sincere upright hearts (I hope) disdain such sordid emoluments, and scorn to appear or be any otherwise than within the COMPASS of *honour, affability*, and *good-nature*.

No doubt the inclusion of such a homily shows that such dreadful warnings were necessary in those days, but it seems strange to tack it on to a dissertation on a masonic implement among a number of others which followed a rather different moral track. But Meeson certainly got home the principle of moderation which he associated with the compasses. This use of the compasses as a symbol of moderation is carried further in the writing of Rev J. T. Lawrence.

Whilst Freemasonry will teach us to act upon the square with our neighbour, it is nevertheless not entirely left to ourselves whether we act up to that injunction or not. Our neighbour may be trusted to look after his own rights in this respect. To procure the most useful and valuable teaching of the compasses, let us find out those aspects of life in which personality has an unfettered freedom of display.

There are first of all the sorrows of life. Bereavement, sickness, the misfortunes of those near and dear to us, temporal loss. How do we bear these? It is the habit of some to be loud and obtrusive in their expressions of grief. Instead of waiting for the bestowal of a sympathy that has been evoked and that cannot be restrained, they seek it. Every little trouble and ache and pain is loudly advertised. Do they wear crape or sackcloth? Then they take care that all shall see it. Are they reduced to rags? They will even make an extra slit in them rather than that the fact shall not be noticed. Are they unhappy? They are not content until all around them have been made unhappy also. They resent any suggestion that others have suffered. All this is evidence of a lack of self-control. The really great nature bears its sufferings in silence.

The really deserving poor do not advertise their poverty. They resort to a hundred pathetic little ingenuities to hide it. They draw sympathy, they do not ask for it. The first lesson, therefore, taught to us by the compasses is that the accidents of life ought to be treated as such, and not allowed to obsess the whole nature.

The Freemason is taught to control his emotions and to keep them within due bounds, and if the depths of his nature are to be stirred up let it be with sympathy for the troubles of others.

And human emotions are not alone those of sorrow, but they are ofttimes of joy. It is perhaps natural that we should seek to make other partakers of our feelings of gratitude to the Giver of all good things. But we are warned against undue elation, carried possibly to an extent that arouses in those around us feelings of discontent and envy rather than those of sympathetic joy. In any event of Divine Providence a man should possess his own soul.

There are yet other emotions. And in these absence of restraint works out its own cure. Liability to uncontrolled anger, for instance, reduces and ultimately nullifies the effect which it is proposed to have. Undue expressions of appreciation cause those upon whose efforts they are bestowed to ask what is the worth of such appreciation when conferred indiscriminately and unreservedly.

It is the brother who has not learnt the full value of his obligation who injures the whole fraternity, and through one member the whole body suffers.

By his very separation from the popular and uninstructed world, the Freemason invites criticism. He has not only entered into the light of

Freemasonry, but he stands out in the light and more than ever is circumspection needed.

As newly admitted brother gazes with newly opened eyes upon the compasses let him remember that the honour not only of the lodge but of the whole craft has been committed to his keeping.

The same emblem that restrained any rash advance when he first entered a lodge is now exposed to his gaze as one of the great lights of his future life, and it not only keeps him to a fixed point of departure, but describes for him the full round of his masonic duties, limited only by the compass of his attainments, just as the radius of the circle to be described is limited by the extent to which the compass can be opened.

The geometrical figure described with the aid of the compasses is a circle, a figure which presents no points nor angles. It is not only a perfectly symmetrical figure in itself, but it is the test of symmetry in other figures, for a perfectly symmetrical figure is one that can be described in a circle or about a circle. The teaching of the symbol in this respect is obvious. A man who possesses perfect self-control presents no points and obtrudes no angles. His personality is neither assertive nor aggressive. He maintains the same front under all conditions.

William Meeson, whose works were published two hundred years ago although probably written and collected very much earlier still, has been freely quoted in this chapter because he is one of the first who wrote on the moral symbolism of the implements of masonry. Let him then have the final word:

Mafonical Aphorifms, &c.

THE mighty PILLARS on which MASONRY is founded, are thofe whofe BASIS is *wifdom,* whofe SHAFT is *ftrength,* and whofe CHAPITER is *beauty.*

The *wifdom* is that which defcends from above; and is firft *pure,* then *peaceable, gentle and eafy to be intreated,* full of *mercy* and good *fruits,* without *partiality,* and without *hypocrify.*

The *ftrength,* is that which depends on the living GOD; who refifteth the mighty, and fcattereth the proud in the imaginations of their hearts: who giveth us power to refift and to efcape all temptations, and to fubdue our evil appetites. A ftrength, which is a refuge to the deftreffed; a bond of unity and love amongft brethren, and of peace and quiet in our own hearts.

Our *beauty*, is fuch as adorns all our actions with
holinefs; is *hewn* out of the *rock*, which is CHRIST,
and raifed UPRIGHT by the PLUMB-LINE of the *gofpel;*
SQUARED and LEVELLED to the *horizontal* of *God's
will*, in the *holy lodge* of *St. John:* and fuch as becomes
the *temple*, whofe maker and builder is GOD.

On fobriety your pleafure depends; on regularity,
your reputation.

The ungovernable paffions and uncultivated nature
of man, ftand as much in need of the SQUARE and
COMPASS to bring them into order, and to adorn us
with the beauty of holinefs, as thofe inftruments of
MASONRY are neceffary to bring rude matter into
form, or to make a block of marble fit for the polifhed
corners of the temple.

Thofe *focieties* dwindle away and vanifh, which are
not contrived, fupported, and adorned with the *wifdom, ftrength*, and *beauty*, of our moft ancient and honourable order; where nobility is ennobled; where
knowledge is improved, and where converfation is
rendered ufeful; as MASONS and rational creatures
draw no *define*, but on the TRASEL-BOARD of a *good
intention*.

Though we are all *free* and on the LEVEL, yet it is
our duty to keep always within COMPASS, and to conduct ourfelves according to the SQUARE and PLUMB.

There is no converfation more ufeful, than that
which promotes morality, charity, good-fellowfhip,
good nature, and humanity.

Society has harmony in the very word; but much
more in the application of it. For it is to it we owe
all arts and fciences.

Until the duft and cobwebs of a man's ftudy are
brufhed off him by converfation, he is utterly unfit
for human fociety. A good genius not cultivated
this way, is like a rich diamond, whofe beauty is in-
difcernable till polifhed.

Prudence is the queen and guide of all other virtues; the ornament of our actions, the SQUARE and
RULE of all our affairs.

Faith, hope, and *charity*, are the three principal

graces, by which we afcend to the grand celeftial
LODGE, where pleafures flow for evermore.

Let every true MASON *knock* off every *evil dif-
pofition*, by the GAVEL of *righteoufnefs* and *mercy:*
meafure out his actions by the RULE of one *day:* fit
them to the SQUARE of *prudence* and *equity:* keep them
within the bounds of the COMPASS of *moderation* and
temperance: adjuft them by the true PLUMB-LINE of
gofpel fincerity: bring them up to the juft LEVEL of
perfection; and *fread* them abroad with the *filent*
TROWEL of *peace,* &c. &c. &c.

INDEX

q indicates a quotation
AQC = Ars Quatuor Coronatorum

Aaron's rod *Plate 10*
Accepted 15–16
'Acception, The': in the London
  Company 15–18; safeguards of
  membership 19; religious connections
  42
Adam brothers 46
Age of Reason 15, 35, 43
Ahimon Rezon 39
Alchemical influence 44
Allegory 27–28
All Souls Lodge No 120 description of
  working tools q170
Anderson, Dr James
  Book of Constitutions 10, 15, 16, 17,
  38; on Christian faith 52; on Jewish
  influence 39; The Mysteries 33; the PM
  jewel 147; Sir Christopher Wren 16
Antients' Grand Lodge (*see also* Grand
  Lodge 1717) 62, 107, 129; Coat of
  Arms 29; Laurence Dermott 39;
  exposures 29; formed 47; Royal Arch
  Degree 137; the Square 153;
  symbolism and the Union 28–29; the
  third degree 137; three great lights 107,
  115, 120–121; twenty-four inch gauge
  159; the working tools 149
Antiquity, Lodge of 100
Antiquities of the Jews, Flavius Josephus
  39, 73
Apron (*see also* Scripture references)
  Book of Constitutions description 147;
  colour 142, 145; design 56; flap
  position 142–143; Hutchinson on moral
  significance q143–144; in Ladd's *The
  Science of Freemasonry Explained*
  q142; in *Leaves from Georgia Masonry*
  q146; Installed Masters 'Levels'
  146–147; uniformity and distinction of
  rank 141–142; in Oliver's *Signs and
  Symbols* q144–145
Ashlar, Rough and Perfect 93–94
Ashmole, Elias 18
Arms adopted by Grand Lodge 1717, 18

Bacon, Francis 44
Beehive 43, Dr Oliver on q104

Bell, Dr J. P. 163
Beswick, Samuel, *The Swedenborg Rite*
  q44, q45
Bible (*see also* Scripture references)
  ceremonies based on 122; Ephraimites
  49; first great light 107, 115; in
  Lawrence's *Sidelights on Freemasonry*
  q116–118; on Masters pedestal
  120–121; the Sacred Law 116
Blazing Star 113–114
Bowring, Josiah, 97
Bridewell 17
Browne, John, *A Master Key* 30; on the
  letter G q86; on Geometry q90; on
  point within a circle q98–99; on light
  105–106; on the blazing star q113–114
Builders, The, Fort Newton 15, 33
Bunyon, John 123

Cabala (Kabbala) 40–41, 54, 55, 66
Cabalists, Jewish sect in *A Defence of
  Masonry* q37; 39–40, 54; influence on
  use of numbers 55
Cagliostro 44
Calcott, Wellins *A Candid Disquisition* on
  hieroglyphics q22
Carpet of lodge, J. S. M. Ward on q79–80;
  W. L. Wilmshurst on q80–81
Carr, Harry, *The Letter G—AQC Vol 76*
  89, 90
Cathedral Builders, The, Leader Scott q15
Ceremonies: not principal work in early
  lodges 61–62; symbolic progression
  towards east 67
Chetwoode Crawley MS (c1700) 32
Chippendale 46; *Gentleman and Cabinet
  Maker's Directory* (1754) 78
Chisel 150; in Old Lectures q151, 154; in
  Meeson's *An Introduction to Free
  Masonry* (1775) q157–158; Stability
  Lodge of Instruction 160
Christian influence: Anderson on 52; on
  lodge layout 65
Circle as symbol in third degree 137–138
Clarke J. R. *External Influences on the
  Evolution of English Masonry* (1969
  Prestonian Lecture) 43
Clare, Martin 16
Cockburn, Sir John, on the Square and
  letter G 88
Cockeburne, Rev L. D. H. 100
Coffin as a symbol, Dr Oliver q103

College of Arms 18, 166
Collars, J. S. M. Ward q148
Columns (see also pillars) 72; confusion
  with pillars 78
Comacine Masters in *The Cathedral
  Builders*, Scott q15
Compasses (see also Square) one of three
  great lights 107, 115; jewel of Grand
  Master 171; in Hutchinson's *The Spirit
  of Masonry* q172; as symbol of
  moderation Lawrence 174, q175–176;
  Meeson, q172–174; Dr Oliver
  q171–172; in old Lectures q151; as
  working tool 150; significant to third
  degree 137–138, 171
*Complete Concordance of the Old and
  New Testaments* Alexander Cruden 46,
  53, q54
Concord, Lodge of 31
Conder, Edward, 15
Constitutions, Book of Anderson 1723,
  1738 and *Cooke MS* 10; 'Concerning
  God and Religion' 52; and *A Defence of
  Masonry* 13, 38; Euclid's 47th
  Proposition 147; continuous existence
  of freemasonry 15; first published 10;
  Ghiblim 148; Grand Lodge 17; Jewish
  history and KST 39; Masters and Past
  Masters apron 147; the Mysteries 33;
  Sir Christopher Wren 18; the working
  tools 149
Constitutions, Book of Entick 1756, 17,
  lodges built symbolically east and west
  q64
Constitutions, Book of Noorthouck 1784,
  17; speculative and operative masonry
  q35; three pillars q75; Faith, Hope and
  Charity 97; frontispiece illustration
  Plate 2
Constitutions, Scotland 147
Cooke MS c1400, 10, 11
Corinthian order 72
Corn as symbol of plenty 59
Coustos, John q89
Crane and Pulley in old Lectures q152
Cruden, Alexander 46, 53, q54
Custom House 17

Defence of Masonry, A (1730) 13; the
  Essenes 40; Jewish influence 39; the
  Mysteries q35–37, 38; the numbers
  three and seven q51, odd numbers 53
Dermott, Laurence 39
Dictionary of Antiques (1770) George
  Savage on Allegory q27–28
Dictionary, Dr Johnson's (1751) 46
Doric Order 72, 78–79
Downing, George q33
Dring, E. H. q45–46
Druids, *A Defence of Masonry* 37, 38
Dumfries No 4 Manuscript (c1710) 32, 51
Dunkerley, Thomas 30, 110

Early Masonic Catechisms, The Knoop,
  Jones and Hamer (1943) 32
Edinburgh House Manuscript (1696) 32;
  use of numbers q53
Eleusinian Mysteries, The Taylor (c1793)
  45
Emulation Lodge of improvement 87
Encyclopaedia Britannica 46
Encyclopaedia Judaica (1971); the
  number three and seven 54; temple
  entrance 66; inscription on columns
  q74; structure of KST 123
Entick, Rev John *Book of Constitutions*
  (1756) 17, q64
Ephraimites 49
Essenes, Jewish sect 37, 39–40, 54
*External Influences on the Evolution of
  English Masonry* J. R. Clarke (1969) 43
Euclid 133

Fellows, John, on the point within a circle
  q100
Finch, William *A Masonic Key* (1801) 30
Free: the word 9–10; 'open only to free
  men' 10; by free-stone 15
Free and Accepted, Geometry as
  free-science 11; freedom of the Guilds
  12; rise and development 19, 35; as
  alternative to speculative 20–21; as two
  degree system 16
Freemason, free mason 9, 12
Freemasonry, speculative, the Acception
  17; development 9–21; in Ladd's *The
  Science of Free Masonry Explained* q20;
  from Preston's Lectures q20; use of
  symbols 20; Wren 18
Freemasons' Guide and Compendium
  B. E. Jones 13
French masonry 70; Coustos and the
  letter G 89

'G' the letter 84–90: in Browne's *A Master
  Key* q86; John Coustos and letter 'G'
  q89; earliest reference 89; the gallows
  square 88, J. S. M. Ward q164–165; and
  Geometry 85, 86; Ghiblim 148; from
  Gimel 90; John Harris and 'G' denoting
  God 85, 87, 89, 90; Jewish influence
  86–87; William Preston and 'G' 89–90;
  in Rylands' *Notes on Some Masonic
  Symbols* q87; on Scottish PM jewel
  148; in second degree 84–85; and
  threefold sign 132
Gainsborough 46
Gauge (see Twenty-four inch gauge)
Gavel, Common gavel 149, 154; Hiram
  150; in Meeson's *An Introduction to
  Freemasonry* q157–158, 162; Stability
  Lodge of Instruction 160
Genesis of Freemasonry, The Knoop and
  Jones (1949) q42–43

Gentleman and Cabinet Maker's Directory Chippendale 78

Geometry, in Browne's *A Master Key* q86, q90; John Coustos q89; and letter 'G' 85, 86; in Preston's *Illustrations* q90–91; synonymous with masonry 10–11; Wilmshurst on Geometry q91–92

Germany 17

Goldsmith 46

Gould, Robert Freke, *History of Freemasonry* (1886) 12, 13, 15

Grand Lodge 1717—the premier Grand Lodge known as 'Moderns' (*see also* Antients Grand Lodge); architectural symbols 72; arms of Masons Company adopted 18; similar to Square 165; Bible as furniture of lodge 114–115; early development 17–18; entrance to the lodge 69; 'excellent mason' 85; exposures 29–30; James Hestletine 46; the Irish 47; Jacob's Ladder 97; layout of lodges 64; use of Lectures 28–30; William Meeson 156; the Royal Arch 137; Sandby's Grand Temple 65; Square and Compasses as furniture of lodge 114–115; three degree system 136–137; three great lights 106–107, 120–121; tracing boards 152; the Union and differences in symbolism 28–29; effect on tracing boards 94, 152; uniformity in regalia 141; working tools 149

Grand Mystery of Free-Masons Discover'd, The (1724) q53

Guilds (*see also* London Company) 11–12; membership of 19

Guildhall 17

Harris, John 87; illustration of first degree T. B. *Plate 8*; illustration of second degree T.B. *Plate 9*

Haunch, T. O., 97

Hawksmoor 46

Heseltine, James 46

Hieroglyphics, Calcott on the meaning of 22

Hills, G. P. G. *Notes on Some Masonic Personalities at the End of the Eighteenth Century—AQC Vol 25* 45, 46

Hiram, another name for Gavel 150, 154

Hiram Abiff 71, 152

Hiram King of Tyre 71

History of Freemasonry (1886) R. F. Gould 12

Horne Alex, 43, q44

Hutchinson, William *The Spirit of Masonry* (1775); the ceremonies 123, q124, 125; on the Compasses q172; on the Apron q143–144, 145; on the letter 'G' 85, 87, 89, 90; valley of Jehosaphat q68–69; lectures 31; on the lodge q62; on the old Mysteries q38; the two pillars and their names q74; on the Square q166; the entrance to the Tabernacle 65

Illustrations of Masonry Preston (1775) q21 30–31, q90–91, q115, 125, q150, 155

Interpretation of our Masonic Symbols, An Ward q22–23, 88, 146

Introduction to Freemasonry, An Meeson (1775) 156, q157–159

Ionic Order 78–79

Ireland 47

Jachin 73–74

Jackson A. C. F. 30

Jacob's Ladder 95–97

James, Percy q41

Jewels, Movable and Immovable 92

Jewish encyclopaedia (1903) 54, q66

Jewish influence on letter 'G' 86–87

Johnson's, Dr, *Dictionary* 46

Jones, Bernard E. *Freemasons' Guide and Compendium* 13

Jones, Inigo 78

Josephus, Flavius; *Antiquities of the Jews* 39, 65, 73

Kent, William 78

Keystone, The Rev J. T. Lawrence q75–77

Kevan Manuscript (c1714) 32

King Solomon 15, 66, 67, 69, 71

King Solomon's Temple 39, 49, 62–63, 65, 69, 72, 122, 128, 130–131, 133–134; in *Leaves from Georgia Masonry* q63–64; built east and west 65; the entrance 65–66, 69, 123, 134

Kipling, Rudyard, *The Mother Lodge* q156

Klein, Sidney T. 162, q163

Knoop and Jones *The Genesis of Freemasonry* (1949) q42–43

Knoop, Jones and Hamer *The Two Earliest Masonic Manuscripts* (1938) 10; English medieval industry q13–15; The Early Masonic Catechisms 32

Ladd, John *The Science of Freemasonry Explained* (1770) q20, 31, q142

Lawrence, Rev J. T. the Compass as a symbol of moderation 174, q175–176; the level q167, q169; on lodge layout 64; on the pillars *The Keystone* q75–77; on the point within a circle q102; on the Sacred Law *Sidelights on Freemasonry* q116–118; on the Square *The Perfect Ashlar* q163–164; on the Square and Compasses q119

Leaves from Georgia Masonry q23–24, 25, q26; on the apron q146; on the movable jewels q170–171; the numbers three, five and seven q56–57

Lectures (or Catechisms) 28, 55, 59–60, q67–68, 72, q81–83, 105, 108, 109, q114–115, q123, q134, q140
Leslie, Charles 90
Level as a working tool 153, 167–170
Light 105–106
Livery Companies 11
Lodge layout 58, 59, 64, 65, Dr Oliver q60
London Company of Masons 12–13, 15, 17
London, and the great fire of 1666, 16–17
Lovejoy, frontispiece of *Masonic Miscellany*, *Plate 4*

Mallet (*see also* Gavel) 150, 152, 154, 159
Masonic Confession, A (c1727) q53, 156
Masonic Key, A Finch (1801) 30
Masonic Miscellany Stephen Jones (1797) illustration *Plate 4*
Masonry Dissection Samuel Pritchard (1730) 13, 32, 38, 89, 106
Master Key, A John Browne (1802) 30, 105, 106; on the blazing star q113–114; on the letter 'G' q86; on geometry q99; on the point within a circle q98–99
Maul 149, 154
Maurice, Rev Thomas 33
Meaning of Masonry, The W. I. Wilmshurst (1922) 33, q34
Meeson, William *An Introduction to Freemasonry* (1775) 156–157; the Compasses a symbol of moderation q172–174; the Gavel and Chisel q157–158; the level q168; the plumb line q168; the Rule 158–159; the Square q162–163, q168; symbolism q176–178; the trowel q155–156
Mesmer 44
Milton, John 31
Moderns Grand Lodge (*see* Grand Lodge 1717)

New Standard Jewish Dictionary (1970) 67
Netherlands 47
Newton 46
Newton, J. Fort, *The Builders* 15, 33
Noorthouck, John *Book of Constitutions* (1784) 17
Notes on Some Masonic Personalities at the End of the Eighteenth Century AQC Vol 25 G. P. G. Hills 45
Notes on Some Masonic Symbols AQL Vol 8 Rylands (1895) q25
Numbers, significance and use of, 50–55; W. L. Wilmshurst q55–56; *Leaves From Georgia Masonry* q56–57

Ode to Masonry, An Bancks (c1738) 58
Oil as symbol of peace 59
Oliver, Rev George, 38, 48, 55, 62, 135; on the coffin, skull and cross bones

q103–104; on the compasses q171–172; on the first degree q130; on King Solomon's Temple q63; on the lodge room q59–60; on the master representing King Solomon q67; Movable jewels q166–167; on the pillars q70, q74–75; on the point within a circle q102–103; separate meaning of degrees q125–127; the Square q166; on the tracing board q93; *Signs and Symbols* (1837); the apron q144, q145; on the ladder q95, q96
Theocratic Philosophy of Freemasonry (1840); on light q110–113; on the twenty-four inch gauge q160–161

Palladio 78
Parallel lines 98, 99, 100
Payne, George, 10
Pencil as a symbol 153, 154, 171
Perfect Ashlar (*see* Ashlar)
Perfect Ashlar, the Rev. J. T. Lawrence q163–164
Perjured Free Mason Detected, The q16
Pilgrim's Progress 123
Pillars (*see also* Columns) 67–73, 78, 135
Plumb 149–154, 156, 157, 170–171, 172
Pocket Companion for Freemasons Smith (1738) 13
Point within a circle 97–103
Pope 40
Pot of Manna *Plate 10*
Preston, William, architectural orders q79; on the blazing star 114; Cabalistic influence 41; on the letter 'G' 85, 87, 89–90; on Geometry q11, q90–91; membership of Guilds 19; and James Heseltine 46; miscellaneous references, 30, 31, 38, 46, 97, 109, 137; parallels q98; pillars 70; on Sacred Law 115, q116; the second degree 131–132, 134, and speculative masonry q20, q21; on the Square q161; the third degree q127; on the trowel 155, 156; on the twenty-four inch gauge q159; on the working tools q150–152, 153
Prichard, Samuel *Masonry Dissected* (1730) 13, 32, 38, 51, 89, 96, 106
Pythagoras 36–38, 40, 147

Rainsford, General 146
Reconciliation, Lodge of, 27
Regius MS (c1390) 10
Revelations of a Square q63
Reynolds 46
Rocques's Map of London (1776) *Plate 1*
Rosicrucian influence 44
Rough Ashlar (see Ashlar)
Royal Arch degree 137
Royal Exchange, the 17

Rule 150, 'masonic line and rule' 153,
Meeson's *Introduction to Freemasonry*
q158–159
Rylands, W. H. q87

St Clement Danes 64
St John 68, 98–99
St John's Day 10
St Martin 44
St Paul's Cathedral 18, 64
Salt a symbol of friendship 59
Sandby, Thomas, 65
Savage, George *Dictionary of Antiques*
q27
Scandinavia 47
Science of Freemasonry Explained Ladd
(1770) q20, 31, q142
Scott, Leader, 15
Scripture references
Acts 2:1–4 on light q106
II Chronicles 3: 15–17 on the pillars 73
II Chronicles 4 the pillars 72
Deuteronomy 27:5–6 on tools 49, 50
Exodus 3 removing shoes 49; lodges on
Holy Ground 68
Exodus 4 on the signs 49
Exodus 20:25 on metal tools 49
Exodus 27 on the structure of the
Tabernacle 65
Ezekiel 8:16 entrance to KST q65, 73
Genesis 1:3 on light 106
Genesis 3:7 and 21 on aprons 48, 142
Genesis 21:9–10 'free man' 49
Job 9:23 'free men' 49
Joshua 5 removing shoes 49; lodges on
Holy Ground 68
Judges 12 on test word 49
I Kings 6:2 dimensions of KST 62
I Kings 6:7 building of KST 49
I Kings 6:8 entrance to middle chamber
q134
I Kings 7:15–22 the pillars q72–73
I Kings 20:22 the c t q128
I Kings 8 dedication of KST 68
Numbers 15:37–40 on aprons q48–49,
142
Ruth 4:7 removing shoes q128
St John 1 on light 106
Seven liberal arts and sciences 10, 11
Shakespeare, William *Coriolanus* q141
Shekinah 87, 113, 114
Sheraton 46
Sheridan 46
Sherwood, L. M., 25
Signs and Symbols Oliver (1837) q95,
q96, q144, q145
Sidelights of Freemasonry Lawrence
q116–118
Skirrett 154, 171
Skull and cross bones q103–104
Sloane Manuscript, The (c1700) 32
Smith's *Pocket Companion for
Freemasons* (1738) 13

Somerset House *Plate 3*
Spectale de la Nature or Nature displayed
(1757) q49
Speculative masonry (*see* Freemasonry,
speculative)
Speth, G. W. 11
Spirit of Masonry, The Hutchinson (1775)
31, q38, q62
Square (*see also* 'G'); and the apron 146;
arms of Grand Lodge 165–166; letter
'G' and gallows square 88–89; same
shape as Gamma 164–165; Hutchinson
on, q166; Klein on, 162, q163;
Lawrence on, q119, 163–164; *Leaves
from Georgia Masonry* q170–171;
many references in lodge 153, 156, 161;
from old Lectures q151; in Meeson's
Introduction to Freemasonry
q168–169; Dr Oliver on 166; in second
degree 132, 161; and compasses
115–118, 120, 150; and level 156; one
of three great lights 107, 115; Ward on
q119; Wilmshurst on q119; as working
tool 118–120, 121, 149, 150, 156, 161,
162, 167, 170
Stability Lodge of Instruction 160
Stationers Company 19
Stow's *Survey of London* 12
Sussex, Duke of, 39, 40, 55, 99
Swedenborg Rite, The Beswick (1870)
q44, 45
Scythe as a symbol 103–104

Taylor's *The Eleusinian Mysteries* c1793,
45
Temple, Masonic (see also King Solomons
Temple), place for the worship of God,
62; Grand Temple of Moderns G. L.
(1776), dimensions, 65.
Thorpe, John 87
The Letter G, AQC Vol 76, Harry Carr,
89
Tracing Board, 59, 64, 84–5, 92–5, 152;
Grand Lodge certificate based on, 95;
Harris Boards of Emulation Lodge of
Improvement, *Plates 8 and 9*; Effects of
Union on, 94–5; dual tracing board,
Plate 5; and letter G, 84, 87, 148;
Master t/b *plates 5, 6, 7*; second degree
133; third degree, 138, 148; Tresal or
tracel board, 92; winding staircase
representation 135
Trassel Board, old lectures q152
Tresham, Sir Thomas, Triangular lodge at
Rushton, 51
Theocratic Philosophy of Freemasonry,
Oliver 1840, Light q110–113
Trinity College Dublin MS, The, 1711, 32
Trinity, Triune God of Orthodox
Christians, 51, 87
Trowel, *Plate 10*, 149, 150, 151, 154, 155,
156, 172

Twenty-Four Inch Gauge, 149, 150, 153,
  Dr Oliver on q160
Two Earliest Masonic Mss, The, Knoop,
  Jones and Hamer, 10

United Grand Lodge of England (see also
  Antients', Moderns, Grand Lodge), 9,
  27, 141
United States of America 56

Vanburgh 46
Vatcher, Dr Sidney, on John Coustos 89
Vulgate on triangular buildings 52

Ward, Rev J. S. M. *An Interpretation of
  our Masonic Symbols*, speculation and
  symbols q22–23, Columns q77–78,
  Carpet and tassels q79–80, Square and
  Gamma G 88, 89, q164–165, parallel
  lines & point within circle q101, Square
  & Compasses q119, 'levels' on IPM
  apron 146, PM Jewel and 47th
  proposition q147–148, collars q148.
Warrington, Lancs 18

Wardens, identified with pillars 69, 71, 72
Webb, *The Mysteries of Freemasonry* 100
Westcott, Dr William Wynn 40, on the
  figures five and seven 54, on the letter G
  90
Whiston, Translation of *Antiquities of the
  Jews* q73
Wilmshurst, W. L. *The Meaning of
  Masonry* 33, q34, development 41, use
  of numbers q55–56, pillars 73, 74,
  carpet q80–81, geometry q91–92,
  Square & Compasses q119–120, the
  Winding Staircase 135, second degree
  q136, third degree q138–139, q140, the
  apron 145
Wilkinson Ms, 106
Wine 59
Winding Staircase 65
Wordsworth 46
Wren, Sir Christopher 16, 17, 18, 46
Working Tools (see also under individual
  names) 149, 150, q150–152, 153, 156,
  Dr Oliver on q167, third degree 171,
  William Meeson q176–178.

Lewis Masonic

Also of interest

I Just Didn't Know That
Revd Neville Barker Cryer

A collection of talks which explain many of the fundamentals of Freemasonry, which should inform, encourage, entertain and extend the knowledge of the Craft.

Ref: L048 | 210mm x 150mm | 104pp | SB | **£9.99**